Exploring Language Assessment and Testing

D1259008

The *Routledge Introductions to Applied Linguistics* series takes an innovative 'practice to theory' approach, with a 'back-to-front' structure. This leads the reader from real-world problems and issues, through a discussion of intervention and how to engage with these concerns, before finally relating these practical issues to theoretical foundations.

Exploring Language Assessment and Testing offers a straightforward and accessible introduction that starts from real-world experiences and uses practical examples to introduce the reader to the academic field of language assessment and testing.

Extensively updated, with additional features such as reader tasks (with extensive commentaries from the author), a glossary of key terms and an annotated further reading section, this second edition provides coverage of recent theoretical and technological developments and explores specific purposes for assessment. Including concrete models and examples to guide readers into the relevant literature, this book also offers practical guidance for educators and researchers on designing, developing and using assessments.

Providing an inclusive and impartial survey of both classroom-based assessment by teachers and larger-scale testing, this is an indispensable introduction for postgraduate and advanced undergraduate students studying Language Education, Applied Linguistics and Language Assessment.

Anthony Green is Professor in Language Assessment at the University of Bedfordshire, UK. His other publications include *IELTS Washback in Context* (2007) and *Language Functions Revisited* (2012). He has taught courses in Language Assessment around the world and has extensive practical experience of testing and assessment – including working as a test researcher, developer, item writer and language teacher.

Routledge Introductions to Applied Linguistics

Series editors:

Ronald Carter, *Professor of Modern English Language*
University of Nottingham, UK

Guy Cook, *Professor of Language in Education*
King's College London, UK

Routledge Introductions to Applied Linguistics is a series of introductory level textbooks covering the core topics in Applied Linguistics, primarily designed for those entering postgraduate studies and language professionals returning to academic study. The books take an innovative 'practice to theory' approach, with a 'back-to-front' structure. This leads the reader from real-world problems and issues, through a discussion of intervention and how to engage with these concerns, before finally relating these practical issues to theoretical foundations. Additional features include tasks with commentaries, a glossary of key terms and an annotated further reading section.

Exploring Digital Communication
Language in Action
Caroline Tagg

Exploring English Language Teaching 2ed
Language in Action
Graham Hall

Exploring Intercultural Communication 2ed
Language in Action
Zhu Hua

Exploring Language Assessment and Testing 2ed
Language in Action
Anthony Green

'The innovative approach devised by the series editors will make this series very attractive to students, teacher educators and even to a general readership, wanting to explore and understand the field of applied linguistics. The volumes in this series take as their starting point the everyday professional problems and issues that applied linguists seek to illuminate. The volumes are authoritatively written, using an engaging "back-to-front" structure that moves from practical interests to the conceptual bases and theories that underpin applications of practice.'
Anne Burns, *Aston University, UK,*
University of New South Wales, Australia

For more information on any of these and other titles, or to order, please go to https://www.routledge.com/Routledge-Introductions-to-Applied-Linguistics/book-series/RIAL

Additional resources for Language and Communication are available on the Routledge Language and Communication Portal: http://dev.routledgetextbooks.uk.corplan.net/textbooks/languageandcommunication

Exploring Language Assessment and Testing

Language in Action

Second edition

Anthony Green

Routledge
Taylor & Francis Group

LONDON AND NEW YORK

Second edition published 2021
by Routledge
2 Park Square, Milton Park, Abingdon, Oxon, OX14 4RN

and by Routledge
52 Vanderbilt Avenue, New York, NY 10017

Routledge is an imprint of the Taylor & Francis Group, an informa business

© 2021 Anthony Green

First edition published by Routledge 2014

British Library Cataloguing-in-Publication Data
A catalogue record for this book is available from the British Library

Library of Congress Cataloging-in-Publication Data
Names: Green, Anthony, 1966– author.
Title: Exploring language assessment and testing : language in action /
    Anthony Green.
Description: Second edition. | Abingdon, Oxon ; New York, NY :
    Routledge, 2021. | Series: Routledge introductions to applied
    linguistics | "First edition published by Routledge 2014" | Includes
    bibliographical references and index.
Identifiers: LCCN 2020039446 | ISBN 9781138388772 (hardback) |
    ISBN 9781138388789 (paperback) | ISBN 9781003105794 (ebook)
Subjects: LCSH: Language and languages—Ability testing. |
    Language and languages—Study and teaching.
Classification: LCC P53 .G675 2021 | DDC 418.0028/7—dc23
LC record available at https://lccn.loc.gov/2020039446

ISBN: 978-1-138-38877-2 (hbk)
ISBN: 978-1-138-38878-9 (pbk)
ISBN: 978-1-003-10579-4 (ebk)

Typeset in Sabon
by Apex CoVantage, LLC

For Richard, Maria and Alexander

Contents

Figures

Tables

Permissions

The publishers and I would like to thank the following copyright holders for permission to reprint material:

Oxford University Press for extracts from *Oxford Applied Linguistics: Language Assessment in Practice* by Lyle Bachman and Adrian Palmer (2010).

Taylor and Francis for extracts from 'Evolution of a test item' by Mary Spaan from *Language Assessment Quarterly*, vol 4, issue 3 (2007), www.informaworld.com.

Pearson Education Inc. for extracts from the Versant Pro Writing Test (2009) and Versant Aviation English Test (2008).

Cambridge English Language Assessment for extracts from *Examining Speaking: Research and Practice in Assessing Second Language Speaking* edited by Lynda Taylor (2011); *IELTS Washback in Context: Preparation for Academic Writing in Higher Education* by Anthony Green (2007); *Preliminary English Test Information for Candidates* (2006); *Cambridge Young Learners Tests Sample Papers* (2010); *Cambridge English Business English Certificates Handbook for Teachers* (2012); *Continuity and Innovation: Proficiency in English Examination 1913–2002* edited by Cyril Weir and Michael Milanovic (2003).

The British Council for extracts from *English Language Testing Service Specimen Materials Booklet* (1987).

The Language Policy Division of the Council of Europe for the scale for 'Qualitative aspects of spoken language use' from the *Common European Framework of Reference for Languages: Learning, Teaching, Assessment* (2001).

English Language Testing for extracts from the *Password* test (2012).

It has not always been possible to identify the sources of all the material used and in such cases the publishers would welcome information from the copyright holders.

Acknowledgements

This book would never have been possible without the inspiration, help and support of many people. First, I am very grateful to the series editors, Ron Carter, for giving me the opportunity and for their encouragement and advice. Thanks also to Eleni Steck at Routledge for all her help in guiding the book along to publication.

My thanks also go to Nick Saville, John Field and Liz Hamp-Lyons, and to other anonymous reviewers who read all or part of the manuscript and offered insightful suggestions; to Cyril Weir, Roger Hawkey and Barry O'Sullivan who have done much to shape my ideas on language assessment; to Lynda Taylor, Fumiyo Nakatsuhara, Sathena Chan, Stephen Bax and Angela Mugomezi at the University of Bedfordshire for their support and to the many others who have helped with enquiries or suggestions. My thanks also must go to the wider community of language educators and assessment professionals around the world from whom this book has drawn.

I am, of course, indebted to my doctoral students, especially Carolyn Westbrook and Daniel Waller, and the many other students and trainees over the years, too many to mention by name, who have raised those difficult or unanswerable questions that have helped me to refine my thinking.

I very much appreciate the people and institutions that have contributed or helped me to source materials and to track down copyright holders. Special thanks are due to Martin Eayrs, to William Bonk of Pearson Knowledge Technologies, Ed Hackett and Alison Sharpe at Oxford University Press, John Savage at Cambridge English, Eileen Tyson, Xiaoming Xi and Anthony Ostrander at the Educational Testing Service.

Of course, involvement in a project like this leads to the neglect of other commitments and adds to the burdens of others. The book would never have been possible without the patience and unfailing support of my family. Thanks are especially due to Sachiyo for keeping me on track.

Series editors' introduction

The introductions to applied linguistics series

This series provides clear, authoritative, up-to-date overviews of the major areas of applied linguistics. The books are designed particularly for students embarking on master's level or teacher-education courses, as well as students in the closing stages of undergraduate study. The practical focus will make the books particularly useful and relevant to those returning to academic study after a period of professional practice, and also to those about to leave the academic world for the challenges of language-related work. For students who have not previously studied applied linguistics, including those who are unfamiliar with current academic study in English-speaking universities, the books can act as one-step introductions. For those with more academic experience, they can also provide a way of surveying, updating and organising existing knowledge.

The view of applied linguistics in this series follows a famous definition of the field by Christopher Brumfit (1995, p. 27) as:

> The theoretical and empirical investigation of real-world problems in which language is a central issue.

In keeping with this broad problem-oriented view, the series will cover a range of topics of relevance to a variety of language-related professions. While language teaching and learning rightly remain prominent and will be the central preoccupation of many readers, our conception of the discipline is by no means limited to these areas. Our view is that while each reader of the series will have their own needs, specialities and interests, there is also much to be gained from a broader view of the discipline as a whole. We believe there is much in common between all enquiries into language-related problems in the real world, and much to be gained from a comparison of the insights from one area of applied linguistics with another. Our hope therefore is that readers and course designers will not choose only those volumes relating to their own particular interests, but use this series to construct a wider knowledge and understanding of the field, and the many crossovers and resonances between its various areas. Thus, the topics to be covered are wide in range, embracing an exciting mixture of established and new areas of applied linguistic enquiry.

The perspective on applied linguistics in this series

In line with this problem-oriented definition of the field, and to address the concerns of readers who are interested in how academic study can inform their own professional practice, each book follows a structure in marked contrast to the usual movement *from* theory *to* practice. In this series, this usual progression is presented back to front. The argument moves *from* Problems, *through* Intervention, and *only* finally to Theory. Thus each topic begins with a survey of everyday professional problems in the area under consideration, ones which the reader is likely to have encountered. From there it proceeds to a discussion of intervention and engagement with these problems. Only in a final section (either of the chapter or the book as a whole) does the author reflect upon the implications of this engagement for a general understanding of language, drawing out the theoretical implications. We believe this to be a truly *applied* linguistics perspective, in line with the definition given previously, and one in which engagement with real-world problems is the distinctive feature, and in which professional practice can both inform and draw upon academic understanding.

- theory should come from application of language, not viceversa

Support to the reader

Although it is not the intention that the text should be in any way activity driven, the pedagogic process is supported by measured guidance to the reader in the form of suggested activities and tasks that raise questions, prompt reflection and seek to integrate theory and practice. Each book also contains a helpful glossary of key terms.

The series complements and reflects the *Routledge Handbook of Applied Linguistics*, which conceives and categorises the scope of applied linguistics in a broadly similar way.

Ronald Carter
Guy Cook

Reference

Brumfit, C. J. (1995). Teacher professionalism and research. In G. Cook & B. Seidlhofer (Eds.), *Principle and practice in applied linguistics* (pp. 27–42). Oxford: Oxford University Press.

Part I

Part I of this book is intended as a practical resource to help teachers, students, trainees and anyone interested in language education to understand more about the practice of language assessment and testing. A better understanding of the qualities of good assessments and of processes and techniques for improving helps practising teachers and other educators to make more effective use of assessment in their professional lives.

The first two chapters set out the core functions of language assessments. Chapter 1 outlines what is meant by language assessment and its place in language education. Chapter 2 considers some of the many reasons that people have for assessing language abilities. It shows how the practice of language assessment needs to be closely linked to the ways in which results will be used and interpreted. In educational settings, this means there must be an interdependent relationship between teaching, learning and assessment.

Chapter 3 explains a practical and widely applicable approach to building quality assessments for use in the classroom or in testing programmes. Chapter 4 describes the qualities of useful assessments and ways of evaluating them. These chapters introduce the reader to ways of working that have been shown to improve the quality of assessment materials and procedures.

Supplementary resources are available on the companion website (www.routledge.com/cw/rial). There you can find three additional documents that extend what is available in this book: *Illustrative Assessment Cycles* and *Statistical Tools* accompany Chapter 3, giving examples of assessment cycles and introducing statistical procedures that can help in improving the quality of assessments.

Part II introduces the reader to relevant theoretical insights and shows how the processes described in Part I are used in developing tests and assessments. Chapters 5 and 6 offer straightforward guidance on designing and developing more effective assessments and preparing appropriate materials for the purpose.

On the companion website, the document *Task Types* accompanies Chapters 5 and 6. It sets out a wide range of options for people involved in preparing assessment tasks.

Part III introduces the reader to the study of language assessment, tracing its emergence as a distinct field of inquiry. It outlines developing trends and points to areas of controversy and debate. This aspect of the book not only helps to contextualise and deepen understanding of the practices described, it also opens up avenues for the reader to explore through further study.

The focus throughout is on assessing peoples' ability to use foreign, second or additional languages and reasons for studying this. The principles and techniques described apply to the assessment of any language, but the examples are mainly taken from the assessment of English. This is partly because my own experience is mainly in teaching and assessing English, but also for the very good reason that this book is itself written in English and so the examples should be accessible to all readers.

Technical terms that are covered in the Glossary are identified where they first appear by bold type. Additional resources on the internet can be found via the *Links* button on the companion website (www.routledge.com/cw/rial). For each section, sources are recommended for the reader who wishes to explore the issues further.

1 Putting language assessment in its place

Personal reflection

What do you understand by the term *language assessment*? How is it different from *language teaching* or *language learning*?

What do you think are the main differences (if any) between *assessments*, *tests* and *examinations*?

What do you understand by the terms *language skills*, *language knowledge* and *language abilities*?

Think about an experience you have had of a language test.

Did you find the experience enjoyable? Why (or why not)? *when I did "well," yes*

Do you think that the test helped you to learn the language? In what ways did it help?

Language as evidence about people

It is a natural reaction to hearing or reading any fragment of language to treat it as evidence about the person who produced it. When we speak on the telephone to people we have not met, we may use the sound of their voice, its accent and pitch to give us clues about whether they are native speakers of our language, which country or region they come from, their gender, age, social class and profession, and their mood and attitudes.

It seems that we can't help forming an opinion about people according to the kind of language they produce. Americans tend to connect British accents with intelligence while British people associate American accents with wealth and high levels of success. Stereotypes like these may be unreasonable, but we are more likely to listen to and believe messages delivered by voices that we find pleasing and dependable. Businesses know this and carefully choose actors with suitable accents to deliver their advertising messages. Language learners tend to adopt similar opinions, preferring the prestige of standard accents found in textbooks.

If we receive a letter or email from someone, we base similar judgements on their choice of words and written style. We may even begin to form ideas about their appearance and personality. As you read this, you are probably already building up a picture in your mind of the writer of this book. When you do this kind of thing, you are using the language that a person produces to make **inferences** or draw conclusions about them. Note that when a word appears in this book in bold type (as **inferences** does here), you will find a brief definition in the Glossary in Chapter 8.

Linguistic evidence can sometimes be used quite formally to give insights into a person's identity or personality. Experts in forensic linguistics often try to establish where a suspect comes from by studying his or her accent or speech patterns. Sometimes employers look at the size and shape of job applicants' handwriting because this is supposed to give insights into their personalities. However, these kinds of inferences about people's regional origins or personal characteristics are not usually what is implied by the term language assessment. In this book the focus is on assessments where knowledge about language, the ability to use language or skill in applying these are measured or evaluated.

In everyday life, we not only make judgements about people on the basis of how they use language; we also make judgements about the qualities of the language that they use. We notice when they make grammatical errors or choose an inappropriate word; when they appear impolite or overly formal; when they are very hesitant; when they are being unclear or imprecise or, on the other hand, when they seem to express their ideas or communicate particularly well. We also judge our own use of language. As we speak or write, we monitor and correct ourselves. We put right our slips of the tongue and fix our spelling mistakes (with or without the help of our word processing software); we rephrase the things we say if people misunderstand us; we reorganise our written texts to try to make our ideas clearer to our readers.

What does it mean to use a language?

The nature of the **knowledge, skills** and **abilities** involved in learning and using a language is a matter of debate. An introduction to some of the contentious issues that have excited language assessment specialists is given in Part III. Briefly, **knowledge** about language may include recognizing a word written in a foreign language and knowing a translation equivalent (*bird* in English can be translated as طائر in Arabic, 鸟 in Chinese or *Vogel* in German), or knowing a grammatical rule: the past participle in English regular verbs is formed by adding –*ed* to the stem: look – look*ed*), or knowing pragmatic conventions. For example, in most circumstances *How are you?* spoken by an acquaintance is likely to be intended as a conventional greeting.

The anticipated response might be, *Good. You?* rather than details of the other's feelings or of any medical conditions.

A distinction is often made in language education following Hymes (1972) between knowledge of the rules governing language as a system and the **ability** to use language in unrehearsed interaction. Learners may know a good deal about a language but be unable to access the words or phrases they know in the course of a conversation or be unable to pronounce them accurately. Conversely, many people can communicate effectively in a wide range of situations with little or no explicit knowledge of the systems of rules that govern the language they are using. Language **skills** involve drawing on language knowledge and language abilities in order to read, listen, write, speak, to interact with others, or to mediate between them. The evidence we have of a person using a language may be very limited – a few telephone conversations and a handful of emails, perhaps – but based on what we observe in these few instances, we often make inferences about their more general knowledge of a language, their ability to use the language and their skill in carrying out language-related **tasks**. We may hear them speak for just a few minutes but reach conclusions such as: 'Adel knows more Albanian than I do' or 'Bonita can get by in Bengali.' We see a few examples of their writing and we make statements such as: 'Carole can write very polished business letters in Chinese' or 'Dai finds it really difficult to form questions in Danish.'

This book will focus on the relationship between how a person performs on an assessment, the inferences that users of the assessment make about them and the impact that the process has on the people involved. The emphasis will be on the use of language assessment in educational contexts. This setting for language assessment is unusual in some important ways. Firstly, language teachers, unlike most of us, are actually expected to voice their judgements about other people's language use and are generally rewarded (rather than resented) for pointing out and correcting errors. If you have worked as a language teacher, you will probably have experience during the natural course of any lesson of deciding whether one of your students has produced accurate and appropriate language, and perhaps putting right mistakes they have made or asking them to try again. You have probably asked them to read or listen to a text in the foreign language and then asked them questions about it to check their understanding. As I define language assessment in this book, examples can range from informal classroom activities to well-known national and international language tests.

So, here is a simple definition: *key word*

Language assessment involves obtaining evidence to inform inferences about a person's language-related knowledge, skills or abilities.

The *evidence* comes from the performance of tasks that involve the use of language. The *inferences* are what we interpret the performance to mean based on our beliefs about the nature of language and its role in the life of the person being assessed.

Using evidence from assessments

The inferences we make about **assessees** (the term I will use in this book for the people being assessed) are generally used to inform **decisions** – decisions that can range in magnitude from whether it would be better for them to use another comma in a sentence or practice saying a certain phrase again, to whether or not they should be given a job or given permission to make their home in a certain country.

In language education, teacher training programmes tend to give assessment rather little attention. Assessment is often the topic of just a few sessions: apparently an issue of little direct concern to the teacher, perhaps better left to expert specialists. On the other hand, it sometimes seems to take on overriding importance in the lives of teachers and learners. Many school children, if asked why they are learning a foreign language, would answer that they are doing it mainly to pass a public test, often known as an **examination** (distinctions between tests and examinations are discussed in Chapter 7). Most language teachers spend a good deal of time assessing their students and, especially when the day of an important national examination is getting close, many dedicate most of their classes to preparing their students to take these tests.

In this book I argue that language assessment is inseparable from the teaching and learning of languages. This challenges the more traditional view in teacher education that assessment is a distinct activity: one that is marginal to the main business of the language teacher. In my view, teachers need to develop what is sometimes called **assessment literacy**. They not only need to understand something about how language assessments are made, scored and interpreted by others, but also to be able to make, score and interpret the results of useful assessments themselves. Experience suggests that low levels of assessment literacy can lead to bad educational decisions and to teaching and learning that are less effective than they could be.

Assessment and testing

The traditional view that separates assessment from teaching may result from the identification of the word *assessment* with the narrower activity of **testing**. A test is an event that is especially set up to elicit a performance (usually within a predetermined time frame) for the purpose of making judgements about a person's knowledge, skills or abilities. In the course of a language test the person being judged (the assessee – a 'test taker,' 'testee' or 'candidate') will respond to a **prompt** (e.g., an essay title; questions asked by an interviewer; a set of choices on a test paper). The test taker's response is judged or scored according to a mark scheme. This is a predetermined procedure such as identifying and calculating the proportion of correct answers: 14 out of 20; counting the number of errors in a piece of writing; assigning points or marks to an essay to match descriptions presented on a scale, etc. The outcome is a **score** or **grade**, which is then formally recorded. The formalities and rituals of formal testing and the penalties associated with failure can make them an intimidating experience for the test taker.

For some commentators, **assessment** is distinguished from testing because it covers a much broader *cycle* of activities. In addition to the test event (which involves eliciting a performance as evidence of language abilities), these activities include:

- deciding on the content of the test;
- scoring the performance;
- deciding on the meaning of the scores obtained;
- decisions that the scores are used to justify (such as choosing which students to admit onto a course or deciding whether to award certificates).

In this view, the test is just one step in a sequence of events which together make up a **cycle of assessment**. This assessment cycle will be discussed in more detail in Chapter 3.

From another point of view, the word 'testing' can refer to this entire cycle of assessment events, but tests are understood to make up a relatively small set of controlled procedures among a much broader *range* of options. Assessment is a more general term than testing and takes in many different methods of obtaining and evaluating language data, including less formal procedures with fewer controls and restrictions than tests.

While it can be helpful to remind ourselves that assessment involves a whole cycle of inter-related activities, it is the second of these distinctions – the range of options for obtaining information – that is more often made in discussions of language assessment and so is the one used in this book.

In contrast to tests, other forms of assessment may involve such activities as:

- informal questioning in class by teachers;
- semi-formal **exercises** and **quizzes** carried out in class;
- learners judging each other's performance – **peer assessment**;
- learners reflecting on their own use of language – **self-assessment**;
- the collection of samples of language that have not been elicited according to any fixed or formal plan. Examples of this include **observations** and some forms of **portfolio assessment**.

Observations involve teachers watching and recording student performance in classroom activities. Portfolios are collections of student work that may showcase their best achievements or represent progress over a period of time.

Task 1.1

Have you ever experienced peer assessment or self-assessment?

Was it a positive experience?

Make a list of the main advantages and disadvantages of these techniques.

Compare your list with the task commentary.

Note that commentaries on this and other tasks can be found in Chapter 8 on p.234.

Other approaches to assessment that do, like tests, involve specific prompts (e.g., classroom exercises of the kind found in most textbooks) may not be carried out under controlled conditions (such as set time constraints or curbs on discussing answers with fellow students). Scores may not be formally recorded as evidence of the students' abilities. In fact, reporting does not need to involve the award of grades or scores at all, but may, for example, involve highlighting errors or giving descriptive commentaries on performance.

It is important to understand that tests are not the only means of judging learners' language knowledge, skills and abilities; and that not all language assessments are **formal** procedures that lead to scores or grades. On the contrary, most language assessments are **informal**, unobtrusive, involve no special arrangements and do not cause particular anxiety or fear in the people who are being assessed.

Assessment, teaching and learning

There are a number of different strategies we can use when we learn a new skill from another person. Perhaps the simplest of these is imitation; one person, the learner, watches what another person does and then attempts it for him or herself. When animals learn skills, this often appears to be how they do it. We know that some, chimpanzees, for example, can learn how to carry out quite sophisticated tasks, such as using a stick as a tool to catch insects, by copying the actions of other members of their group. They carefully observe what the skilled chimpanzee does, recognizing that one set of actions – such as shaping a stick – is related to another – poking the stick into a tree trunk – and that these actions together bring a reward – a meal of insects. They then try to recreate the same series of actions themselves to get the same reward. Chimpanzees are very good at imitation and they often perform better than humans in carrying out intricate imitation tasks.

Assessment of this kind of learning can be straightforward. Combining imitation with a process of trial and error, learners either succeed in accomplishing the **task**, or repeatedly fail and eventually give up.

Although it is possible to build knowledge by observing and copying, imitation alone is a limited way of passing on skills, and the more complex the skill, the less effective imitation seems to be. A child can watch an adult driving a car and try to copy the movements she sees, but that will probably not make her a safe and effective driver when she has the chance to take the wheel. When learning a language, I can try to imitate the sounds that speakers of that language make, to memorise words and grammatical patterns; but that is not likely to be enough to enable me to communicate effectively.

Learning complex skills like these is much more effective if we understand something about *why* people perform certain actions and how those actions help them to accomplish the tasks they want to carry out. This level of understanding is easier to achieve if we have another person to *teach* us.

In order to teach, people need both to understand that others can't do what they themselves can do, and to be motivated to pass on their own knowledge. When a person has mastered a new skill, they often share their newfound ability not only by showing – inviting others to watch as they perform the skill – or telling – explaining to the learners how to do it – but also by attending to the learners and judging how well they have understood and how close they are to being able to carry out the task independently.

Human learners do not usually simply imitate their teacher, but actively try to make sense of what they are learning: not only to notice that carrying out a sequence of actions leads to a particular outcome, but to understand *why* it does so. The teacher can support the learner by observing the learner's efforts and providing **feedback**: pointing out what they are doing well and what they are doing poorly in order to help them to improve. As humans, our willingness to teach each other in this way is one reason why we are so much more efficient than animals at preserving and developing our collective knowledge and technologies.

Understanding the gap between what learners can do now and what they need to be able to do or understand in order to fulfil a task successfully requires a sophisticated awareness of the task and of the learner. In the case of language learning, learners need to build an understanding of how people can use language to accomplish tasks such as establishing a rapport with another person, buying clothes or getting their hair cut. Assessment that takes account of this requires more than simple judgements of success or failure.

As well as having a good mastery of the skill themselves and the ability to model the skill in ways that make it more accessible to the learner, good teachers break down complex skills into the different elements that contribute to success. The teacher recognises which of these the learners can do independently, which they can do with some help or prompting, and which remain well beyond their abilities. The teacher may allow learners to carry out parts of a task that they are already able to accomplish but offer help with the more challenging stages. Think of how a mother might help a child

[handwritten margin note: primary role of feedback in learning]

to assemble a model or cook a meal. She lets the child carry out the task, but asks questions, points out mistakes and perhaps actually carries out some of the most complex steps in the process herself. Finally, she asks the child to try to replicate what she has done, giving feedback at the same time on what the child is doing well and how he might do better.

Another way in which people learn new skills is through working together to solve problems. By acting as a team, people can do things that no individual member could do when acting alone. Think of teams of engineers or medical researchers developing innovative machinery or new treatments. The members of the group create new forms of knowledge by participating together in activities. The relationships between them can be very important to the learning that occurs.

This kind of collective social learning can be challenging to assess, especially when using traditional tests, grades and scores, because it is difficult to establish what contribution each group member has made to the outcome. In order to achieve better results, members of the group may need to come to understand for themselves what aspects of the activity they might be able to carry out in different, more effective ways. Because assessment is used for a wide variety of purposes, it is quite easy to conceive of assessment taking place without teaching – one reason why many learners don't like public tests is that the test providers do not often give them any advice on which questions they answered correctly or incorrectly. The test teaches them nothing. On the other hand, it is almost impossible to imagine any form of teaching that does not involve assessment. Even in the most traditional classrooms, based on a transmission model of teaching (which assumes that learning is mainly or wholly dependent on the teacher telling a group of students new information), the content of the lectures is intended to fill a gap between what the students are believed to know already and what they need to know in order to succeed.

To be really effective as teachers, we need to find effective ways of assessing learners. We need to use what we learn from assessment to decide on actions to take that will help learners to improve their knowledge of the language or their skill in using it. A major challenge for language educators is that the process of learning a second language is still rather poorly understood. **Second language acquisition** (SLA) researchers, who investigate this process, disagree about the fundamental mechanisms of language learning and a number of competing theories can be found (see Cook, 2008; Lightbown & Spada, 2012; Mitchell, Myles, & Marsden, 2012; Ellis & Shintani, 2013). In assessing learners, we need to be clear about how we believe languages are learned; what kinds of evidence we might be able to collect to show us what learners know about a language; what they are able to use the language to do; what they have difficulty with; and how we can help them to expand their abilities.

Another troublesome issue in assessing language learning is the extent of disagreement about the purposes for learning languages. For some,

why even try?

languages should be taught in schools as a necessary basic skill. Just as we need to learn arithmetic in order to operate in the modern world – shopping, using banking services, checking our taxes – so we need foreign languages to do business and to interact with people from other countries. There are said to be economic benefits for countries with a linguistically adaptable labour force. For others, the primary advantage of learning languages has more to do with what Cook (2008) described as 'brain training.' Languages help us to develop our intelligence or adopt more flexible ways of thinking. Traditionally, a major purpose for learning languages was personal development through the understanding of classic works of literature and so becoming more 'cultured.' What we choose to assess will, of course, reflect what we think are the key purposes for language learning. These issues will be explored in more detail in Part III.

People generally tend to believe that language assessments give them pertinent information that can help them to make good decisions. If they are right, assessments may be useful tools that improve teaching and learning and serve society more generally. On the other hand, a lack of assessment information, poor information from badly conceived assessments or even poorly understood information from well-conceived assessments may lead to regrettable decisions. Teaching and learning will suffer, able people will be denied opportunities and society will experience the negative effects. It is very important that we carry out language assessment as well as we can and use the results in a well-informed manner.

2 Purposes for assessment

Task 2.1

Here are some reasons for giving language assessments. In each case . . .

Who would need the information?

What would be the best way to find the information? Is an assessment really needed?

1   How long is it likely to take this person to learn to speak Portuguese at an advanced level?
2   What sounds does this learner find it most difficult to produce?
3   Is this learner going to benefit more from an elementary or an intermediate-level language class?
4   Has this student learnt enough to progress to studying at the next level?
5   Has this student learnt the definitions of the 20 words I assigned as homework?
6   Does this person speak Chinese well enough to be able to work effectively with Chinese colleagues at our office in Beijing?
7   Will this student be able to write effective essays in English when she studies at an Australian university?
8   Has this learner reached a high enough level in Italian for us to award him an intermediate-level certificate?

What other kinds of reasons for using assessments can you add to this list?

Read the following section on 'Purposes for assessment.' Which purpose or purposes are involved in each situation?

Purposes for assessment

People most often use language assessments to collect two kinds of data. One relates to the learning of languages, with assessing the degree of progress towards a learning goal. These purposes are important in schools and other educational settings and so the assessments used to collect the data come under the heading of **educational assessment.**

Educational language assessment usually takes place within language programmes. The procedures are usually based on content that has been (or will be) taught; are frequently developed and carried out by teachers; and can often be flexible, allowing for the use of observational techniques (watching and recording what learners do), portfolios (collections of learners' work), self-assessment (learners making judgements about their own abilities) and informal tests or quizzes, as well as formal tests administered under more strictly controlled conditions.

The second kind of information is connected with whether or not a person's language ability is adequate to satisfy some predetermined need or standard. This is known as **proficiency assessment.** The assessment of language proficiency is usually connected to the language and related skills that are needed to carry out a job, study an academic subject or fulfil other kinds of roles. Because the focus is not on what the assessee has been taught, this kind of assessment is less likely to be carried out by teachers and more likely to involve formal tests administered under controlled, uniform, **standardised** conditions and produced by national or international agencies.

Proficiency assessments are distinct from educational assessments because they do not centre on learning processes or the outcomes of a particular course of study. Proficiency assessments are connected with a person's current functionality rather than with their learning: what the assessee can accomplish through their use of language now, not how they reached this point, or how long it might take them to arrive at a higher level of ability. In proficiency assessments the issue is whether or not the person being assessed has sufficient language ability to satisfy certain needs.

Proficiency assessments are often used for **gate-keeping** decisions: immigration, access to employment and educational opportunities. These may relate to a relatively **specific purpose** – such as using the language in leading groups of tourists around a city, working as a dentist, steering ships in international waters or studying marketing at a university – or it may be for less specialised or less clearly definable **general purposes** that might apply to a very wide range of language users. Tasks that many language users might need to carry out at some point might include reserving a room in a hotel or guest house, filling in forms with basic personal information, buying food, following television news programmes, reading articles in popular magazines or holding conversations about personal experiences.

Educational assessment in teaching and learning

Assessment can take place at different stages during the learning process. Before they begin a course in a new language, we may be interested in the learners' **aptitude** for language learning: their potential to learn. Although we know that almost anyone can learn a foreign language, given the time and motivation, some people may be predisposed to make faster progress than others.

A sports coach looking for someone with the potential to be a good basketball player may try to find someone who is tall and able to jump high, with quick reactions, good coordination and a competitive spirit. In the same way, some selective language training programmes, such as those organised by the military, need to pick from a large group of applicants those with the greatest potential to learn a language quickly. The Pimsleur Language Aptitude Battery (Pimsleur, Reed, & Stansfield, 2004), for example, set out to identify as potential language learners individuals with a good memory for word shapes and sounds who are good at discriminating between similar sounds, good at identifying grammatical patterns, and who have an interest in other cultures.

Partly because motivation is now widely regarded as more important than aptitude in shaping language learning success and partly because most language courses cater for learners who already have some knowledge of a language, aptitude tests are not as widely used as they used to be. It is more often the case that course providers wish to find out how much of the content of the course language learners already know before they begin, or how much they have learnt by the end. In this case, assessments may be **prognostic** – looking forward to the content planned for the course and deciding on priorities – or concerned with **achievement** – looking back to what the learners have been taught to find out how much they have absorbed and what might need to be covered again.

Aptitude and prognostic assessments are used to inform selection decisions – deciding which learners might require language courses or choosing those most likely to succeed. They may also be used to inform **placement** decisions: decisions about which of the available classes best matches each learner's needs. During a course, achievement assessments (as **progress** tests) might be used to gauge the ongoing improvement made by learners. At the end of a course (as **exit** tests), they are often used in making pass/fail decisions or in assigning grades. In using achievement assessments, the teacher may be interested in obtaining detailed **diagnostic** information about which parts of the material the learners have taken in and which parts will need more work.

In assessing learning, a distinction is often made between more **formative** uses of assessment that immediately guide what teachers and learners will do next and more **summative** uses, which focus on a retrospective picture of what has been learnt. Another way of expressing this distinction is to call the former **assessment *for* learning** and to contrast this with **assessment *of* learning** (Black & Wiliam, 1998). In other words, in Wiggins' (1998) terms, summative assessment *audits* learning; formative assessment *informs* it.

An example of the use of formative (and diagnostic) assessment would be a teacher observing that some students are having difficulty in distinguishing between *for* and *since* when talking about time in English. The teacher might decide to intervene by asking questions and providing examples to help build their understanding of the distinction. This kind of assessment informs learning because the teacher is able to adjust the content of her classes to take account of the students' performance. The focus is on what should happen next in the classroom to bring about learning.

Task 2.2

Look at this extract from a job advertisement placed by the British government. What kind of language assessment do you think they might use in selecting suitable people for the job?

> You won't need any specific language skills for a career in the Foreign Office, although they'll certainly be an advantage in your career. Where an overseas position requires language skills you'll receive intensive tuition to get you up to the right level. So if you need to speak fluent Russian for a press and public affairs role in the British Embassy, Moscow, we'll make sure that the full-time language training is in place for you.

An example of a more summative assessment would be an end-of-year test based on the topics taught during the year. The test audits learning by providing evidence of what the students have learnt and how well they have met the course objectives. The focus is on finding out how much learning has happened. Like the formative assessment described previously, such a test might include questions dealing with specific points of grammar, such as the *for/since* distinction found in the diagnostic test; but the results may not be available until the school year has finished and there is no immediate opportunity to work on improving performance as all the students have left. In this case, the results might be used for programme **evaluation** or judgements about the effectiveness of the language course rather than on the abilities of individual learners.

Assessment and learner motivation

Gaining an awareness of how well the learners are progressing is, of course, easiest when the learners are also involved and interested in the process and share their insights with their teacher. Good learners are self-regulated: they set themselves targets, think about how best to learn (trying out and evaluating new techniques), and often reflect on their own progress towards their goals. Self-assessment and peer assessment (in which learners assess their own and each other's performance) have emerged as powerful means of engaging learners in these processes and helping them to take more control of their own learning.

Of course, teaching can become more challenging when the learners do not want to learn or are unwilling to communicate. This brings us to another reason for using assessment: motivating learners. Because assessments are often associated with rewards – access to opportunities such as courses or jobs, prizes, certificates, grades, praise and attention from the teacher – they can serve as a powerful motivation for learners. However, using assessment in this way is risky and potentially very damaging. In some cases, it can even have a negative effect on a learner's motivation. The learner who repeatedly fails to gain good grades or pass tests will sooner or later become frustrated, conclude that language learning is not worth the effort and give up even trying to learn.

Formative diagnostic assessment, by providing helpful feedback (using information about performance to help learners to improve), promises to guide learners in their studies. However, for many learners, especially those in formal schooling, success on tests, especially major proficiency tests, may come to seem more important than successful communication in the language they are learning. Where this happens, the content of the test can take over from the official curriculum and learning goals that are not covered on the test may get pushed aside and ignored. Teachers may teach and students may try to learn only the material that they think will be assessed. The changes in teaching and learning that may come about in response to an upcoming test are known as **washback**, and this has emerged as an important area of language assessment research. Feedback and washback are discussed in more detail in Chapter 4.

Different worlds or shared spaces?

Educational assessment, on the one hand (particularly formative assessment), and proficiency assessment, on the other, are often seen as distinct, even incompatible areas of specialization, conducted by different people employing different techniques, informed by different theories and embracing different values. For this reason, they are often treated separately and the relationship between them ranges from mutual indifference to sometimes heated conflict. This conflict is most often played out in the field of summative assessment where the role of the teacher as the facilitator of learning (the world of formative assessment) comes up against the need to account for what has been learnt in terms of the general standards set by employers, governments or other external agencies (the worlds of summative assessment and proficiency assessment).

Although the differences between what teachers do in the classroom and large-scale testing are important, there is also a good deal in common between them. To be effective, both depend above all on well-crafted questions or other techniques that will provide useful evidence of learners' abilities. Task types used in large-scale tests can be adapted for use in the classroom while innovative ideas first tried out in class can find their way into more formal assessments. Both classroom assessments and large-scale tests can be improved by careful and critical review and through experience. The results from an assessment given on one occasion inevitably point to improvements to be made the next time it is used. Achieving good quality in both requires collective and systematic effort. Ways of checking and improving language assessments are described in Chapters 3 and 4.

Perhaps the strongest argument for treating assessment in the classroom and in the examination hall in the same book is that in a healthy educational system, both should work together. If teachers understand how tests work, they will be more effective at preparing their students to take examinations. On the other hand, as Alderson (1999) remarked, testing is too important to be left to testers. It is essential that educational tests should reflect the curriculum and the needs and interests of learners. Teachers are familiar with their learners and with the reality of how the curriculum is delivered in practice. They are therefore well placed to judge the content of tests and to hold the test makers to account.

3 The practice of language assessment

Building quality systems for language assessment

Personal reflection

Would you buy this car?

> The engine is uneconomical, and running costs are surprisingly high for such a cheap car. Safety and security are poor and drivers report frequent mechanical problems.

Does this seem like a good hotel?

> The hotel was within an easy walk to all the main tourist sites. The rooms we had were spacious and modern with free bottled water in the fridge alongside tea and coffee. Staff at the hotel were friendly and helpful. We will definitely come back again soon.

What makes a good language assessment? What facts might you want to know about a language assessment before deciding whether or not to use it in a school?

If you have taken a test recently, what was the experience like? How do you think it could have been improved?

What do you think other people expect of language assessments? Parents of students in a school? Teachers? Employers? Immigration authorities?

When we say that any product or a service is of 'good quality,' we generally mean that it consistently lives up to (or is better than) what we expect. For many people a good quality car is safe and comfortable and always starts when we want it to. A good quality hotel has clean, quiet and comfortable rooms with equipment that works well and staff who respond promptly and politely when we have a request. When thinking about buying a new product or using a new service, people often want to find out something about its quality. They may read reviews on websites or in magazines or ask their friends about it, or they may try using it for a short period to find out if they like it.

The expectations people have of any service or product will depend partly on their needs. People look for different things in a hotel depending on whether they will stay there alone on a business trip for one night or with their family on vacation for a week. Expectations are also affected by factors such as price. People don't expect five-star luxury in a cheap hotel, and they don't expect a small cheap car to go very fast or to be as smooth and comfortable as a limousine.

Similarly, it would be unrealistic to expect teachers working under strict time pressures to produce assessments with the same qualities that are demanded of tests made by large national or international testing agencies. Equally, large testing agencies can't be expected to produce assessments that take into account what an individual teacher has chosen to cover in class over the past few weeks (Gronlund, 1989). But what expectations *should* assessees, on the one hand, or users of assessment results, on the other, have of different types of assessment? And as producers of assessments, what can we do to ensure that the assessments we make are as good as they can be: that they are of high quality?

According to White (1998), ideas about quality borrowed from business management have become increasingly influential in language education. Two concepts of particular importance to language assessment are **standards** and **quality management** (Saville, 2013). Standards describe desirable characteristics of products and services such as consistency, environmental friendliness, safety and economy. When products or systems work well and safely at an economical cost, it is often because they meet predetermined standards. Quality management is a means of achieving and surpassing standards and involves continuous improvement in the effectiveness and efficiency of an organization and the processes it carries out.

This chapter will look at quality standards for language assessments and steps that can be taken to build the principle of continuous improvement into their development and ongoing use. Chapter 2 showed that the concept of assessment includes practices that are carried out to meet a very wide variety of different purposes. It is inevitable that 'high quality' should have different meanings for a classroom teacher experimenting with new approaches to formative assessment, a programme leader asked to develop achievement tests for use in a college, and a ministry of education or testing agency developing a new test for use nationwide.

Different uses of language assessments are sometimes seen to be mutually incompatible (Teasdale & Leung, 2000). Some commentators suggest that large-scale proficiency tests and classroom assessment should each be approached in a different way. The resources available in each setting, the kinds of information needed and the implications of the decisions that will be made are certainly quite different. On the other hand, assessments of all kinds are about obtaining good quality evidence of assessees' knowledge, skills or abilities. The principles presented in this chapter are based on the practical advice offered in a range of language assessment textbooks and are intended to be relevant across the broad spectrum of language assessment contexts.

Putting quality into practice in language assessment

Task 3.1

If you were asked to prepare a language assessment to use in a school, what would be your first step?

What kinds of expertise do you think you would need?

What steps could you take to make sure you produce a good quality assessment?

What factors might prevent your assessment from being as good as you would like?

Read the rest of this chapter before looking at the task commentary.

Projects to develop a new assessment, especially at the classroom or programme level, are often seen by those involved as one-off linear exercises with clear-cut beginning and end points. It is decided that an assessment is needed. The content is settled on, procedures are sketched out and the questions, or **items**, are written (often within a very tight schedule). Or perhaps a test is bought in from a publisher or other external organization. The assessment is administered to a group of learners. Scores are awarded, decisions are taken and certificates are handed out. The work is complete. Sometimes an assessment is used once and then discarded: the next time everyone starts again from the beginning. Sometimes the same assessment is used again, unchanged (even when it has obvious shortcomings).

The first of these choices is an obvious and impractical waste of resources: rather like buying a new car each time you need to travel somewhere. The second is irresponsible and potentially dangerous: like buying a new car, suspecting there is a serious problem with the brakes, but instead of taking it back to the dealer for investigation and repairs, ignoring the problem and continuing to drive around in it. Poor quality assessment practices may not cause physical injuries, but they do produce misleading results and so can have damaging **consequences** both for the assessees and for the people who use the results as a basis for decisions.

Popham (2001) argued that in addition to the familiar problems of limited resources and lack of time, many teachers suffer from a lack of assessment literacy: they have not received training in basic assessment principles and do not understand how assessment and teaching can complement each other. Coniam (2009) cited a number of shortcomings in teacher-made language assessments that could result from this lack of assessment literacy. Tests made by teachers are often too easy or too difficult for learners, fail to reflect what learners have achieved, and contain content that has not been taught or is not included on the syllabus.

Effective assessment comes at a PRICE

Not every institution has the resources to employ the full array of trained language assessment professionals listed by Buck (2009), including specialist assessment writers, psychometricians (or statisticians trained in educational measurement) and graphic designers. Nonetheless, all institutions certainly do have the capacity to improve on their current practice. Fortunately, acknowledging a few basic principles can help to develop assessment literacy and improve the quality of practice.

These principles can be summed up by the acronym *PRICE*: *Planning* and *Reflection* lead to *Improvement*, when supported by *Cooperation* and informed by *Evidence*:

- *Planning* should always be built into the development of any new project and assessments are no exception. The more thorough the plans, the better the assessment is likely to be.
- *Reflection* and review are fundamental to good quality systems. The effectiveness of planned and current materials and practices in fulfilling their purpose should constantly be questioned and evaluated.
- *Improvement* on current materials and practices is always possible and should be the constant aim of any assessment system. Reflection is directed towards making improvements.
- *Cooperation* and teamwork are essential to the development of good assessment materials and practices. Shared ideas and shared criticisms aid reflection and inform improvement.
- *Evidence* is the basis for good decision-making. Reflection based on good evidence is much more constructive than prejudiced guesswork as a means of improving quality. Effective record-keeping helps everyone involved to understand where procedures and materials could be made better. Systematic analysis informs effective improvement.

Planning, reflection and improvement

The first three PRICE principles – planning, reflection and improvement – suggest a regular *plan – do – review* schedule in which current assessments are evaluated and ideas for improvements put forward for integration within the plans for the next time the assessment will be used.

These principles do not only apply to locally developed material. Assessments that have worked well in one location with one group of learners may not work equally well in another. Material that is bought in from publishers or external agencies should be subject to the same process of critical review as locally developed material. The checklists provided in the next three chapters are intended to help in this process. The last two of the PRICE principles – cooperation and evidence – are the conditions required to make planning, reflection and improvement effective.

Personal reflection

Have you been involved in preparing or administering a test?

Were there any problems with the content of the test or with the administrative procedures?

How did you identify these problems?

Were any steps taken to fix the problems?

How could you make sure the same problem would not happen again?

Cooperation

One cause of poor assessment practices is a mistaken belief that individual expertise or experience can guarantee quality. An experienced teacher is trusted to produce and carry out assessments in a better way than a novice (although this doesn't always mean that novices will be given any help with the job!). An expert in assessment is assumed to produce better material than a teacher with no specialist training. This may seem reasonable, but even assessment materials produced by the most skilled, best-trained individuals have faults and idiosyncrasies.

Weir (1993, p. 19) stressed the point that developing assessments should be 'a group activity.' Individuals acting alone are very unlikely to be able to plan, design and put into practice a really effective assessment system. In fact, teamwork of various kinds is essential to good assessment. First, it is important at the planning stage to agree on standards that the team will work towards. If individual teachers or testers each use very different approaches either in creating assessments or in judging performance, learning can become a disjointed and confusing experience.

Davidson and Lynch (2002) argued that good assessments are developed by consensus rather than by imposition. When people combine their efforts and everyone involved has a say in the development of an assessment system, there is a much better chance that it will run successfully and that problems will be minimised. If teachers are able to work together to contribute to a shared collection or bank of assessment material, the system can become more efficient as well as more coherent and effective. The following chapters of this book suggest ways of organising and coordinating this shared activity.

Another aspect of cooperation is linked to reflection. The work of team members should be checked and repeatedly evaluated. A second opinion on assessment materials is always necessary (and having a third or fourth opinion is even better). Someone with a different point of view is often able to spot problems and errors that one writer or one scorer may have missed. Wherever possible, classroom teachers should work with their colleagues in regularly reviewing their overall approach to assessment, the specific techniques and materials they intend to use, and the decisions they make when awarding scores.

At the programme level, enough resources must be made available to allow for regular review of all assessment materials and procedures. It should also be kept in mind that effective reflection and review needs a supportive and professional environment in which criticism is objective and is not taken to be personally malicious. As one teacher involved in developing assessments said of the experience of team work: 'I . . . learnt to be open to, and . . . willing to accept group mates' criticism' (primary school teacher from Hong Kong quoted by Coniam, 2009, p. 233). Willingness to accept sincere criticism is vital to good quality assessment systems.

Personal reflection

Have you ever been involved in making changes to a teaching or assessment system?

Why was the change felt to be needed?

Did everyone affected support the change?

What kinds of evidence were used to support or oppose the arguments for change?

Collecting evidence

A very widespread shortcoming in much assessment practice is, paradoxically, that the assessment itself often goes unexamined. It is surprisingly rare for assessment users to attempt in any systematic way to find out whether the decisions taken based on assessment results were the right decisions. Precautions may be taken to guard against obvious disasters: questions that are all too difficult for the students, test papers getting lost or stolen, recording equipment breaking down; but few people or institutions seriously try to answer the important questions of whether the assessment has really provided information that is as comprehensive and useful as it could be and whether things might be done better next time:

- Were language learners really placed into the most appropriate classes on the basis of a placement test?
- Were insights from self-assessment used effectively to improve learning?
- Following a university entrance test, were the best suited people accepted onto the course?
- Were new employees hired after taking a proficiency test really able to use the foreign language to carry out their work?

Adequate answers to questions like these will only be found if evidence is collected rigorously and systemically. However, in many educational systems, apart from scores or grades, very little information of any kind is ever collected about assessments. In these circumstances, it is impossible to be confident that an assessment has provided relevant and adequate information about the assessees.

Evidence is also important at the planning stage, informing the initial design of an assessment. Proficiency assessments should be planned on the basis of evidence about how assessees may need to use the language in the world beyond the test. In assessing achievement, evidence is needed about what learners have been studying. Developers will additionally need data on a wide range of practical issues, such as how long it takes to prepare and score the kinds of tasks envisaged, how many computer workstations (or other equipment) can be made available for an assessment and so on.

As another vital source of evidence, every language assessment handbook insists that material must be tried out or trialled in some way, particularly if it is to be used in any **high-stakes** assessment: one that leads to decisions with serious consequences for the assessee. Without compromising the security of any confidential test material, assessees who are as similar as possible to those who will take the operational assessment (the one that will be used as a basis for decision-making) are given tasks that are under development. Their responses to each question are recorded and scored and the results are analysed statistically to learn whether the material is really capable of providing the kinds of information it is designed to collect. Reports about the experience collected from test takers and those involved in administering the assessment can also help in identifying problems.

Statistical analyses play a particularly important role in the practice of language assessment – particularly in support of formal testing. At least a basic understanding of statistics is needed to appreciate how tests are made and how results should be interpreted. A brief overview of key techniques and their applications can be found in the document titled *Statistical Tools* on the website that accompanies this book (www.routledge.com/cw/rial). Fuller treatments are to be found in Bachman (2004) and Green (2013).

During the initial development of an assessment, the focus is on the types of task that will be used. Does this task format work? Do the tasks elicit useful information about the assessees? The terms vary, but this trialling process is sometimes called **piloting** (Alderson, Clapham, & Wall, 1995, p. 74).

Once the system is in operation, the focus is on fresh material that will go into new **forms** of the assessment – are these particular questions good examples of the established type? Do they provide the same kind of information as the prototype tasks? This trialling process is sometimes called **pretesting** (Alderson et al., 1995, p. 74). In addition to the piloting of task types and pretesting of new material, after each administration of an operational assessment, there should always be a process of reflection or **item** and **assessment review** so that lessons can be learnt and improvements made.

When intentions are not stated or understood, procedures not consistently followed and evidence not carefully collected, it is impossible to tell just how good or bad an assessment has been at fulfilling its purpose (although experience suggests that the quality is likely to be very poor).

If nobody explains just what the assessment is supposed to measure, it is impossible to judge whether or not it has been successful in measuring or capturing anything meaningful. If nobody keeps a record of the answers that assessees gave to each question, it becomes impossible to tell whether some of the questions are problematic. If nobody provides guidance on which answers can be accepted and which are incorrect, when different people score an assessment each one may judge the same answer differently. If nobody sets out how much time each assessee should be allowed or what sources of help they can use, some may unfairly be given more time or receive more help than others. In these circumstances – in the absence of **standards for language assessment** – the results may be meaningless and so cannot be useful. Practices will certainly need improvement, but without evidence, it will not be clear how they should be improved.

The assessment cycle

When improvement is sought, assessments and assessment systems should not be seen just as products (such as test papers) or as events (such as a role plays or one-hour written examinations), or even as a series of linked events that lead to a decision about the assessee. Instead, assessments should be viewed as continuous and repeating cycles of activities. The process does not end when a decision about an assessee is made but can be modified and improved before the cycle begins again. The next time around, the quality of assessment will be better.

Task 3.2

Stages in developing and implementing an assessment

Make a list of the activities (such as preparing the assessment, taking the assessment, etc.) that might be involved in developing a language assessment system.

What documents are used to guide or record each activity?

Which people are involved in each activity?

Are all of these activities essential? Which activities would be important in developing an assessment for use in the classroom?

Compare your list with Figure 3.1.

Within the overall cycle, it is useful to identify a sequence of activities, each associated with a particular function or role. Each role may be carried out by a different person or group of people and some may even be carried out automatically by machines. On the other hand, one person or group may carry out several roles. In large-scale assessment programmes, each activity will involve detailed documentation so that different groups of individuals can coordinate their contributions.

Teachers, especially if working more or less independently on classroom assessment, will not be able to keep such extensive records, but will need to consider efficient ways of keeping track of and communicating the progress that their students are making in their learning, how well their approach has worked and how their assessments fit into an overall school programme. Breaking down the cycle into the different stages involved can help them to do this.

Figure 3.1 represents the different roles involved in the assessment cycle and the various documents used to record each stage. The roles and their associated documents are discussed in the paragraphs that follow.

Stage 1: designers, objectives and specifications

As we saw in Chapter 1, and as Hughes (2003, p. 59) insisted, 'the essential first step in assessment is to make oneself perfectly clear about what it is

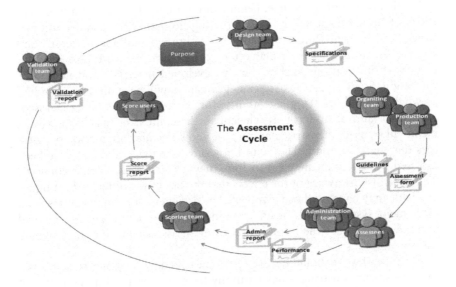

Figure 3.1 The assessment cycle: roles, responsibilities and documentation

one wants to know and for what purpose.' Fulcher (2010) compared the designer of an assessment to the architect of a house. The architect begins with an understanding of the purpose of the building that he or she is going to design, considers (among other things) the location and the available budget, and turns this into plans for the construction of the building. The architect provides detailed drawings and instructions for the builders. These plans include the materials to be used, the precise layout of the rooms and so on.

Just as the architect needs to know before beginning the design whether the building is intended as a family home or as a shopping centre, the designers of an assessment need to be clear about the decision (or decisions) the assessment is intended to inform. Many assessment projects fail before they begin because too little attention is given to what the people who will use the results to make decisions – the assessment users – really need to know about the assessees. Often at the outset, the users themselves may not be very clear about what kinds of information they really need. This reinforces the need for cooperation. The designers of the assessment will need to consult closely with the users and to be sure that they build a shared understanding of the intended purpose. From the outset, as part of the planning process, it is necessary to decide who will be involved in each stage of delivery and administration and to take account of their views in developing the assessment.

Architects do not, of course, begin from nothing. They can draw on centuries of human experience in constructing homes, offices, shops and factories, and longstanding knowledge of traditional building materials and techniques. In making their plans, they can combine the established traditions with innovations such as newly developed materials and new ideas for design. Similarly, good assessment designers will have an understanding of what they believe 'language ability' (or whatever else is being assessed) consists of and of how this is relevant to the context in which the assessment will be used, the particular purpose and particular population of assessees they have in mind. They will know how language abilities have been assessed by others in the past, or how they are assessed in other contexts. They will also be aware of the effects that the use of the different techniques available may have on those involved. The designers of formative classroom assessment systems need an understanding of how languages are learned and how best to use the information from an assessment to guide ongoing learning.

The issue of what should be assessed or measured by language assessments – the assessment **construct** – has naturally been the centre of a great deal of debate between people who favour one approach or another. Part III will look at the impact that some of the different theoretical approaches to defining constructs have had on language assessment design.

Task 3.3

Should all teachers in a school base their grades or scores on the same assessments?

Why or when might it be important to give learners the same assessment?

Why or when might it be important to have different assessments for different learners?

As one means of ensuring a coherent system with consistent results, it is important that the procedures followed in making a useful product or carrying out a project can be repeated. The steps in the process have to be recorded rigorously enough to make replication possible. This also helps in identifying the likely sources of any problems when they do occur. According to the purpose and formality of the assessment, different aspects of the content and administration may need to be more or less strictly replicable.

Standardised testing

Large-scale tests are often standardised – both the content of the test and the conditions for administration are carefully delineated and controlled so that each assessee will have the same test-taking experience. For reasons of security, the same questions can't be used every time a test is given. To avoid this, different forms (sets of assessment material that follow exactly the same design but include different content) are produced. These are intended to be similar enough to give comparable results when the assessment is given to different groups of people at different times and in different places. Assessees who score 57 percent on Form A of a test should also score very close to 57 percent on Form B. If two forms include very different material and are administered under different conditions, the results will not be directly comparable.

In many kinds of formative assessment, standardization is unnecessary and could be counterproductive as teachers may wish to adjust procedures according to the needs of their students. Nonetheless, some degree of replication is important even for informal classroom questioning and self-assessment. The successful use of formative assessment depends on embedding regular procedures in the classroom. Teachers need to have a consistent approach to questioning and feedback so that students become familiar with the techniques and understand how to benefit from them. Learners need to be trained to follow set processes if they are going to be effective at self- and peer assessment. The descriptive reporting of results needs to be carried out consistently so that users can develop a clear understanding of their meaning.

Specifications

The key document that communicates standards and guides how an assessment is to be produced, administered and replicated is known as the **specifications**. The specifications set out the plan for collecting observable evidence that will inform judgements about how much knowledge, skills or abilities a learner has, connecting theoretical understanding of language with the decision that the users will make about the assessees. Specifications typically include three elements: a **design statement**, an assessment **blueprint** and task specifications. The specifications may cover a single assessment event – e.g. a summative educational test or proficiency test – or take the form of an *assessment plan* that covers a sequence of linked events, providing a picture of the assesses' abilities that develops over time – for example, through continuous classroom assessment.

The design statement

When considering the design of a new assessment or of an approach to assessment with a school curriculum, it is important for those involved to begin by considering, discussing and collectively answering some fundamental questions:

- The purpose of the assessment: what decision needs to be taken? Who should take the decision? What effects will this decision have on the assessees and on others?
- Who will be involved in developing the assessment? In addition to the decision-makers and assessees, who else has an interest or stake in the assessment? How will their views be taken into account?

- Who will take the assessment: who will be the assessees?
- If some assessees have special requirements (e.g., deaf learners taking a speaking test, partially sighted students taking a test of reading skills), how will these be met? How will any adaptations affect the decision?
- What aspects of language (and which curriculum objectives) are relevant to the decision?
- How are these aspects of language believed to connect to the decision?
- How much information about the assessees' knowledge, skills or abilities will be needed to support the decision?
- Is an assessment the *only* way to obtain relevant information? What other sources might be used? Is another suitable assessment already available?
- Is an assessment the *most efficient* way to obtain the relevant information? Could other sources be used to supplement the assessment?
- In classroom assessment, should the focus be on the whole class or on groups of students/pairs of students/individuals? Will all students be assessed or only a subset?
- What is the best way to report the results so that they are as helpful as possible to users?
- What effects is the implementation of the assessment intended to have on teaching and learning? What unintended negative effects might it have and what will be done to prevent these?

Large-scale assessment programmes will document the answers to questions such as these in the form of what Bachman and Palmer (2010, p. 143) called a '**design statement**' and Fulcher and Davidson (2009, p. 123) called a 'statement of test purpose.' The design statement usually comes at the beginning of the specifications and sets out the designer's understanding of the purpose of the assessment: 'the decision to be made, stakeholders affected by the decision and individuals responsible for making the decisions' (Fulcher & Davidson, 2009, p. 270). It provides a definition of the assessment construct, a description of the assessees and an explanation of why the approach adopted by the designer is appropriate.

Classroom teachers will not need to publish a design statement for each assessment they use in class, but they will nonetheless need to have a clear understanding of the 'theoretical justification for the content: what theories of language and proficiency underpin the test, and why the test is the way it is' (Alderson et al., 1995, p. 10). And this is as true for other forms of assessment as it is for tests. Within teaching programmes, an explicit statement of the overall approach to assessment and its relationship to learning should be included among the key curriculum documents.

Blueprints

Just as builders need detailed plans or **blueprints** in order to construct a building, so those involved in preparing an assessment need more than a design statement if they are going to produce material that matches what the designer intended. Assessment blueprints include clear statements about 'what content is to be covered, what methods are to be used, how many papers or sections there are, how long the test takes, and so on' (Alderson et al., 1995, p. 10).

Teachers often work with blueprints that set out what kinds of assessment they may use to account for student learning over the course of a semester or term or other period of study. All tests and assessment procedures should have a clear and defensible rationale. External audiences such as administrators, parents or employers will set greater store by results if they have some understanding of how grades are arrived at. The use of consistent routine procedures in class within a coherent overall scheme for assessment can help teachers to better understand their learners' abilities and can help learners to appreciate what is expected of them and to keep track of their own progress towards longer-term goals.

Questions that should be answered in an effective blueprint include the following (Bachman & Palmer, 2010; Fulcher, 2010):

Assessment content

- How many components (sections of a test, class quizzes, homework assignments, etc.) are included?

- What is the function of each component? What knowledge, skills or abilities is it designed to assess?

- How are the components and tasks ordered?

- How many tasks are included in each component?

- How much time is allowed for the assessment? How much for each component?

- The assessment will be administered . . .:
  - How (on paper, via computer, by the teacher)?
  - When (point in the school calendar, day of the week, time of day)?
  - Where (in class, in a computer lab, in an examination hall)?

Reporting results

- How are results reported?
- If scores are awarded:
  - How many points are awarded for each component?
  - How are overall scores calculated?

- If scores are not awarded, in what form will results and feedback be provided?

- How are any pass/fail or grading decisions made?

Task 3.4

Look at this extract from public information about a test. This has elements of a test design statement and a blueprint (more information can be found on the Danish immigration service website).

Who do you think the information is intended for?

Which of the previous questions about design statements and blueprints does it answer?

What decision do you think this assessment is designed to inform?

Do you think this test is likely to provide a reasonable basis for that decision?

Is this the kind of decision that governments *should* make?

About the immigration test

You must pass the immigration test (testing your Danish language skills and your knowledge about Denmark and Danish society) unless you are a citizen of a country whose citizens are not required to take the immigration test (Australia, Canada, Israel, Japan, New Zealand, Switzerland, South Korea and the USA).

The immigration test is an oral test consisting of two parts: a language test testing your Danish language skills and a knowledge test testing your knowledge about Denmark and Danish society. The two parts of the test are taken in succession, without a break in between. You must pass both tests in order to pass the immigration test. The entire test takes approximately 30 minutes.

The test contains 70 questions: 40 questions designed to test your Danish language skills, and 30 questions about Danish society. In order to pass, you must have at least 28 correct answers in the language test and at least 21 correct answers in the knowledge test.

Please note that **all questions** in both the language and knowledge tests are asked in Danish, and that you must **answer in Danish**.

In the **language test** you must understand and answer simple questions as well as understand everyday terms and a number of standard Danish expressions:

Section 1: presentation. In section one, you will be asked to answer questions about yourself in Danish. You will be asked five questions in Danish.

Section 2: stories. In section two, you will listen to five stories in Danish. You will hear each story twice. The first time, the entire story will be played without pause. The second time, the story will be played in three parts, with a pause after each part. After each part, you will be asked one question in Danish.

Section 3: conversations. In section three, you will listen to six short conversations in Danish. You will hear each conversation twice. After each conversation, you will be asked to answer one question in Danish.

Section 4: words. In section four, you will be shown seven pictures of things and people. After each picture is shown, you will be asked to say in Danish what the picture shows. You will then be shown six pictures of people doing something. You will be asked to state what the people in the pictures are doing.

The **knowledge test** contains questions about Danish norms, values and fundamental rights, such as the principles of democracy, the personal freedom and integrity of the individual, gender equality and freedom of expression and religion.

(Further details of the knowledge test are provided on the Danish Immigration Service website.)

Tables of specification

Miller, Linn, and Gronlund (2012) suggested that a variation on the blueprint – a **table of specification** – could be a helpful tool in developing assessments to ensure that all elements are given a degree of attention that reflects their relative importance in the curriculum or in the contexts where learners will need to use the language.

In a table of specification, the knowledge, skills or abilities to be assessed can be plotted on the horizontal axis and different task types can be plotted on the vertical. When assessing achievement:

> The final distribution of items in the table of specification should reflect the emphasis given during the instruction. Objectives considered more important by the teacher should be allotted more test items. This applies not only to the items on classroom tests but also to **performance assessment** tasks. The weight given to the performance of such assessment

tasks should reflect the importance of the objective. Similarly, areas of content receiving more instruction time should be allocated more test items and assessment tasks.

(Miller et al., 2012, p. 147)

In the example provided in Table 3.1, the content of a series of assessments of speaking skills is based on the objectives of the school curriculum expressed as **Can Do statements**. These objectives include greetings, exchanging personal information and simple social interactions. Assessed tasks are carried out periodically during the course and include a range of role play tasks or simulations.

The table provides a convenient way of showing which objectives (or areas of knowledge, skill or ability) are dealt with in each assessment and identifying any gaps. Tables can be used flexibly for a variety of other purposes. For example, in a classroom assessment plan, a table could be used to map out how a series of assessments conducted over the course of a semester will assess different listening skills or, in a summative test of writing, to indicate which text types should be included.

Task and item specifications

In addition to determining what decisions need to be made; the nature of the knowledge, skills or abilities that should be assessed; and what weight

Table 3.1 An example table of specification for a sequence of assessment tasks

Objectives	Can introduce self and others	Can spell out personal details: name, address, phone number	Can make simple social plans with a friend or colleague	Can express likes and dislikes using basic expressions	Etc.
Task 1 (Week 2)	Introducing self to teacher and two student partners. (c. 5 min.)	Spelling own name, town and telephone number to partner. (c. 2 mins)			
Task 2 (Week 6)			Making plans together for the weekend – in pairs. (c. 4 mins.)		
etc.					

to give to each component of the assessment system, developers also need to select the most appropriate item and task formats to elicit evidence of the knowledge, skills or abilities that they want to investigate.

For Brown (2005), the assessment item is the basic unit of assessment, like the phoneme in phonetics or the morpheme in syntax. The item is the smallest unit that produces distinctive and meaningful information on an assessment: information that can be captured in the form of a score, rating or description of performance. An item could be anything from a single grammar question on a test or a question asked in class to an extended essay scored on a **rating scale**: *poor – moderate – good – very good – excellent*.

An assessment **task** is the means of eliciting a response from the test taker. A task may consist of a single item or several linked items (as in a reading passage accompanied by a series of questions, or an open-ended discussion rated using separate scales for *fluency*, *accuracy* and *appropriacy* – each one of these scales would be treated as a separate item).

All tasks involve some form of prompt, stimulus or **input** – such as a set of instructions and a reading passage or a recording – and an **expected response** on the part of the assessee. Following Brown and Hudson (1998), we can classify responses into three types:

1 *Selected response* involves choosing the correct answer from a set of choices, as in true/false or multiple-choice questions.

A selected response task

Look at the map and answer the following question:

The post office is located ___ the mall.

(a) next to
(b) opposite
(c) inside

2 *Constructed response* formats range from more *limited* fill-in (gap filling, table completion) and *short answer* (a phrase or sentence answering a question) responses to more *extended* performance responses (role playing, essay writing, etc.).

A (limited) constructed response task

Look at the map and answer the following question using no more than ten words:

Where is the post office located?

An extended performance task

Write a letter to a friend in Brazil to invite them for a holiday in your town. Give him or her some details about your town and what he or she can do there.

3 The distinguishing feature of *personal response* formats is that the focus is *not* on the assessee's language abilities, but on the assessee's personal reactions or feelings towards the input or task. Personal response formats are usually associated with reflective assessments such as self- or peer ratings of performance, commentaries on portfolios of work and teacher conferences.

A personal response task

Did you find the letter easy or difficult to write? Why?

How many times did you revise the letter before handing it in?

What suggestions did you receive from the teacher?

Did you try using any new words or expressions or new sentence patterns?

What did you learn from writing this letter?

Designing effective item types is an essential element in the development process. It follows that the process of building specifications is vitally important in clarifying the ideas of the assessment designer(s) and testing these against the perceptions of teachers and other users.

Task and item specifications should be comprehensive because they are intended to communicate the intentions of the test designers to the people who will put the assessment plans into action: the test writers. If test writers fail to follow the specifications, the assessment that is actually used will not be the assessment that was planned. A strong argument for including assessment writers and teachers in the development process is that this can make them intimately familiar with the philosophy and aims behind the assessment.

Reflecting different perspectives and different purposes for assessment, item and task specifications have been developed to fulfil different functions. Two approaches that have been particularly influential in language assessment involve task specifications as learning objectives and as a means of capturing important features of real-life language use.

Task specifications as learning objectives

Language teaching often involves setting objectives for learners expressed in terms of realistic tasks that a learner should be able to accomplish following instructions: *at the end of this course, learners will be able to use past tense forms to report events* (Brown & Abeywickrama, 2010; Genesee & Upshur, 1996). Task specifications can be used to make these often rather vague statements more concrete and, hence, replicable as assessment tasks.

The more detailed the specifications, the easier it is to construct items or tasks that are measuring the same thing (Davidson & Lynch, 2002, pp. 20–21) and so allow teachers to produce different forms of an assessment that will all produce reasonably equivalent results. On the other hand, very detailed specifications can become unwieldy, constraining and impractical for teachers.

Davidson and Lynch (2002) built on an approach to task specifications developed for general education by Popham (1978). In addition to a title and indications of how it connects to other related specifications, their task specification has five elements (the following is largely based on Davidson & Lynch, 2002, p. 14):

1   General description:

   • A brief statement of the behaviour or skill to be assessed, perhaps in terms of a Can Do objective such as 'Can ask for and give directions referring to a map or plan.'
   • A brief explanation of the purpose for assessing this objective (e.g., relates to Unit 3 in the Year 2 syllabus).

2   Prompt attributes:

   • A detailed description of the input given to the assessee. This might include key features of the text in a reading task, maps and instructions given to the assessee in a speaking task involving giving directions, etc.

3   Response attributes:

   • Details of how the test taker will respond to the item or task. This would indicate whether the task requires a selected, constructed or personal response and the expected extent of the response. It should also explain how the degree of success or adequacy should be judged: how the score should be decided.

4   Sample tasks:

   • These provide a model or (better) several models to illustrate the kinds of task that would match the specification. Davidson and Lynch (2002) make the point that providing a variety of sample tasks can help to reduce the risk that teaching of transferable *skills* gets reduced to the teaching of one very specific *task*: the task that always appears on the assessment.

5   Specification supplement

   • This is an open-ended element that allows the developer to add any further information that seems essential to generating suitable tasks. Davidson and Lynch (2002) suggest vocabulary lists or grammar points to be covered, or sources that could be used in finding inputs to tests of reading.

Davidson and Lynch (2002, Chapter 2) and Fulcher (2010, Chapter 5) provided detailed examples of this approach in language assessment contexts.

One attraction of this approach to task specification is the potential it offers for ordering tasks according to how well learners perform them. This is a way to integrate teaching and assessment and to motivate learners by giving them a series of meaningful and attainable targets to work towards. Curriculum objectives and assessment tasks may be linked together to form a series of structured targets for learning. These can be ordered and organised into an overall framework, such as the Canadian Language Benchmarks (Pawlikowska-Smith, 2000). The use of specifications as objectives in this kind of **mastery learning** and criticisms of the approach will be discussed in Chapter 7.

Task specifications and real world language use

Bachman and Palmer (2010) presented a much more detailed framework of language **task characteristics.** Where Davidson and Lynch's (2002) approach is primarily intended to be used within language teaching programmes for the assessment of achievement, Bachman and Palmer's is particularly relevant to proficiency assessment because it facilitates comparisons between assessment tasks and the tasks learners need to carry out in what Bachman and Palmer called the **target language use (TLU) domain.** This TLU domain refers to the **settings** beyond the language classroom where learners will use the language.

Bachman and Palmer's framework has been used to inform assessment design. Relevant TLU tasks that assessees may encounter in their future lives can be described in detail and the descriptions then used to reproduce key characteristics of these tasks in an assessment. The framework can also be used retrospectively to evaluate how closely tasks currently used in assessments resemble the tasks that assessees might need to carry out in the TLU domain. Green (2007), for example, used the framework to compare the writing tasks that students need to carry out at university when they study subjects such as business or engineering with tasks included on a test of academic writing (the International English Language Testing System – IELTS – Academic Writing component).

Bachman and Palmer (2010, pp. 66–68) proposed five sets of **task characteristics** for specification:

1   **Setting:**

- physical;
- participants;
- time of task.

2 **Rubric:**

- instructions (procedures to be followed, language used, channel of presentation – aural/written);
- structure (number, sequence, relative importance of parts/tasks);
- time allotment;
- recording method (scoring/recording/describing).

3 **Input:**

- spoken/visual/written;
- controlled/impromptu;
- length/complexity/number of speakers/live or recorded;
- topic, genre, function;
- planning time.

4 **(Expected) response:**

- length;
- selected/short answer/extended response;
- form (language/non-language, interactive/monologic);
- text type/genre;
- functions;
- linguistic features (vocabulary, phonology, grammar, discourse);
- purpose.

5 **Relationship between input and response:**

- reactivity: degree of reciprocity/interaction involved;
- scope: amount and range of input to be processed in order to respond;
- directness: extent to which response can be made using information in input by or whether test taker must also rely on contextual information/ real world knowledge.

> (Reproduced by permission of Oxford University Press from Language Assessment in Practice by Lyle Bachman and Adrian Palmer © Oxford University Press 2010, p. 66.)

The characteristics of the **setting** include the *physical characteristics* of the setting for performing the task (the location, noise level, temperature, seating arrangements, lighting, materials provided), the *participants* involved (assessee, interviewer, etc.) and the *time* when the task is carried out.

The characteristics of the **rubric** refer to a range of practical issues. These include *task instructions* (explaining the task, telling the test taker what to do, procedures for administering the assessment: these are largely implicit in TLU tasks). Instructions on assessments should be readily comprehensible to the assessees. The *structure* refers to the place of each task in the structure of the test (or sequence of activities). The rubric also covers the *time allotment* or duration of the task and the *recording method*: procedures for scoring, describing or evaluating the performance. These include the criteria used for judging correctness and the people who will make these judgements.

The characteristics of the **input** refer to the material that the test taker is expected to process and then respond to (e.g., a reading text or recording for listening, an essay question, a picture to describe orally). These are similar to the *prompt attributes* in Davidson and Lynch's 2002 specifications. Bachman and Palmer (2010) listed a range of parameters that could be specified under the headings of *format* (including characteristics such as the *form* of the input – is it presented through language or through pictures sounds, etc.; *language* – if the input is presented through language, is this the assessee's native language or the language being assessed, or both; and the extent or *length/time* of the input), *language characteristics* (i.e., the grammatical, textual and pragmatic characteristics of the input) and the *topical characteristics* (the nature of the topic: personal, technical, cultural, etc.).

The characteristics of the **expected response** (raising a hand, ticking a box, presenting a written argument, describing a picture to the teacher). These are similar to the *response attributes* in Davidson and Lynch's (2002) specifications. Responses may be selected or constructed and limited or extended and can be classified in similar ways to inputs in terms of form, language and topical content.

The **relationship between input and response** may involve different levels of *reactivity*. Reading is typically a *non-reciprocal* task as the reader's understanding of a text does not affect the input. A conversation, in contrast, is *reciprocal* as one person's contributions influence what the other people say. A conversation or interview may also be *adaptive* or adjusted to suit the level of one or more of the participants as this becomes clearer. In an interview test, a confident response from the assessee may influence the assessor to follow up with a more difficult question, while an unsure response or silence might be followed by an easier question. The *scope* of the relationship between input and response may be *broad* (the response draws on all or most of the input: e.g., a question calls for a summary of a reading text) or *narrow* (the response only refers to a small part of the input or the input itself is only very short: a question covers just one point of detail in the text). The relationship may be *direct* (the response is closely based on the input: the content of a picture is described in detail) or *indirect* (the input is only indirectly related to the response: the picture is used as a starting point in talking about a related theme).

Comprehensive task specifications of this kind can also be used as a basis for relating assessments to wider frameworks and systems of levels. For example, specification 'grids' resembling Bachman and Palmer's framework have been produced for use in relating test content and procedures to the Common European Framework of Reference for Languages (CEFR). They can be found as Appendices B1 (Reading and Listening) and B2 (Writing and Speaking) of the *Manual for Relating Language Examinations to the Common European Framework of Reference for Languages*, freely available from the Council of Europe website www.coe.int.

Summary: specifications as tools for communication

Although their primary purpose is internal to an assessment programme – to make replication possible and promote consistency in the way that assessments are developed and conducted – Alderson et al. (1995) suggested that different versions of the specifications may be used to communicate more widely about relevant aspects of an assessment or assessment scheme. Whether for large-scale tests or for classroom assessments, simplified selections from the blueprint and task specifications, together with sample items, can be used to help to familiarise assessees and teachers with the kinds of tasks they will encounter and to inform them about what knowledge, skills or abilities are being assessed. A version of the design statement can provide users of assessment results with a fuller picture of the intended meaning of scores and grades.

Specifications reflect planning and guide the work of test writers. They provide an explicit basis for judgements about how well assessment materials correspond to the developers' intentions. Specifications promote cooperation because they force developers to be explicit about the purpose and content of their assessments. They provide a focus for discussion and debate both during the development process and during regular reviews. Ideas for improvement lead, in turn, to revision of the specifications. Chapters 5 and 6 will look at task design for different language skills and explore in more detail features of tasks and items that can be specified.

Stage 2: producers and assessment forms

Personal reflection

Have you ever taken an assessment and found a mistake in one of the questions? What was done about the mistake? Were scores changed when the mistake was found?

What steps could teachers take to detect and prevent problems in assessments before giving them to students?

Item writing and review

Specifications are invaluable in setting out what is to be assessed and how the assessment should be conducted, but well-crafted specifications alone will not ensure that assessment material will be of good quality.

Even though they are mass produced to the same design, it would be unthinkable to sell machines like cars to the public unless they had been thoroughly inspected and tested in the factory and found to be free of defects and working satisfactorily. If a problem is found before a new car is sent out for sale, a component can easily be replaced or a few adjustments made and the customer will receive a properly functioning vehicle. Inspection is also helpful during the working life of a car to ensure that it continues to work safely and efficiently. Regular inspections of safety features such as tyres, brakes and windscreen wipers are carried out by the governments of many countries and dramatically reduce road accidents.

This contrasts with the situation for most of the tests in use in schools around the world. It is probably fair to say that faulty tests are the norm. Experience shows that when it is checked, even following careful review, some test material simply does not work. In other words, it is not good enough to give test users the information that they need. Inspection and adjustment at every stage are essential to the production and ongoing operation of quality assessment materials and processes.

Like the overall development process, the routine production of assessments can be viewed as a cycle with a series of stages (see Figure 3.2).

Figure 3.2 The assessment production cycle

Item writing, or turning specifications into working assessments, is 'a unique skill that must be learned and practised' (Downing, 2006, p. 11). Training and experience are both helpful. Research into item writing for tests by Green and Hawkey (2012) and Kim et al. (2010, p. 161) has revealed how item development can be 'both a consensus-building process within a team and an individual creative process.'

The collective aspect is vital to successful outcomes. Not every teacher is a gifted item writer, and even gifted item writers who have been well trained can produce flawed material. Like cooks working from the same recipe, individual item writers can work conscientiously from the same specifications but produce very different results. Other people who have not been involved in writing the material are often able to spot errors or notice that a certain activity is unlikely to provide the kinds of information that it is intended to collect.

All material should pass through at least one round of item review (or item moderation, as it is sometimes called) before it is used in earnest. In a review, a team (that may include assessment developers, item writers and other educators) attempts the tasks, looks at the material and considers how well it matches the specifications, identifying problems and suggesting changes. If formal reviews are not always feasible, as in many classroom settings, it should at least be possible for teachers to exchange materials with colleagues and offer each other comments and suggestions for improvement. Chapters 5 and 6 provide checklists that can be used (together with the assessment specifications) in reviewing assessment material.

The importance of trialling all assessment material has already been mentioned. The same general principle of trial and review applies equally both to less formal classroom procedures and to formal tests. Neither test tasks nor innovative assessment techniques are likely to work optimally the first time they are used. Assessees may find instructions difficult to follow, especially when they are unfamiliar with the format or overall approach. Tasks may prove to be much more difficult (or easier) for the assessees than expected. It can take a very long time for students to learn how to use techniques such as peer and self-assessment.

Unlike formal tests, conditions for informal assessment do not need to be standardised. Adjustments can be made as things happen. The task can be explained again, hints can be given to make the tasks easier, or the exercise can simply be abandoned and the class can do something else. On the other hand, assessments will be more effective if everyone is clear from the outset about what is expected. Based on careful reflection on the experience of using a technique, improvements can always be made. Again, this can be facilitated when others are involved. Colleagues may inspect materials and observe classes either directly or through video recordings, evaluating what they have seen and suggesting improvements.

With more formal testing, trialling becomes a more difficult challenge. When preparing tests, piloting can be carried out in one year or in one class and operational testing can take place in another, although this takes long-term planning. Security is a concern and steps such as accounting for all test materials and keeping them in secure storage must be taken to ensure that no material goes missing.

Another difficulty sometimes found with item trials is that learners do not take them as seriously as the operational test. To avoid this problem, Alderson et al. (1995) and Brown (2005) suggested that material for pretesting could be added as a 'caboose' to an operational test so that, for example, 90 questions are operational and count towards a final score and ten are pre-test items that will not be counted towards the final score. Assessees do not know which questions belong to the caboose and so take all tasks equally seriously. If there are enough assessees involved, several variations of the test can be prepared, each with a different caboose. In this way a large amount of test material can be trialled in the course of a single administration.

Although piloting and pretesting can be challenging, the difficulties are not insurmountable. Trials are vital to the quality of any kind of assessment and should always be carried out to the extent that is possible. The following suggestions are based on Alderson et al. (1995), Davidson and Lynch (2002), Hughes (2003) and Brown (2005).

Trialling test material

1   Trial substantially more material than will eventually be needed (the more material that is trialled, the greater the chances of producing enough really good material to use in the operational assessment). As a rule of thumb, it is sensible to prepare 50 percent more material than will eventually be needed.
2   Pilot or pretest the material on groups of students that are as similar as possible as the group that will take the operational assessment.
3   Record all responses and use questionnaires to collect feedback from assessees and administrators on the quality of the material.
4   Always analyse the assessment results and feedback both qualitatively and statistically: even results from a handful of learners can be revealing.
5   Review the results to identify why problems might have occurred.
6   Choose only the best material for the operational assessment; return other material to writers for improvement or discard it.
7   If changes are made as a result of a review, always pilot the material again before using it in an operational assessment.

If trialling shows that assessment material meets quality standards, it can be passed as fit for use. It can then be compiled, following the assessment blue-print, into an operational or 'live' form of the assessment. But accepting the material for use on one occasion does not imply that it will always remain equally useful. Over time, circumstances change and material must be constantly monitored to check that it continues to be effective.

One constant concern for developers of high-stakes assessments is security. Once a task has appeared on an assessment, assessees may share details of the answers and it will lose its value as a result. If a teacher uses exactly the same writing tasks as the basis for a writing portfolio each year, students may get away with submitting copies of work done by their friends who took the course the year before.

With regular reviews, assessments evolve over time and material that matched the specifications when an assessment system was launched may no longer match the improved specifications when, after a few years, a new version of the assessment is released (Fulcher, 2010). Unlike different forms of a test, different versions are constructed to a different design (although they may appear under the same name). For example, the version of the International English Language Testing System (IELTS) used in 2010 was based on somewhat different specifications than the versions used in 2000 or 1990, but in each of these years several forms of the test appeared, and these forms were intended to produce interchangeable results.

Occasionally, material that seemed effective when it was trialled just doesn't work as well on the operational assessment. Following each administration, results should be analysed and reviewed, following similar techniques as those used for piloting and pretesting, in order to check that the material continues to function satisfactorily. Material that is not up to standard should not be included when results are calculated.

Stage 3: organisers and guidelines

As well as setting out the content of an assessment and the conditions under which it is to be administered, it is equally important to be clear about practical management issues. It must be unambiguous who is responsible for ensuring that everything runs smoothly when preparing for an assessment event as well as during and after the event.

In standardised assessments it is particularly important that every assessee gets an equivalent experience; but any assessment programme that includes more than one classroom or examination hall will be confronted with issues of comparability. Professional testing agencies devote a great deal of time, energy and paperwork to training and coordinating staff, securely transporting, storing and accounting for all test materials, configuring rooms so that test takers will not be able to see each other's work, marshalling and supervising the test takers, processing results within a set period, accommodating test takers with special needs (such as physical disabilities), anticipating and preparing for attempts to cheat and for every conceivable emergency, complaint or appeal. Procedures for addressing these kinds of logistical issues are dealt with in documents known as **guidelines for administration** or administration handbooks.

The conditions for carrying out informal assessment in the classroom do not need to be standardised. Indeed, standardising them would work against the effective use of many formative techniques. These require flexibility. Teachers may change the assessment conditions in order to adjust the difficulty of a task and reveal more about what learners are able to accomplish. On the other hand, all assessments do have logistical requirements that need to be planned for. Teachers and learners will need to be well prepared, having materials ready, anticipating and planning for possible problems, establishing clear policies to deal with them, providing timely feedback, recording any issues that occur.

Assessment procedures that involve maintaining and adding to records over time, such as learning journals and portfolios, and those that involve complex extended tasks, such as projects and presentations, require particularly careful planning. For portfolios, in addition to choices about the number and types of tasks to be entered, there are decisions to be made about the division of responsibility between students and teachers for selecting, responding to and scoring the portfolio entries.

Hamp-Lyons and Condon (2000, p. 5) argued that the greatest benefits for student learning come when students are responsible for choosing, and justifying, what goes in to their portfolios because the process of 'collection, selection and reflection' serves to raise awareness of the nature of successful performance. However, learners need to be trained to take on this level of responsibility for monitoring their own work. Especially when students first start working with portfolios, clear and frequent guidance from teachers is needed. This generally means planning and organising classes in a way that will allow the teacher to spend time with individual students or small groups for **teacher conferences** while the remaining students work on other things.

Just as it is in designing and producing materials, cooperation is helpful when organising and managing assessment. Organisers can share ideas, discuss issues and anticipate problems. Following the assessment, time should be set aside to review organizational issues as well as issues concerning the material.

Making arrangements: generic considerations for guidelines for test administration

Preparing for the test

- What would be suitable/unsuitable locations for the test?
- How should seating be arranged (distance between desks/workstations, interviewer and interviewees)?

- What audio or video equipment, recording devices, PCs, software will be used?
- What arrangements need to be made for assessees with special requirements (such as temporary or permanent disabilities)?
- Are all copies of any confidential materials stored in a secure location?
- Are all the necessary materials ready in the right quantities to be distributed to test rooms?
- Are arrangements in place for transporting materials securely (e.g., sealed packages)?
- Have suitable invigilators (proctors) and supervisors been identified and trained?

Informing the assessees

- Have the assessees been informed about the purpose and content of the test?
- Are the assessees clear about the procedures for administration?
- Where do assessees need to go on the day?
- What do they need to bring (identification/pencils/ paper)?
- What items are prohibited during the test? Where can these be stored?
- What regulations will assessees need to follow? Have they been informed of these?
- When will assessees get their results? How will they receive them?
- What are the procedures if assessees want to appeal their results?

On the day of the test: Making ready

- Has the test room been set up correctly?
- Is the room bright and heated or cooled to a comfortable temperature?
- Will all assessees be able to see a clock and the test finish time?
- Have 'Silence: test in progress' notices been posted in the area around the test room?
- Will it be impossible for assessees to read material on other assessees' desktops or workstations?
- Have any potentially helpful posters or displays been removed from the walls?
- Has all technology required for the test (PCs, recording devices, playback equipment, clocks) been checked and found to be in full working order?
- Are there enough invigilators (proctors) to supervise the assessees effectively? A minimum of two for each room?
- Have the invigilators been informed how to request assistance if needed?
- What checks are made to ensure that the test is administered and invigilated in accordance with the guidelines?
- What procedures are there to deal with staff who fail to follow the guidelines?

Generic instructions for administrators

In the test room

- Allocate the assessees to seats/workstations. Prepare a seating plan showing the name and location of every assessee. To reduce the risk of collaboration between friends, assessees should not be seated in a predictable pattern, such as alphabetical order, and should not know in advance where they will be seated.
- All toilets should be checked for crib sheets or other materials before the test. If an assessee needs to use the toilet during the test, an invigilator should make a note of the time and accompany them from the test room to the toilet door and back again. The toilet should then be checked again.
- Arrive in the test room at least 15 minutes before the test begins.
- Check the identification of each assessee and direct them to their seat.
- Remove any mobile phones, cameras or other forbidden materials from assessees.
- Switch off your own mobile phone.

The test begins

Give your full attention to invigilating the test. Do not use invigilation as a chance to catch up on your marking or reading the news.

- Unseal the package of test papers and distribute the test materials, recording the number of test papers that have been distributed.
- For computer-based assessments, assist assessees with logging into the test delivery system and entering their passwords.
- If an assessee asks for help, respond quickly, but only answer questions about procedures. Do not answer questions about the test content.
- If you suspect a test taker of cheating or other breaches of the test regulations:
    - Take immediate action to prevent a recurrence. Remove and keep any incriminating evidence such as prohibited materials. Move the assessee to another part of the room to prevent further collusion or copying.
    - Make a clear record: what did you observe? At what point in the test did it happen?
    - If the assessee's behaviour is distracting other assessees, take him/her out of the room until the situation is resolved. Call for assistance from a senior colleague.

If you do suspect cheating, be cautious. It is possible to misinterpret an assessee's behaviour and accusations of cheating can be very damaging.

- If there is an emergency such as a fire alarm:
    - Ask all assessees to stop the test and give the order to evacuate the room.
    - Record the time, leave all test materials in the room and lock the door.
    - On your return, indicate the point on the test paper where the emergency occurred, note the length of the interruption then allow the assessees to continue.
    - Revise the finish time to take account of the length of the interruption.
    - Record the details of the incident.

At the end of the test

- Do not let candidates leave the room until all the materials have been collected/everyone has logged off from the test delivery system.
- Count the papers and sort them into the order shown on the attendance register.
- Record the number of papers and check that this matches the number of papers distributed at the beginning.
- Never leave the papers unsupervised.
- Seal the papers in the envelope provided, together with the seating plan, and note the number of papers on the cover.
- Sign over test materials to the coordinator.

Stage 4: assessees and performance

The quality of any assessment very much depends on how the assessee responds to the assessment material. The assessee must be able to follow the guidelines – arriving in the right place at the right time, carrying any necessary materials – and be able to engage with the assessment format – responding (or attempting to respond) in the expected way within the allotted time.

If the assessee is absent or unaware of how he or she is expected to respond, the results will not reflect his or her true abilities and so cannot be interpreted. The question of how well responses to assessment material can represent an assessee's knowledge, skills or abilities is taken up in the discussion of **validity** in Chapter 4.

Stage 5: administrators and reports

The administrator is the person responsible for conducting and delivering the assessment. In some forms of assessment, such as teacher – student interactions and face-to-face interviews, the administrator may play an active role in delivering the input. In other cases, the administrator remains in the background as an invigilator or proctor. He makes sure everything has been prepared according to the guidelines and that any equipment is working. He distributes and collects assessment materials, supervises the assessees and controls the timing.

The administrator of a formal test will be responsible for confirming that everything was carried out in line with the guidelines, recording seating plans and noting start and finish times, numbers of papers distributed and collected, and details of any problems that cropped up such as malfunctioning equipment, incidents of misbehaviour or suspected copying. This kind of information will be crucial if assessees want to appeal against their result or if someone is later accused of cheating.

Naturally, the more official the assessment, the more formal the administrator's report will need to be. Formal tests often have set forms designed for the purpose, but it is equally useful in ongoing classroom assessment to keep notes on how well everything has gone. Informal procedures such as the **observation** of students in class can be challenging to manage and teachers may need to experiment to find the most effective ways of organising activities. Keeping effective records will assist the process of reflection and improvement.

Stage 6: scorers and results

Personal reflection

What are some different ways of reporting the results of an assessment?

When you were at school, how did your teachers report on your performance in class?

If you have taken a language test recently, how were the results reported to you? Did the results help you in any way in your language learning?

Scores for each item are usually combined to represent the performance on the task and task scores are combined to show the overall quality of performance on the assessed material as a whole. The overall score may be calculated by simply adding up points awarded for each item to arrive at a total or **raw score** for each assessee. However, if particular emphasis is to be given to one aspect of the performance, a **weighting** may be applied. For example, O'Malley and Valdez Pierce (1996) suggested that when assessments are aggregated to arrive at an overall grade for a course, weighting should be applied to reflect the attention given to the various activities in class. The results of a speaking test scored on a five-point scale might be multiplied by four to give it similar weight to a 20-item dichotomously scored test of listening comprehension. When scoring an essay, if organization is valued more than grammar, it may be decided that ten points should be awarded for organization, but only five points for grammatical accuracy.

There are various ways of representing scores either as a proportion of the maximum possible score or in relation to how well other assessees have performed. *Percentages* (%) offer one way of placing scores from several assessments scored out of different totals onto an equal scale: the speaking test score of three out of five and listening test score of 12 out of 20 would both become 60 percent, which makes it easier to calculate aggregated totals that give similar weight to different assessments.

A *percentile* rank score, on the other hand, is a more sophisticated variant on the rankings used by some teachers to place all students in order from 'top of the class' to 'bottom of the class.' It shows the percentage of assessees who scored lower than the assessee in question: a percentile score of 95 or greater shows that her score is among the top five percent of learners taking the assessment, while a percentile rank of ten would mean she scored higher than ten percent and lower or equal to 90 percent of them. Percentiles are often reported for large-scale national or international tests in comparing the performance of different groups. *Standardised scores* such as *z*-scores and *t*-scores combine aspects of proportions and ranks to show how well an assessee has performed in comparison with the average. Details of how overall scores are calculated and used can be found in Bachman (2004) and Green (2013).

Anyone who has grappled with a piece of student work knows that scoring is rarely quite as simple as it first appears. Even for selected response items with dichotomous scoring – where assessees just tick a box or choose a letter to indicate their answer and the **scorer** compares these against the **answer key** or list of correct responses – decisions will need to be taken and mistakes will inevitably be made.

Answer papers may be filled out incorrectly – assessees sometimes choose two answers where only one is called for; or they choose the correct answer to Question 30, but mistakenly mark their choice next to Question 31 on the answer paper. The American presidential election in the year 2000 illustrated in dramatic fashion that computer technology does not eliminate this kind of problem. In the state of Florida, the voting system required voters to mark their choices on paper forms. The forms were then read by computers, which counted the votes automatically. Many voters had difficulty understanding the rather complex method for marking their choices and, as a result, unusually large numbers of votes were ambiguous and could not be counted. The confusion may even have affected the result of the national election, handing victory to the Republican George Bush rather than his Democrat rival, Al Gore.

The consequences are not usually so momentous, but errors in reading answer papers and totting up scores are a regular problem. Even when the assessees fill in the answer papers correctly, humans get tired and misread answers. Mechanical scanners have to be carefully programmed. If they are oversensitive they will register smudges on an answer sheet as the intended response. If they are not sensitive enough, they will fail to register some responses. Mistakes of this kind distort the picture that an assessment can give of an assessee's true level of ability. Classroom teachers are sometimes (but not always) able to pick up mistakes and can ask students what answer they intended to give, but scorers working on external tests do not have the same flexibility.

Seven ways to reduce scoring errors

1   Instructions to assessees and scorers are fool proof:

- Give explicit, unambiguous instructions and provide examples showing how responses should be made. In the classroom, teachers should aim to use simple and consistent verbal instructions. All test instructions should be trialled and standardised (always use the same instructions for a given task type).
- Avoid complexities such as asking assessees to copy their answers from a question paper to an answer sheet as this introduces an opportunity for errors to occur.

2   Assessees have opportunities to review and confirm their responses before moving on:

- Computer-based assessments should make it very clear to assessees whether or not they will have a chance to navigate back to revise their answers.

3   Answer papers and answer keys are simple and clearly laid out:

- The layout of the test material should make the responses easy to see and score. For example, answers to gap fill items should be written at the edge of the page, not embedded in the text where they are harder for scorers to find.

4   Instructions, answer papers and keys are discussed and trialled with the people who will have to use them:

- Computer-based assessments should go through extensive usability testing to ensure that assessees find the interface easy to navigate.

5 Scorers follow standard rules for the treatment of ambiguous responses (such as the selection of two options):

  • There need to be clear procedures for the treatment of any ambiguous responses so that scorers make consistent decisions.

6 Answer papers are marked independently by two people and disagreements investigated:

  • At least a proportion of the responses should be scored by two people so that it can be established whether or, rather, how often mistakes have been made and corrective action can be taken. Computer as well as human scoring should be checked. Scanners may be mis-calibrated, scoring keys wrongly programmed.

7 Scorers are supervised and monitored:

  • Mistakes should be identified and dealt with as early as possible.

Occasional errors are inevitable for selected response item types, but the more open-ended the response, the greater is the scope for variability in scoring. Even single word response items pose numerous problems – see Task 3.5. Issues connected with scoring extended performance responses are dealt with in Chapter 6.

Task 3.5

As an example of the issues involved in productive response items, look at this apparently simple one word gap-fill item:

  Can you help me to ___ a new jacket for the awards ceremony?

What issues does this present for scorers?

1 Here the answer intended by the item writer was *choose*, but you can probably think of many other words that could fill the gap: *select*, *pick*, *find*, *get*, *make*, *buy* or *design*, etc. Although the task instructions might call for a single word answer, how should a correct multiword answer such as '*pick out*' be treated? This would break the rules set by the designers, but would be evidence of knowledge of vocabulary: the intended focus of the item. Spelling and typing

errors raise further issues: should correct spelling be required? Is *'choos'* acceptable? Or *'chuze'*? How about *'chose'* or *'choice'*? How should scorers deal with barely legible handwriting?

2   If the intention of the item is to test knowledge of the word *'choose,'* could you design a limited response item that would not have the same problems?

Whenever more than one person is involved in scoring, they should never have to fall back on their 'common sense' to make judgements. When items are piloted or pretested, the scorers should agree on a list of acceptable responses and include this in the answer key. Where possible, scoring should be carried out collectively by all of the scorers so that any issues that arise can be discussed and decisions recorded on a shared list for future reference. If the assessment is delivered and scored by computer, all responses can be collated and the list of all possible answers reviewed by the scorers. Answer keys can be adjusted as necessary before the final scores are calculated and reported.

Although numeric total scores and letter grades are relatively easy to generate, they do not have great formative value because they do not, by themselves, provide any information about how performance could be improved. Within a teaching programme, decisions on procedures for aggregating scores and arriving at final grades should be made collectively so that everyone involved is as clear as possible on their meaning. It is also beneficial if teachers sometimes score work by students in classes other than the ones they teach and discuss any disagreements. This helps to promote consistency and fairness across a programme and helps both teachers and students to understand the expected standards.

If all teachers use the same rating scales to judge performance – scales which define and communicate the meaning of scores or grades – results become easier to interpret. The provision of comments and feedback will also help students to understand how their grades have been arrived at and what they can do to improve. On the other hand, including factors other than achievement (such as improvement, effort or behaviour) in calculating student grades can confuse learners because they dilute the power of the grade as an indication of how far the learner has actually achieved the goals of the programme (Brown & Abeywickrama, 2010). For more on grading in language programmes see Brown and Abeywickrama (2010, Chapter 12) O'Malley and Valdez-Pierce (1996, pp. 29–31) and Cheng and Fox (2017, Chapter 7).

Stage 7: users and decisions

The users of assessment results base decisions about assessees on what they assume the results mean. For example, a learner finds that he doesn't know what to say when he answers the telephone in a foreign language and decides, on the basis of this self-assessment, to consult a teacher or look in a phrase book and learn some suitable gambits. A teacher observes that a student hasn't used a topic sentence to introduce the main idea of her essay and decides that the student doesn't have a good understanding of topic sentences and so plans to spend time talking about this in their next teacher conference. An employer decides that a score of at least 630 on their language test shows adequate language ability to enable a trainee to work in their international division.

To make sensible, justifiable decisions, users need to understand what the results can and cannot tell them about the assessees' abilities. Especially where users of results are people outside the school system with limited knowledge of language education, assessment developers have a responsibility to explain in straightforward terms how the results should be interpreted. The steps involved in justifying the uses of assessments are considered in Chapter 4.

All stages: validators and useful assessments

Validators are the people responsible for evaluating the overall qualities of an assessment system and suggesting ways in which it can be improved as a means of informing the decisions made by users. Validators will need to make regular reports on all aspects of the system, including recommendations for improvement. Their task is not to serve as an apologist for the assessment, defending it from criticism, but to scrutinise it for any possible shortcomings so that improvements can be made.

Every individual performing a role in the assessment cycle has some interest in fostering the quality of the system as a whole. Users need adequate and relevant information to help them arrive at good decisions. Assessees want to know that the assessment provides an accurate and fair estimate of their knowledge, skills or abilities. Test designers, producers, organisers, administrators and scorers want to know that their procedures are working effectively: that they are doing a good and effective job. In this sense, all involved have a stake in ensuring that the cycle, as a whole, is operating smoothly and in making improvements in quality wherever possible. All have a part to play as validators.

On the other hand, taking a more sceptical view, those involved in an assessment may have conflicting interests and there are often incentives for resisting change and for hiding or overlooking negative aspects. The people and organizations who produce assessments may need to present them in the best possible light in order to sell them or to persuade their employers that they are doing an excellent job. Exposing any flaws in the system may undermine these goals. Making improvements is costly, so item writers and administrators may wish to ignore minor faults to avoid additional workload and possible recriminations. Teachers may not want to devote their time to reforming familiar assessment practices. Some assessees, particularly those belonging to groups that tend to do well in the current system, may not wish to see changes introduced, even if these improve the quality of the assessment. Users may be looking for the cheapest and most practical ways of arriving at their decisions and may not wish to invest in more expensive alternatives even when these promise to provide more useful information.

In some educational systems there are independent organizations tasked with evaluating assessments and setting minimum quality standards. In others, there is no regulation of assessment and it is up to the stakeholders involved to decide how to judge the quality of the available alternatives, perhaps consulting independent reviewers to help them. Professional organizations such as the International Language Testing Association (ILTA) and the European Association for Language Testing and Assessment (EALTA) have published quality standards to support those who want to promote good practice (see Chapter 7).

The job of evaluating and improving an assessment is ultimately shared between those involved in developing and using assessment information. It is another reflective and cooperative enterprise involving a range of stakeholders. Working cooperatively to agreed principles helps to keep the process transparent and honest. The next chapter will look in more detail at the qualities on which assessments can be judged.

Summary: stages of the assessment cycle

Table 3.2 Stages of the assessment cycle

Role	Documentation: output	Function
Designer	Specifications: • design statement • blueprint • task specifications	According to the purpose of the assessment, sets out what knowledge, skills or abilities will be assessed, how this should be done, and the intended effects of using the assessment.
Producer	Assessment form/ scoring procedures	Follows the specifications to create an assessment form and appropriate scoring procedures.
Organiser	Administrative guidelines/assessment procedures	Decides how the assessment should be managed and conducted, sets this out in the form of guidelines that need to be consistent with the specifications.

Role	Documentation: output	Function
Administrator	Administration report	Conducts the assessment according to the guidelines and produces a report on the assessment event.
Assessee	Performance/script	Responds to the assessment form to produce a performance or script that can be described, evaluated or scored.
Scorer	Score/grade/report	Describes or judges the performance or script by comparing the assessee's response with the key or other scoring instrument, such as a checklist or rating scale.
User	Decision	Interprets the score as a basis for a decision involving the assessee's knowledge, skills or abilities.
Validator	Review	Reports critically on the qualities of the assessment as a basis for informing the user's decision. Recommends improvements for future cycles.

Examples of how these roles are performed in three different kinds of assessment are given in the document *Illustrative Assessment Cycles* on the website for this volume (www.routledge.com/cw/rial).

4 The qualities of effective assessment systems

The last chapter looked at the steps that developers can take to embed continuous improvement within their assessment procedures. This chapter examines in more detail the qualities of a good system of assessment: the characteristics that users look for when choosing assessments or that educators look for when evaluating an assessment system – in other words, the characteristics that make the assessment **useful**.

Four qualities of useful assessments

The four elements represented in Figure 4.1 represent a broad (but by no means universal) consensus on the essential qualities that make up useful language assessment systems. I would not wish to downplay the importance of other qualities that have been proposed such as **authenticity** (Bachman & Palmer, 1996) or absence of **bias** (Kunnan, 2004), which are discussed in Chapter 7, but I would argue that they are reasonably well accounted for within this four-quality framework.

Presenting the four qualities in Figure 4.1 in the form of a cone with **practicality** at the base and beneficial consequences at the top is intended to convey something about the relationship between them. Practicality is found at the base because it is a necessary condition for all assessment. An impractical assessment will simply not survive for very long whatever its other distinctions.

Beneficial consequences that might flow from use of a language assessment are at the apex of the cone because they are the ultimate objective of any assessment system. These hoped-for consequences may include teaching and learning becoming more effective; opportunities opening up for language learners; and employers finding suitably qualified staff to carry out linguistically demanding tasks. Their position in Figure 4.1 reflects that they are supported by the other qualities. Beneficial consequences are not guaranteed by the presence of the other three qualities but are very unlikely to follow if an assessment system lacks practicality, **reliability** and validity.

Movement up the cone also represents increasing controversy. Judging the practicality of an assessment system is a relatively straightforward matter. Its validity and consequences will be much more open to dispute.

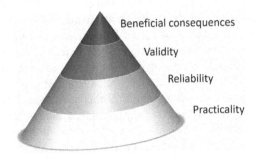

Figure 4.1 Four qualities of useful assessments

Practicality

Personal reflection

If you have ever prepared or administered an assessment, what practical problems did you face?

How did you cope with those problems?

What do you think are the biggest practical problems facing the developers of large-scale international tests? How are these similar or different to the problems facing teachers?

Practicality was described by Bachman and Palmer (2010, p. 262) as 'the difference between the resources that will be required in the development and use of an assessment and the resources that will be available for these activities.' It is self-evident that an assessment that lacks resources will not be sustainable. If there is not enough time, equipment, money or expertise to operate an assessment, it may never be used and certainly will not survive in use for very long.

In reality, assessment is always in competition for resources. In any language-teaching organization, informal assessment in the classroom has to compete for time and attention with other day-to-day activities, while at the more formal, summative end of the continuum, assessment has to compete for funding with libraries, computers, software, teacher salaries and all the other essential requirements of a functioning school, college or national education system. Where quality assessment is made a priority, resources can often be found to support it.

Practicality can be thought about in terms of efficiency: the extent to which the commitment of resources to a system of assessment is justified by the benefits it brings. As in other areas of expenditure, assessment choices involve a complex balancing of benefits and costs. As Weir (1993, p. 22) put it: 'We have to be sure that the tasks we are using are the most efficient way of obtaining the information we need.' Equally, it is important to ensure that all of the activities involved in an assessment, including development, scoring, giving feedback, reporting results and monitoring quality, are taken into account and that they are carried out as efficiently as possible.

Educational managers need to weigh up the gains from investing in assessment against the other demands on their budgets. Teachers need to think about how much of the limited time they have with their students should be spent on assessment and how best to integrate and balance this with other activities. Assessment systems cannot and should not continue to be used unless a compelling case can be made that the benefits of maintaining them outweigh the costs.

Personal reflection

The place of assessment in the classroom

Add your own ideas to this list of language teacher responsibilities:

- keeping administrative records;
- planning lessons;
- being accessible and caring towards students;
- effective classroom management;
- assessing student progress and achievement.

Professional development:

- developing knowledge of the language;
- developing knowledge of teaching principles and techniques;
- making topics interesting and engaging for students.

Put the responsibilities in order of importance.

Where does assessment appear on your list?

How does assessment support or conflict with the other responsibilities?

It is not easy to find the right balance. Teachers may enthusiastically take up new ideas only to find that they cannot keep up with the additional workload. Or they may resist new forms of assessment because they worry that the new system might involve extra tasks that they cannot fit into their already busy schedules. Often managers underestimate the amount of time and the commitment of resources required to support good quality systems and so fail to invest enough. Alternatively, they may overestimate the costs, conclude that they are prohibitive and fail to invest at all.

Many assessment projects fail because planning only allows for the costs of development and not the substantial additional resources needed to keep the system going. It can be difficult to persuade managers and policy-makers that it is not enough just to be seen to have a test or assessment in place: that it is vital that it should also be useful as a basis for making informed decisions about assessees. Making it useful will mean allowing for the ongoing costs involved in maintaining, supporting and improving it. As with other areas of policy, good quality assessment often relies on energetic individuals who are prepared to argue for funding, demonstrate the value of good practice, criticise bad practice and recognise what is and is not achievable in their working context.

Table 4.1 suggests a list of illustrative practical issues that may constrain an assessment development and therefore need to be considered (Bachman & Palmer, 2010; Brown, 2005; Buck, 2009). These are organised in relation to the roles identified in Chapter 2.

Judgements about how best to allocate resources usually bring with them disagreements and political controversies. In addition to what he calls 'resource constraints' of the kind presented in Table 4.1, Buck (2009) observes that there are often additional 'system constraints' imposed by established working practices and cultural issues.

In some places performance is traditionally reported in terms of percentages, while in others, teachers tend to use letter grades. Certain approaches to assessment and certain item formats are favoured in some countries but rejected in others. Multiple choice questions and standardised examinations are well established in Turkey, for example, but are seen as controversial in the Russian Federation, where assessment by teachers using **performance assessments** is the tradition. It will generally be less contentious to go along with local expectations than to try to take a different direction.

Personal reflection

System constraints

Think about a place where you have taught or learned a language.

What do learners there expect assessments to be like?

What kinds of task do they expect to see on national tests?

What kinds of assessment do they expect from teachers?

How are scores on tests usually reported – as A/B/C grades; as percentages; as verbal descriptions?

What score or grade do learners usually have to get to pass a test or course?

Are grading policies decided nationally; by the school; by individual teachers?

Table 4.1 Practical considerations in the assessment cycle

Resource requirements	Designer	Producer	Organiser	Administrator	Assessee	Scorer	User
Number	How many designers/item writers/organisers/invigilators/interviewers/coordinators will be required? What would be the implications of reducing these numbers?				How many assessees are likely to take the assessment?	How many scorers will be required?	How many users are likely to need to see results from the assessment? How should they access the results?
Expertise	What are the necessary qualifications for each role? What training might be needed?				What do assessees need to know about the assessment in order to perform to the best of their ability? How will they be given this information?	What kinds of training will the scorers need?	What do users need to know about the assessment in order to make best use of the results? How will they be given this information?
Facilities	Where will designers and producers carry out their work?		Where will organisers carry out their work? What are the requirement for (secure) storage and transportation of materials?		Where will the assessment be administered?	Where will scorers carry out their work?	What facilities are available for users to learn more about the assessment?
Equipment	What equipment – computers, printers, telephones, – will be needed to support each role?			What equipment will be needed to deliver the assessment to the assessees? Audio/video playback/recording, computers, phones, clocks, timers?		What equipment will be needed for scorers to access the performances and record their scores/comments?	What equipment will users need, if any, to access results?
Materials	What materials – software, library resources, picture databases, stationery – will be needed to support each role?			What materials will be supplied, what will assessees need to bring to the assessment? ID card, pencil, pen etc. What materials should be forbidden?		What materials – software, library resources, picture databases, stationery – will be needed by scorers?	What materials will users need to inform them of results and how to interpret them?
Timeline	What will be the overall timeline (from start to completion) for development?	What will be the timeline for the operational assessment cycle? How often will new forms be generated? How often will the assessment be reviewed and revised?		When will the assessment be administered? Time of day, week, course, year? How often will assessments be administered?		When will scoring be carried out and when will results be released?	When will users receive the results?
Time allocation	How much time is allocated to planning, development, review, revision? How many hours are allocated to assessment development each week? How will time allocations change between the development phase and operational phase?			How much time is available for the assessment? How should this be divided among tasks and components?		How much time will be required to score the assessment?	How much time will users be expected to spend interpreting results?
Budget	What are the cost implications of the requirements? How much money is/could be made available to support the assessment?						

Advances in computer technology have made some techniques, such as controlling and timing the delivery of assessments, more practical. They have opened up opportunities to capture more kinds of data (such as how long each assessee takes to respond to each item). However, different software platforms also impose their own limitations. It will not be possible to deliver ideas for innovative task formats if the software lacks the functionality – and some techniques are actually easier to manage on paper. Problems with software or with the logistics of delivering material to large numbers of assessees by computer have put an unexpected end to many otherwise promising projects.

While it is not possible for any assessment to be reliable, valid or beneficial if it is not sufficiently practical to get off the ground, it is quite possible to have a practical assessment – one that is administratively manageable – that has very little to recommend it in terms of other qualities. In fact, such assessments are all too common. As Baker (1989, p. 4) rather cynically expressed it in relation to end-of-year examinations, 'all that is necessary is that the exam be difficult or traumatic and have some vague relationship to the course the learners have followed.' Very often, in situations where assessments are used, no information is ever collected that would allow users to tell whether they have any of the qualities that might make them useful. It seems to be enough that students answer questions and that grades or scores are awarded, even if nobody can explain what these might actually mean to learners, teachers, managers or others who may want to use the results.

Reliability

We use various tools every day to measure aspects of the world around us: clocks to measure time, scales for weight, thermometers for temperature and so on. When we use them, we want to know that we can interpret these tools consistently. If the time on your watch was sometimes the same as the clocks on the wall and sometimes very different, or if your scales told you that a bottle of water weighed 500 grams in the morning and two kilograms in the afternoon, you would reasonably conclude that they were faulty and would not trust what they told you.

Of course, many of the tools we do use every day are not very accurate, but they are good enough for our purposes. We generally get to meetings on time; we measure out ingredients and cook food at a suitable temperature. Much more precise tools are available, but there is trade-off between precision and cost. Accuracy and precision are expensive. Most people don't mind arriving a little early or late for a meeting and barely notice if the temperature in the room is one or two degrees warmer or cooler than is displayed on the thermometer.

Measurements of time, temperature or weight involve tangible quantities that most people do not find controversial. Language ability is a much more slippery and less certain concept and this makes it more difficult to define and measure. In most approaches to language assessment, it is assumed that language abilities represent a kind of mental trait or attribute, similar to physical traits such as height or weight. We often describe people as having more or less language ability in rather the same way as we describe them as being tall or short.

Anyone comparing fluent speakers with learners just beginning to grapple with a language may have little difficulty in accepting this idea. On the other hand, all language learners know that they are better at coping with some situations than others. Those who have studied a language as an academic subject to a high level often struggle to communicate when they first travel to a country where that language is spoken. Those who learn a language in the country, becoming fluent through interactions with friends and neighbours, may have more difficulty with formal written language. In these circumstances, it is more difficult to judge reliably who has the greater 'language ability.'

For this reason, it may make more sense to conceive of – and attempt to measure – many different kinds of language ability, depending on the social purpose for which the language will be used. The development of separate assessments of different language skills with one score for listening and another for speaking reflects this point of view. There has also been ongoing interest in assessing languages for business or for medical or academic or other *specific purposes* (Knoch & McQueen, 2019).

Because the definition of language abilities goes well beyond questions of reliability, we will come back to it later in the chapter (see Validity on p. 75). The important point here is that we are simply not in a position to measure hard-to-define attributes like language abilities with the same precision that we can achieve for weight or temperature. Even the very best language assessments cannot come close to the consistency and accuracy of watches or scales. It is inevitable that scores on language assessments will involve substantial uncertainty or **measurement error**. The best we can do is to estimate the impact of this upon the scores we obtain, and there are established statistical tools that allow us to do just that.

Regrettably, users of assessment results often fail to understand the implications of measurement error. They often overlook or ignore it. If Student A has scored 60 points on a language test and Student B has scored 52, users may assume that this is concrete evidence that Student A has greater ability than Student B. As this section will illustrate, however, this is not necessarily a reasonable assumption at all.

There are several potential sources of measurement error and each affects the degree of confidence we can place in the accuracy of results. These sources of error include measurement using different tools, measurement on different occasions, measurement of different groups of assessees, and measurement by different individuals. If they have reasonable estimates of the amount of error, and understand how to interpret this information, users can gain a sense of how accurate scores and grades might be as indications of the assessees' abilities. Without this information, they can only guess.

Measurement using different tools (consistency)

Just as some tape measures or scales are more accurate than others, there can be little doubt that language assessments can also be more or less accurate. Also, unlike tape measures, assessments are usually more accurate along a certain limited stretch of the range of ability than at points above or below this. It is as though a tape measure could gauge distances between 40 and 60 centimetres quite precisely (56.3cm, 48.1cm), but could only provide fuzzy estimates of 'about 25cm or 30cm' or 'at least 80cm' for distances outside this range.

A complicating factor is that we have no dependable yardsticks to help us judge just how accurate our language assessments are. If our watches show different times, we can check them against a world clock on the internet. If our weighing scales disagree, we can use a standard weight to check which is accurate. Sadly, even if we manage to agree on a definition, there is no generally accepted 'gold standard' measure of language ability.

When they measure exactly the same qualities, we can translate results between different measurement scales by applying a simple calculation: kilograms to pounds in weight, Fahrenheit to Celsius in temperature. In contrast to weight or temperature, the concept of 'language ability' itself is understood in rather different ways by individual teachers or test developers. According to their beliefs and intentions, teachers may use different assessment methods in different combinations to measure abilities and arrive at grades. Translating from one perspective to another may not always be possible and this causes obvious difficulties for the users of assessment results.

Content sampling

Even where two assessments are intended to measure the same knowledge, skills or abilities; are built to exactly the same specifications; and are administered to the same people at the same time (in other words, where two forms of the same assessment are combined), there will be differences in the results. This is because each form can only deal with a very limited selection of the language to be assessed, and it is a matter of chance how far the sample that is chosen matches each learner's limited knowledge.

To illustrate sampling issues, let's say a teacher gives Class A – a group of 20 students – an informal test or quiz based on 1,000 words they are supposed to have learned. To check whether the students know the words (leaving aside the tricky question of what it actually means to 'know' a word), he could give them a quiz made up of 1,000 questions. One point is available for each correct response.

If all the students perform to the best of their ability (and manage to stay awake), this quiz would show the teacher exactly which of the words each student knows; but it would also take too much time. Mindful of the need for practicality and efficiency, the teacher might decide that a quick ten item quiz based on a random selection of the words should be enough to tell him which students now know most of the words and which do not.

Task 4.1

How many points would you think a student who knows 50 percent of the words would score? What do you think the teacher should conclude about a student who gets just two points on this quiz? How about one who scores six?

In fact (although the teacher doesn't know this), each student has learned a random selection of exactly half of the words. In this scenario, taking the quiz is rather like asking each student in the class to flip a coin ten times as each student effectively has a 50 percent chance of knowing each of the words on the quiz.

Task 4.2

Figure 4.2 Heads or tails?

Try flipping or spinning a coin ten times. Count how many times the coin lands showing one face – *heads* – and how often it lands showing the other face – *tails*. Count each *heads* as 1 point and *tails* as 0.

What was your total score?

As all the students know 50 percent of the words, you might expect most of them to get five questions right out of the ten. But if you flipped your coin ten times, it's not particularly likely that you got five heads. Only about 25 percent, or one in four people, get this result. Most people (66 percent, or two-thirds) will find they get four, five or six heads. So for most of Class A the scores of four, five or six do roughly reflect that they know about half of the words.

According to the laws of probability, however, there is a good chance that one or two students might score seven points and one or two might score three points. There is also a good chance that at least one could be very lucky (or very unlucky) in the sample of words on the quiz. There is about a 4 percent chance (just less than 1 in 20) that a student who knows just 500 of the 1,000 words would actually score eight out of ten and a similar chance that one would score two out of ten. It wouldn't be astonishing if one scored ten or zero.

Now let's imagine the teacher gives the same quiz to a second group of 20 students – Class B – but in this group each student only knows 250 of the words. Based on probability, each student in this class has roughly a 25 percent chance of success on each question, so we should expect just over half (53 percent, or 11 of the students) to score either two or three. On the other hand, we could expect four or five students to get a score of at least four out of ten and there is a fair chance that one student might be able to score six or more.

If the teacher decides to reorganise his classes on the basis of this quiz, placing those scoring three or below into a lower level and those scoring four or above into a higher-level class, we would expect to see around seven of the 40 students going into the wrong class. Even if we increase the distance in the probability of success in the different groups – let's say that in Class A+ students all know 750 words – there are still likely to be learners in Class B who will perform at least as well on the quiz as the lowest scorer in Class A+ simply because of the choice of words on the quiz.

Happily for the teacher, there are ways to improve reliability. One is to increase the number of questions. Of course, 1,000 questions would make the picture very clear; but even 100 questions would be enough to minimise the possibility that members of Class A might be confused with members of Class B: it is unlikely (but not impossible) that anybody in Class A would score less or that anybody in Class B would score more than 35 out of 100. On the other hand, taking a representative sample of the full range of language abilities is usually a much more complex proposition than the one facing this teacher. Even when every effort is made to maximise quality, precision is very difficult, time consuming and costly to achieve: chance will always play a part.

Measurement on different occasions (stability)

A problem when trying to measure people's physical characteristics like height, weight and foot size is that these can fluctuate significantly. By late evening, people may be as much as two centimetres shorter than when they wake up in the morning. Mental abilities also fluctuate, being affected by the time of day and physical conditions. Performance on tasks of all kinds is affected by alertness, health and mood. This means that even if we were able to administer identical and perfectly accurate language assessments on different occasions (without learners recalling the answers they gave the first time around), we would still see differences in the learners' scores on each occasion.

And it's not only people's abilities that change over time. If we don't very carefully control the conditions on each occasion that we administer an assessment, the experience may be very inconsistent. Uncomfortable heat and traffic noise might make the afternoon's listening test session more difficult than the morning's, when it was cool and quiet. If the teacher of Class K allows her students ten minutes longer to complete their writing assignments than was allowed for students in Class J, they may produce better work, even though they have the same level of ability in writing.

Holding conditions constant can help to make results more reliable, but it can also be very limiting. Using only strictly controlled tasks for assessment in class can rule out the use of more creative, unpredictable task types and restrict the role of the teacher to that of an invigilator: prevented from taking formative opportunities to investigate students' difficulties or to help them learn from and improve on their performance.

In reality, when tasks are used by teachers, there will inevitably be a good deal of variability in conditions. Balancing the negative effects on reliability from this variation, over the course of a few weeks or months teachers generally have numerous chances to observe what students can do. This means that they gather far more evidence of students' abilities than would be available from most tests. It has been argued that this broad sample of an assessee's abilities may offset the limited reliability of the individual assessment tasks made by teachers (Black & Wiliam, 2006).

Measurement of different individuals (test taker characteristics)

Differences in performance over time are closely related to the personal attributes of assessees – what Bachman and Palmer (2010) called test taker characteristics or **assessee characteristics**. These were divided by O'Sullivan and Green (2011) into three categories: physical/physiological, psychological and experiential (see Table 4.2).

Physical/physiological characteristics include, along with short-term illnesses and injuries, longer-term disabilities that might impact upon test performance (such as poor eyesight causing difficulties in reading the test materials) and stable biological characteristics such as gender.

Table 4.2 Characteristics of assessees (adapted from O'Sullivan & Green, 2011)

Physical/Physiological	Psychological	Experiential
	Unpredictable ↑ Short term	
Short term illness/injury	Concentration	Examination preparedness
	Emotional response	Examination experience
	Motivation	Communication experience
Age	Memory resources	TL-country residence
	Cognitive style	Topic knowledge
	Personality	Knowledge of the world
Long term disability		Education
Gender		Language background
	Systematic ↓ Long term	

Source: Adapted from *Examining Speaking: research and practice in assessing second language speaking*, pages 38–39 © Cambridge English Language Assessment 2011.

Psychological characteristics also include relatively short-term issues such as concentration and mood together with more stable characteristics such as personality type. These characteristics can play a major part in performance on assessments. For example, some individuals suffer from such debilitating anxiety when taking tests that they may be unable to participate, while others seem to respond very positively to test conditions. Every effort should be made to put assessees at their ease so that they are all able to perform to the best of their ability.

In Table 4.2, the *experiential characteristics* include language background (speakers of different languages encounter different kinds of difficulty when learning a target language) and educational experiences (such as experience of learning languages or previous practice with a certain type of assessment). General knowledge is also likely to contribute to performance. Knowing something about the topic of a recording might help an assessee to perform well on a listening test. Learners with little experience of using a language for communication will struggle to respond to a self-assessment questionnaire based on real world language use. For example, assessees will find it much easier to respond 'yes' or 'no' to a statement on a self-assessment questionnaire such as 'I can make a complaint about simple matters, for example "The light in my room doesn't work"' (Association of Language Testers in Europe, 2002) if they have experience of similar situations. Contrasting groups of assessees (e.g., men and women; adults and children) may have different amounts and different kinds of knowledge about the world.

Differences between assessees affect estimates of the reliability of measurement. When assessments are administered to more homogenous groups, they produce more reliable results. When different populations of assessees are involved with different areas of strength or weakness, it is not so straightforward to rank them and results tend to be less consistent.

In an assessment that includes the use of articles in English (*a* and *the*), for example, if all the test takers are speakers of French or Spanish (i.e., languages that have article systems), the results are likely to be more consistent than if the French and Spanish test takers are joined by speakers of Turkish and Russian (i.e., speakers of languages that do not have article systems). Generally, low-scoring French assessees may perform rather well on the questions involving articles while otherwise high-scoring Turkish assessees might perform relatively poorly on the same questions.

Some differences in performance associated with test taker characteristics may actually be relevant to the decisions that test users wish to make. For example, a Japanese learner of Chinese is likely to have an advantage over a Thai learner in a reading test because the Japanese writing system is based on Chinese characters, but the Thai is not. However, this advantage also applies in the real world. Japanese people can read and understand many signs written in Chinese without speaking the language. The test simply reflects this natural advantage.

Other characteristics may affect performance on an assessment, but not affect performance in the real world. This will distort the picture given of real world abilities. It has sometimes been found, for example, that teenage boys tend to perform a little better when grades are based on one-off tests that use multiple choice questions, while girls perform better when grades are based on regular homework exercises (Murphy, 1982). A multiple choice test may tend to advantage boys, but real life language use does not usually involve choosing answer a, b or c and so the advantage is probably just down to the test format and not relevant to the purpose of the assessment. Limiting the range of formats used for assessment to multiple choice questions may therefore introduce a small but systematic bias in favour of boys (as a group, but the advantage will not necessarily apply to every individual).

Measurement by different individuals (scorer and rater reliability)

Just as individual assessees perform inconsistently, so individual scorers may award different numbers of points to the same performance. All scoring processes involve a degree of interpretation, uncertainty and inaccuracy (see Chapter 3). However, the form of scorer reliability that attracts the most attention is **rater reliability**: when scoring involves the judgement of extended constructed responses.

If ten teachers or **raters** (as scorers of extended performance responses are known) are all asked to judge the same performance, it is extremely unlikely that they will all award it the same score. When the extent of the variation between the scores they award is at issue, this is *inter*-rater reliability. Even when the same person judges the same piece of work on two different occasions, the score awarded can change substantially. The extent of this variation is a matter of *intra*-rater reliability.

Perhaps the earliest statistical study on the inconsistencies among raters was carried out by the British statistician, Francis Edgeworth (1890). He published a short composition written in Latin and invited qualified examiners to score it on a scale of 1 to 100 as though it had been written for the

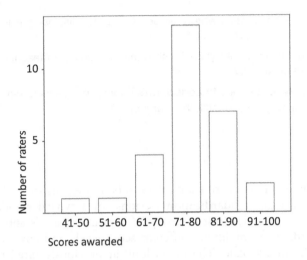

Figure 4.3 Distribution of scores awarded to a Latin composition by 28 expert raters

Source: based on figures from Edgeworth (1890)

prestigious Indian Civil Service examination. He received 28 responses. The number of scores awarded at different levels is shown in Figure 4.3. Two examiners thought the composition worthy of the full 100 marks, but one scored it as low as 45 and three others also gave it a failing score of less than 70. Edgeworth (1890, p. 653) concluded that 'I find the element of chance in these public examinations to be such that only a fraction – from a third to two thirds – of the successful candidates can be regarded as quite safe, above the danger of coming out unsuccessful if a different set of equally competent judges had happened to be appointed.' You might like to try a similar experiment to discover whether the situation has improved since 1890 (Task 4.3).

Task 4.3

(TC)

Find a copy of a foreign language writing task and a text written by a student in response to that task. You may use one from your own teaching context or from a testing organization's website.

Give these materials to as many teachers (or trainees) as you can.

Ask each teacher to read the text independently and to give it a score out of 100, with 60 as the passing score.

Have the teachers each write their score, without disclosing it to anyone else, and give it to you.

Prepare a bar chart like Figure 4.3 showing the number of teachers awarding grades at each level.

Were your results similar to Edgeworth's? If your results were better (more consistent), why do you think that happened?

Standardizing test scores

Fortunately, it is possible to train raters to be more consistent. This is usually done through **standardization** sessions. In a typical standardization session for an interview test, a group of aspiring raters is shown several video recordings exemplifying different score levels and covering the full range of the rating scale. The raters look at previously rated interviews, discuss the rating scales and criteria with the developers, and try to adjust their own interpretations of the scale until they feel they can consistently match the predetermined 'official' scores. The trainees are then asked to work independently to rate more recordings of interviews. Their ratings are compared with the official scores for these interviews. If the new raters consistently agree with the official scores, they are allowed to work as raters on the assessment. If they do not achieve consistent agreement, they are either given further training until they become consistent or they are rejected.

When scoring operational tests of writing or speaking, it is generally recommended that at least two judges should rate each performance independently (without seeing each other's scores) and their scores should be averaged. If the two scores differ by more than one band on the rating scale, a third independent rater (who does not know what scores the original raters awarded) should be used and the average of the two closest scores of the three should be treated as the final score (Luoma, 2004; Weigle, 2002).

Even where extensive training is given, over time idiosyncrasies in rating behaviour tend to recur (Lumley, 2005). Retraining should be carried out before each round of scoring and constant monitoring is needed to check that raters remain in line with the intended standard. One way to monitor raters would be to include some previously rated scripts for which official scores have been fixed and to check that the raters match the official scores on most or all of these.

The same training procedures can be used regularly to encourage teachers to grade learners against comparable standards in their classroom assessments. Of course, teachers who fail to achieve consistency cannot usually be excluded in the same way as test raters, but they can be given ongoing training.

Just as double rating should be used in large-scale testing, grading decisions should be **moderated** by other teachers to ensure fairness. Examples of written work or recordings of performances should be given to other teachers to rate (independently) against the shared criteria. Where disagreements occur, further rating should be carried out.

If a teacher is consistently harsher or more lenient in their grading decisions than his or her colleagues, grades should be adjusted accordingly before they are announced to the assessees. There are statistical techniques such as multifaceted Rasch analysis that can be used to make this kind of adjustment (see McNamara, Knoch, & Fan, 2019).

Seven ways to build reliability into assessment design

The following suggestions are based on Hughes (2003), Brown (2005) and Douglas (2010):

1   Make tasks clear and unambiguous.

> If the assessment is well laid out and clearly explained so that assessees can all see exactly what they need to do, there is a better chance that their performance will actually reflect the intended language abilities. If instructions are not clear to everyone, that is not a problem with the assessees, but with the assessment – which needs to be improved.

2   Add more tasks (or more assessments).

> If you ask one question, a weak assessee may get lucky and give a correct answer. If you ask more questions, luck will be less of a factor and a consistent picture of the assessee's abilities is more likely to emerge. The more often you observe a student during a course, the more likely it is that you will get a reasonable sense of where his or her strengths and weaknesses lie.

3   Limit the scope of what you assess.

> A grammar test with only one format will be more reliable than a test involving a range of language skills and abilities with multiple formats. However, this will also limit what can be learned about the assessee's abilities.

4   Standardise the conditions.

> Results will be more consistent if the conditions are the same for everyone. Although there may be good arguments in favour of offering choices to assessees or giving some assessees more time than others, such variations in conditions will reduce reliability.

5   Control how the assessment is scored.

> Providing clear and comprehensive answer keys, unambiguous rating scales and training for scorers or raters are all likely to lead to more consistent results.

6 Add more scorers (raters of performance).

   If two people score an assessment and the item scores are compared, errors can easily be identified and dealt with. If two scorers or raters score a performance, their disagreements can be settled through a third opinion. The outcome is much more likely to be a fair reflection of the assessee's abilities.

7 Assess learners with a wide range of ability.

   It is much easier to tell the difference between a carving made by an expert master craftsman and one made by a beginner than to choose between two pieces made by experts. In the same way, it is relatively easy to build an assessment that reliably distinguishes between very high and very low ability language users. If all the assessees are at roughly the same level, estimates of reliability are likely to be lower.

Task 4.4

Here are three situations. What problems might each cause for the reliability of the assessment results?

How could you change things to increase reliability in each case?

Are there any reasons why changes that improve reliability might not be good for the overall quality of each assessment?

1 Students are assessed on a research project they carry out outside school. The teacher lets the students choose a topic that interests them. They have to find information about the topic in the foreign language and write a report. Some students come to school from a village outside the city and have a long bus journey each day. Other students live in the city close by the school. There is a good library service at the school with internet access. The teacher scores the projects as A: excellent; B: good; C: satisfactory; or D: fail.

2 Teachers in a foreign language department develop a new test of listening which counts 25 percent of the final course grade. The test involves listening to a conversation between a guest and a hotel receptionist and filling in a form with the guest's personal details. Because there is only one form of the test, the teachers don't feel they need to produce specifications, guidelines or other extra material – just a recording and a question paper. Each teacher gives the test in class, scores the responses (out of 12 points) and reports the scores to the school.

3   During an important one hour writing test, one of the assessees faints
     and falls to the floor, knocking over his chair as he falls. The invigilators
     rush over and manage to help him out of the test room. He sits outside
     with one of the invigilators and soon feels better. After around 20 min-
     utes, he is able to return and complete the test. When the other asses-
     sees have left the room, he is allowed an extra 20 minutes to complete
     his work. The test papers are scored and results reported in the usual
     way.

Validity

It is important for all kinds of language assessment to be reliable. A learner
told by one teacher that she had clear native-like pronunciation would
feel confused and misled if her next teacher commented that that her
strong accent made her speech almost unintelligible and recommended
remedial training. An employer who recruited two trainees with identical
scores on an interview test would lose confidence in the test if one trainee
arriving for work seemed to be very fluent in the language and the other
incapable of connected speech. However, consistency of results is not a
guarantee of their quality. Experience tells us that it is possible to be consistently wrong.

Defining validity

Validity is often seen as *the* essential quality of good assessment. The
classic, century-old definition cited in language testing handbooks such
as Davies (1990), Hughes (2003) and Brown (2005) is that a test can
be considered valid when it 'really measures what it purports to measure' (McCall, 1922, p. 196). McCall went on to explain that ensuring
the validity of a test involves 'securing a close correspondence between
test results and practical life . . . test results are more comparable to life
results the more nearly the test process approaches the character of the
life process.' If the steps that the assessee has to go through to obtain a
high score on the test closely match the processes that language users go
through when carrying out tasks in real life, the assessment accurately
represents relevant features of the assessee's knowledge, skills or abilities
and so must be valid.

The connection between test and real-life abilities identified by McCall
remains central in modern ideas about validity; but his definition is now
seen to be too limited and somewhat misleading. A more current and

comprehensive definition is given in the 2014 *Standards for Educational and Psychological Testing*:

> Validity refers to the degree to which evidence and theory support the interpretations of test scores for proposed uses of tests.
>
> (American Educational Research Association et al., 2014, p. 11)

This definition is not as straightforward, but importantly it recognises that there can be no such thing as 'a valid assessment.' Validity is not properly thought of as a quality of assessments at all, but is a quality of the interpretations that users make of assessment results: these can only be considered valid for a certain purpose. The value of an assessment that is intended to inform one kind of decision and adequately 'measures what it purports to measure' for that purpose may be fatally undermined if results are interpreted to support a different kind of decision.

Task 4.5

Here is an example of a language test being interpreted to inform an employment decision. In what ways might this use of the test be valid?

A language teacher working with young children is asked to take a test in the language she teaches each year (this is a test designed for adult learners based on workplace language skills). The test is used to show that she has enough ability in the language she is teaching to continue being effective. If her score falls below a certain level, she will lose her job.

If you were asked to advise this language school on its assessment of teachers, what changes, if any, would you suggest?

Maybe change test? Not relevant to what she's teaching

A further problem with McCall's (1922) classic definition of validity is that it implies a binary yes/no kind of distinction: results are either valid or invalid. But validity is better seen as a matter of degree. Inferences may be more valid for one kind of decision or for one population of assessees than for another. It follows that when evidence shows that the inferences drawn from the results of an assessment are sufficiently valid to support a decision about one assessee on one occasion, we cannot simply assume that they will be equally valid to support similar decisions taken about different assessees or decisions taken on other occasions.

The process of collecting evidence of the validity of inferences based on assessment results is known as **validation**. Many different approaches can be taken to validation, but the approach adopted should shed light on the conclusions that we wish to make about learners when using the assessment. Ensuring that 'evidence and theory' will 'support the interpretations of test scores entailed by proposed uses of tests' must begin at the design phase. When designing an assessment, we have seen that the first step should be to define and agree on what knowledge, skills or abilities are to be assessed in order to inform decisions about the assessees.

The point has already been made that knowledge, skills and abilities cannot be directly observed and measured in the same way as physical characteristics such as height or weight. However, it is generally assumed that they can be described – either as attributes of the individual human mind or as products of human societies – and that they are variable: some people have more of these attributes and others have less. *assessments based off of what ppl have*

For the purposes of assessment, abstract conceptions of this kind are known as psychological constructs. If we make claims such as 'Your grandmother is the best cook in the neighbourhood,' we are implying that she possesses more of some underlying capacity or trait of 'cooking ability' than the rest of us. But what exactly do we mean by 'cooking ability'? Is my understanding of the concept the same as yours? How could I prove the truth of the claim that 'your grandmother is the best cook'? Is the same ability needed to prepare good Chinese food as is required to prepare good Brazilian food or good Russian food? Do savoury dishes require the same abilities as sweet dishes? By the same token, different uses of language may involve different forms of 'language ability.'

The two threats to validity

Messick (1989) argued that there are two basic threats to the validity of score interpretations. These are **construct irrelevance** (elements are involved in an assessment that are not connected to the knowledge, skills or abilities we intend to measure) and **construct under-representation** (failure to include elements on an assessment that are relevant to the knowledge, skills or abilities we intend to measure).

Construct irrelevance

During the nineteenth century a German doctor named Franz Joseph Gall founded a branch of science known as phrenology. He believed that it was possible to measure a person's mental abilities, including their capacity for learning languages, by measuring the shape of their skulls. Just as lifting heavy weights causes people's muscles to increase in size, Gall believed that someone with a gift for languages would have a well-developed language faculty in their brain. This would cause a certain region of their skull to bulge. A phrenologist's language aptitude assessment would involve making careful (and, no doubt, very reliable) measurements of the shape of a learner's head.

Disappointingly, Gall's theory proved to be mistaken. Skull shape is not connected to language ability. The phrenologist's language aptitude test would therefore be entirely construct irrelevant. The measurement would not really have any association with the ability supposedly being measured and decisions made based on the results would be unsound.

Construct under-representation

Most school language teaching programmes are intended to develop students' abilities in the traditional 'four skills' of reading, writing, listening and speaking. Unfortunately, in many school systems the assessment of speaking is believed to be unmanageable and is often excluded from achievement tests. Scores on tests based on the other three skills are taken to represent learners' overall achievement in their language studies. This means that an important component of achievement is not part of the assessment. The intended construct of language achievement in all four skill areas is under-represented. The picture users are given of a learner's achievements may, as a result, be distorted. A student with good speaking skills but poor writing would be disadvantaged; her friend who writes well but doesn't speak would be flattered by the test results.

Bachman and Palmer (2010, p. 43) suggest that designers 'need to define language ability in a way that is appropriate *for each particular assessment situation*.' Depending on the purpose for our assessment, there are many language-related constructs we might be interested in measuring. These could range from a very broadly defined 'overall language proficiency' or 'reading comprehension' to 'reading for gist,' 'reading for detail' or something as specific as the ability of a language learner to 'ask and answer questions about personal details such as where he/she lives, people he/she knows and things he/she has' (Council of Europe, 2001, p. 24). Of course, even an ability like this is likely to be affected by circumstances. Asking and answering personal questions with new classmates may feel easier or more difficult than doing something similar at a party, in a job interview or at a military checkpoint. Different kinds of validity evidence can be used to shed light on the value of assessment results. The following sections provide a brief introduction to these.

Content validity

If we are going to use the results from an assessment, we should be satisfied that performance on the assessment will really require the targeted knowledge, skills or abilities and that the balance made between components in the assessment will provide a sound basis for the specific decisions that will be made about the assessees. Ideally, the material included in an assessment should represent the full range of knowledge, skills or abilities that the assessment is intended to cover.

Unfortunately, life is not usually that simple. It really isn't possible for any assessment to cover the full range of content that it might be desirable to assess. Limitations on the time available and on the methods that it is feasible to use to administer and score the assessment mean there will always be construct under-representation. These limitations suggest that developers can generally only include a very small fraction of the range of knowledge, skills and abilities that they are interested in. Perhaps the best they can hope for, as Hughes (2003, p. 54) suggested, is to 'sample widely and unpredictably': to assess as wide a range of content as possible and to do this in an unpredictable way so that learners (and teachers) cannot foresee what is likely to be assessed and then concentrate on learning only that relatively narrow area of content.

Regrettably, sampling widely and unpredictably may have a negative effect on reliability as assessees taking different forms of the assessment will be presented with different content. Developing assessments always involves balancing considerations and making difficult choices. Bearing in mind the practical limits on how much material can or should be assessed, tasks should be carefully chosen to ensure that a sufficient range is included. Indications of how far this has been achieved serve as evidence for **content validity**.

The key sources of content validity evidence are reviews of assessment material. Content validation can and should be carried out before an assessment is put into operation through evaluation of the design statement and specifications. Experts in the knowledge, skills or abilities being assessed may be consulted on the content of the assessment. They evaluate how adequately they believe the items assess the intended knowledge, skills or abilities and how comprehensively they cover these. Once the assessment becomes operational, routine checks need to be made to ensure that the forms of the assessment have adequate content validity: does the material assess the intended constructs and reflect the specifications?

Another form of validity often mentioned in language assessment handbooks is **face validity**. This is very similar to content validity, but the judgements are made by non-experts (assessees, parents, employers). The distinction between the two therefore rests on the potentially controversial issue of who should be recognised as an 'expert' judge. Members of the stakeholder groups listed previously are not recognised by measurement specialists as experts with well-informed insights into linguistic theory. This means that <u>face validity is not regarded as a genuine source of validity evidence</u>.

In practice, the reactions of stakeholders certainly do have to be taken into account if only as system constraints (Buck, 2009) that restrict the designer's freedom of choice. If learners, employers and others do not believe that an assessment is credible – that it provides useful information – they may fail to take it seriously or reject it altogether (see Alderson et al., 1995, pp. 172–173).

Criterion-related validity

While evidence about the content of an assessment can be collected before it is ever used, other kinds of validity evidence only become available once results have been obtained from assessees. When test developers first began to talk about validity in the early years of the twentieth century, they were usually referring to the relationship between the results of their assessment and some alternative indicator of the same learners' knowledge, skills or abilities, such as teacher judgements or results from another assessment of recognised validity (a **criterion measure**). This is what would now be termed **criterion-related validity**.

An assessment is said to have criterion-related validity if the results from the assessment and from the criterion measure correspond to each other (i.e., if assessees are ranked from the highest scoring to the lowest scoring, the order will be the same on the assessment and on the criterion measure).

Two different kinds of criterion-related validity can be distinguished. One involves comparing results on the assessment being validated with other indicators of the assessee's current state of ability (test scores might be validated through comparison with teacher grades; grades from one teacher might be compared with grades awarded by others). This is known as **concurrent validity**.

Predictive validity, on the other hand, involves the comparison of assessment results with how well the assessees perform on a criterion measure sometime after the assessment has been given. This shows how useful the assessment is as a forecasting device, telling users how assessees might get along in their future roles.

Examples include validation of a proficiency test through comparing results with judgements of job performance after applicants have been accepted; the academic performance of students studying subjects in a foreign language (see, for example, Cho & Bridgeman, 2012) and validation of a placement test by comparing scores with teacher evaluations after students have spent some time in their classes (Alderson et al., 1995).

Both concurrent and predictive validity have some serious limitations. There are practical difficulties for classroom teachers, in particular, in gaining access to suitable criterion measures.

Concurrent validation is dependent on the quality of the criterion measure. Scores on different assessments may be very similar, suggesting that both are measuring the same thing, but this is no guarantee that they are both measuring the right thing. New assessments are often intended to measure rather different knowledge, skills or abilities than the old assessment, so very close matches are not really desirable. If the level of agreement is low, it is unclear whether it is the new assessment or the criterion measure that better captures the learners' abilities.

With predictive validation, the trouble is that people scoring below a certain level do not often get admitted to the course or accepted for the job to which the assessment relates. Although people achieving passing grades may perform well, there is no evidence about those who failed: perhaps they would have performed just as well (or better), given the chance.

Once accepted for a course or job, people may perform poorly for reasons unconnected to their language abilities: health, finances, family problems and so on. It is often just not possible to track the performance of learners after they have left a school. These difficulties mean that relationships between assessment results and later performance are usually found to be very weak.

Construct validity

It is a fundamental requirement for the effective operation of any assessment system that everybody involved in interpreting assessment results shares at least a basic understanding of the construct or constructs involved. It could be disastrous if a test developer built a test intended to establish whether or not a learner has the language skills necessary to hold a conversation about everyday topics such as entertainment and travel, but an employer interprets the results to mean that the learner is ready to work in a field where knowledge of specialist language is essential (as a nurse, for example, participating in surgical operations or as an air traffic controller with responsibility for the safety of passengers).

Evidence for the validity of the content of an assessment and for its relationship to criterion measures can both help to inform an overall judgement about how well an assessee's performance truly reflects their knowledge, skills or abilities and whether the information provided by the assessment is relevant and adequate to support the intended decision. Ultimately, this is evidence that the theory underpinning the assessment – the construct – provides a sound basis for the decision. *Construct validity* is therefore seen as embracing all forms of validity evidence.

One well-established approach to collecting construct validation evidence is the multi-trait, multi-method approach (Campbell & Fiske, 1959). The validator sets out to discover whether results from the assessment under investigation (*Assessment X*) are similar to results on another assessment (*Assessment Y*) that uses different task types, but addresses the same knowledge, skills or abilities (this is a variation on concurrent validity, sometimes called **convergent validity**).

At the same time, results on other assessments that use the same task types as *Assessment X* but assess different knowledge, skills or abilities should rank the assessees in a different order (**divergent validity**). An application of the multi-trait, multi-method approach in language test validation is the Bachman, Davidson, Ryan, and Choi (1995) comparison between the Cambridge First Certificate in English (FCE) and the Test of English as a Foreign Language (TOEFL®).

Over recent years, complementing statistical approaches such as multi-trait, multi-method, there has been increasing interest in other ways to explore whether the knowledge, skills or abilities that are involved when assessees tackle assessment tasks are the knowledge, skills or abilities intended by the developers. This has been called **cognitive validity** (Baxter & Glaser, 1998; Weir, 2005a). One approach to cognitive validation is to ask the assessees about how they carry out tasks. This is often done using verbal protocol methods that involve assessees reporting on how they found a correct answer or how they decided on the content and structure of an essay (see, for example, Weir, Hawkey, Green, & Devi, 2012).

Task 4.6

Because it is a skill identified with fluent readers, it is quite common for tests of *reading comprehension* to include items that involve 'guessing the meaning of a word based on the context.'
Here is an example from an assessment of English reading skills for high school students of biology:

> What is the meaning of the underlined word in this sentence: 'The rotifer's ciliated <u>trochal</u> disc is used both for locomotion and feeding'?

What does the word 'trochal' mean? Can you find the answer by looking at the context of the other words in the sentence? Here are four answer options. Do these help you to find the answer? What effect do they have on how you choose?

(a) with multiple functions
(b) located on the underside

(c)   broad and flat
(d)   resembling a wheel

How would you establish the content validity of the item? How about its cognitive validity?

It is also possible to observe how assessees perform by analysing their behaviour. Insights have been gained into how readers respond to comprehension questions by recording their eye movements and tracking where they direct their attention while they read (Paulson & Henry, 2002) or by recording each keystroke when they compose their responses to assessment tasks on a computer (Chan, 2012).

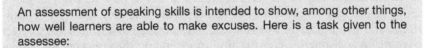

Task 4.7

An assessment of speaking skills is intended to show, among other things, how well learners are able to make excuses. Here is a task given to the assessee:

> You arranged to meet your friend, but you are late. What do you say to her?

Do you think this task will involve assessees in making excuses?

Do you think the assessee will use the same language that she would use outside the classroom?

How would you judge whether the assessee had responded appropriately?

How would you score the response if the assessee did not make an excuse?

Interpretative arguments: assessing the evidence

McNamara (2000) explains that the process of validation is now often likened to a trial in a law court. In trials in many countries, lawyers for each side in the case present a version of events and the judges or jury members make a decision about which seems more plausible. Similarly, the users of assessment results (or those holding them to account) need to weigh up the evidence and judge whether an assessment provides a suitable or adequate basis for decisions about assesses such as whether to admit them to a course, or allow them to work as a professional. Unlike in a court of law, however, the case is never considered closed: more arguments can always be made and new evidence sought. There is always scope to improve the quality of the assessment.

The process of weighing evidence can be conceived as a series of what Kane, Crooks, and Cohen (1999) call *inferential bridges*: links in a chain of argument connecting test performance with 'practical life' and so justifying (or challenging) the use of the assessment as a means of gathering evidence to support a decision. The steps or bridges in the interpretative argument are a series of claims that a test user would want to be able to make about an assessee on the basis of performance on the assessment. Ranged against these claims are credible alternative explanations for the results (or potential **rebuttals** of the claims). Test users and validators need to explore different explanations for an assessee's performance – including both those explanations that support the intended interpretation and those that do not. They collect evidence to establish whether the intended interpretation of an assessment result (e.g. the assessee is capable of writing effective academic essays in English) is justified or whether an alternative interpretation might better explain the result (e.g. the assessee paid someone else to sit the test; the assessee was able to predict the topic and memorised her essay).

Argument-based validation has been applied to a wide variety of educational and psychological assessments, but language assessment researchers have made a distinctive contribution in extending the concept. An **assessment use argument** (Chapelle, Enright, & Jamieson, 2011; Bachman & Palmer, 2010) goes beyond the interpretation of scores to include the impacts of using an assessment. The steps in an interpretive argument are set out in Table 4.3. The final step, utilization, covers the impact of using the assessment.

Assessments as maps

As tools for communicating about the world around us, assessments have been compared to maps (Henning, 1987). Like maps, different approaches and formats for assessment are suited to different purposes and must be carefully chosen. A map that is very helpful for one purpose may be quite useless for another. And an expensive, detailed map is not always the one that best suits our needs. Practical maps often have to be quite limited in size. Designers must be selective in choosing which features to display so that the map gives the user the essential information, but the paper or screen is not so overcrowded that it is difficult to read.

Clear presentation of one set of features such as roads may involve taking away other features such as hills and forests. Walking maps provide a lot of detail, but can cover only a small area (this may make it easier to follow a walking route, but more difficult to locate places of interest). Useful transport maps showing bus or train routes tell us the names of the stops, but do

Table 4.3 Inferential bridges: steps in building a validity argument for a test of language in the workplace

Inferential bridges	Claim	Comment	Some potential rebuttals
Assessment performance ⇧			
Bridge 1 **evaluation**	The performance fairly reflects the assessee's abilities.	The first inferential bridge connects the assessee's abilities to the performance on the assessment and the score (or other result) that was awarded. The quality of this link depends on considerations such as: • the assessee's willingness to perform and awareness of task requirements • the value of the tools used in scoring – scoring keys, rating scales • the qualities of the people (or machines) doing the scoring.	*High score:* The assessee cheated and paid someone to take an assessment for him/her. The scorers/raters were over generous. *Low score:* The assessee didn't understand the instructions and wrote answers in the wrong place. The scorer made a mistake in calculating the score.
Bridge 2 **generalization**	Use of different tasks or different raters would give similar results.	To cross this bridge, we must be satisfied that the scores would have been more or less the same if different tasks had been used, different people did the scoring or different people with the same level of ability had taken the assessment. This involves the reliability of the assessment.	The assessee would get a significantly different score on another form of an assessment. An assessment does not reflect the abilities intended (e.g. the tasks involve discussing topics the assessee knows nothing about, but their failure to respond is taken as evidence of a lack of language skills).
Bridge 3 **explanation**	The assessment reflects a coherent theory of language use that can account for the assessee's performance.	Connects the results of the assessment to a theory of language knowledge, skills or abilities. The theoretical basis on which the assessment has been designed.	The theory an assessment is based on has been discredited. The assessment specifications are not compatible with the theory an assessment is based on.
Bridge 4 **extrapolation**	The abilities measured by the assessment are relevant to the decision being made about the assessee and sufficient to justify that decision.	Connects the theory informing the assessment design to the decisions taken by users of the results.	The language abilities measured by an assessment used in employment selection (e.g. spoken discussion) are different to those needed in the job (e.g. mostly reading written reports and explaining them to managers in the assessees first language). The job does not actually require the use of the target language. The wrong standard has been set: applicants who pass the assessment do not have enough ability/even applicants who fail have enough ability to carry out the work.
Bridge 5 **utilization**	Use of the assessment brings about the intended benefits and minimises damaging consequences.	Links the assessment to the consequences of its use.	Many learners preparing for an assessment of spontaneous spoken language simply memorise their responses. Only wealthy people enter for an assessment because the fees are too expensive for most. People passing an assessment are subsequently unable to perform their jobs because of a lack of language skills.

Source: based on Kane et al. (1999), Chapelle et al. (2011)

not accurately represent the physical distances between them and give no information about the landscape. When we buy a map, we choose one (or a combination of different maps) that is likely to give us the information and level of detail we need and no more.

Like mapmakers working with a small screen display, assessment designers only have a limited opportunity to build up a picture of an assessee's abilities. They need to determine which features of language ability it will be most useful for the user to know about when making decisions. In assessing achievement, the focus will be on what has been taught. In assessing proficiency, it will be on the features that are essential in the real world situations where the assessees will be expected to use the language. When users come to choose a language assessment, they should be clear about the kind of picture of learner abilities they need in order to make reasonable decisions.

Maps must be regularly updated and improved to take account of changes in the landscape, new technologies and the changing needs of travellers. Similarly, we must constantly review and revise assessments to ensure that they continue to give us the right information. The work of validation never ends.

Beneficial consequences

Although maps might appear simply to be neutral descriptions of territory, they are much more than that. They can be powerful tools for control and exploitation. Some of the earliest known maps were used to plan military campaigns, fix land ownership and decide how much tax citizens should pay.

Lines and pictures drawn on maps can become new roads, cities, boundaries and barriers with dramatic transformative effects on the landscape and on people's lives. It has long been recognised that language assessments can also have powerful effects or **impacts** upon the knowledge, skills and abilities they are intended to describe or measure, on individuals (especially assessees) and on society more generally.

Assessments can be life changing. They are used in deciding who should have access to important opportunities in areas such as immigration, further education and employment. They can serve as relatively straightforward gateways to new prospects for some people and stand as impenetrable walls keeping others excluded.

Assessments promise a fairer way of making decisions than the systems of patronage and nepotism that they replaced, but their apparent neutrality can mask continuing injustice. The content, format and administration of assessments can work systematically in favour of one group of assessees and against another. The people who administer assessments and make decisions based on assessment results generally have an official status that gives them power over the assessees and it may not be easy to hold them to account if an assessment is unfair or has been poorly administered (Shohamy, 2001). A truly useful assessment is one that has more benefits than drawbacks for *everyone* involved.

Washback → targeted prep for assessment in classroom

One area of impact that is of particular concern to teachers is known as washback. Washback connects the design and use of an assessment with what teachers and learners do in the classroom when preparing for that assessment. It is often claimed that high-stakes tests, in particular, have a detrimental effect on learning as teachers focus their efforts on the content of the test at the expense of skills that are not tested.

Personal reflection

If you have ever taken a major national or international language test, like thousands of other learners, you might have adapted your learning quite substantially in order to prepare for the test.

Did you make a special effort to study more and intensify your language learning?

Did you give more attention to certain aspects of the language than before? Did you give other aspects less attention?

Did you take extra test preparation classes, look at examples of 'past papers' or try taking one or more sample tests?

What else did you do to help you achieve the score you needed?

How much do you think your changes helped you to pass the test? Did they improve your language abilities?

Do you think the effect of the test on your learning and other aspects of your life was positive, negative or a mix of positives and negatives?

Figure 4.4 sets out how washback is believed to come about. First, the way in which learners respond to an assessment has a good deal to do with the design of the assessment and the content that it covers. In preparing for an assessment, teachers and learners would naturally be expected to focus on the knowledge, skills or abilities that they believe the assessment deals with and give less attention to those that do not seem to be included. In a well-designed instructional programme, consideration is given to the relationship between what learners are intended to learn (the 'focal construct' in Figure 4.4) and the content of the assessment(s).

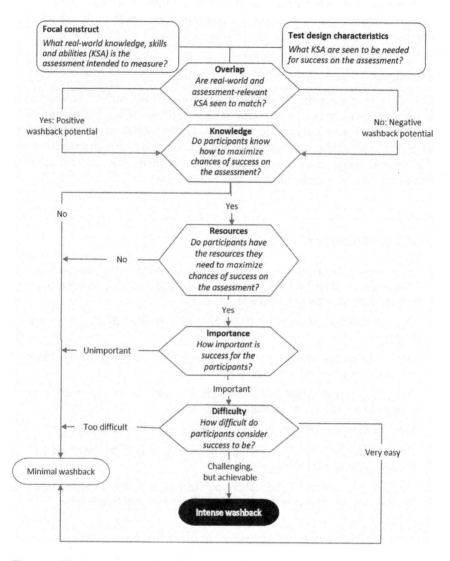

Figure 4.4 Washback causes and effects

The **overlap** shown in Figure 4.4 is closely linked to face validity (see p. 79), as it reflects the point of view of the teachers and learners preparing for the test: their perception of what is being assessed. This influences the **washback direction**, which may be seen as positive or negative. If an assessment validly measures the range of abilities that learners need to acquire, teachers should be encouraged to teach towards that assessment because learning for the assessment will also mean learning for life beyond the test: the direction of washback will be positive. If the assessment appears to cover only a limited amount of content (construct under-representation), or if it assesses abilities that are not included on the planned curriculum (construct irrelevance), teachers may stop teaching important aspects of that curriculum in order to concentrate on the features that they believe are assessed: the direction of washback will be negative.

Historically, arguments about washback have been most intense when there have been disagreements about the nature of language ability and effective language teaching. Groups arguing for a radical new approach come into conflict with assessments that are based on the established old approach. A new curriculum introduces a focus on speaking skills, for example, but the old test is still used and it does not include a component assessing speaking. Teachers feel under pressure from students and their parents to get good results on the test and so focus on the skills that are tested rather than on the speaking skills mandated in the new curriculum. The solution, it has been argued, would be to bring in a new test that does include a speaking component. This would encourage teachers to teach according to the new approach.   *teachers may not be flexible or aware*

More recently, research has highlighted a serious flaw in this line of argument. Teacher and learner behaviour are not as easy to manipulate as it suggests. First, people may not be fully aware of the changes made to the test or of its implications for teaching and learning. Second, they may not be sympathetic to the changes and may resist them. A traditional teacher may not believe that it is possible or desirable to teach speaking skills and may avoid making any changes to her practices. Her colleagues may want to teach speaking, but lack confidence in their own speaking abilities or lack the training to manage speaking activities in the classroom.

The research into washback suggests that teachers tend to pay close attention to the format of a test, rather than considering the underlying construct – the knowledge, skills or abilities targeted by the assessment. Just focussing on practice with the test format might not really help test takers to improve in the abilities being assessed (Green, 2007). A new spoken interview assessment based on personal information intended to assess impromptu conversation skills might, in practice, encourage memorization of formulaic exchanges or short memorised speeches on obscure topics, even though these may be of rather limited value outside (or even inside) the examination room (Shohamy, Donitza-Schmidt, & Ferman, 1996).

Not every learner has the same access to preparation resources: textbooks, sample papers, computers and tutors. Individuals have their own ideas about what might be effective ways of learning and of achieving success. They may or may not be persuaded by advice from testing organizations, teachers, textbook writers and others.

Washback will be more powerful where all of these stakeholders in the educational system share the same beliefs about effective test preparation and work together to achieve it. In practice, washback tends to be highly variable (see **washback variability** in the Glossary). Within a single class, one learner may radically change her language learning behaviours to prepare for a test while another makes no change at all to his.

The variability in the way that people respond to an assessment is linked to their perception of the importance and the level of challenge that the assessment represents. These factors influence the **washback intensity** that each individual experiences. Washback will not be intense – learners are not likely to change the way in which they learn in order to prepare for the assessment – if doing well doesn't really matter to them. This could be because they think success is likely to be embarrassingly easy or, on the other hand, because they think they stand no chance of getting a good score. Washback is likely to be more intense if learners do value success and think that achieving it is challenging, but realistic. In these circumstances, learners are likely to do whatever they can to prepare for the assessment. They might increase the amount of studying that they do or they might be prepared to change their study methods.

To limit the intensity of the washback from any single assessment – so that no one assessment comes to dominate teaching and learning – it may be wise for test users to base decisions on as wide a range of evidence as possible and make it very clear to the test takers that this is their policy. The strategy for improving validity advocated by Hughes (2003, p. 54) of sampling 'widely and unpredictably' is also relevant to washback as it means that learners (and teachers) cannot foresee what is likely to be assessed and so concentrate their efforts on learning only that relatively narrow area of content.

All assessments have consequences for at least one person. The impact is unlikely to be really beneficial unless the assessment is practical, reliable and valid. If the information gained from an assessment is misleading, it is likely that many of the consequences flowing from it will be damaging. That is not to say that beneficial consequences will automatically come from good assessments. Potential benefits will only be fully realised if all participants in the educational system work together.

Feedback

While washback from tests can have a powerful effect on the behaviour of teachers and learners, the consequences of formative classroom-based procedures are more immediate and potentially more far reaching. Such assessments must, of course, have practicality, reliability and validity. The scorers and users – usually the teachers and learners themselves – need a clear and accurate picture of what it is that learners are or are not able to do. This will not be possible unless the tasks and questioning techniques they use are of good quality. However, understanding something about a learner's knowledge, skills or abilities – correctly inferring what they can or cannot do – is not enough.

To be useful, the insights obtained through formative assessment procedures must inform effective action. The main priority of formative assessment is therefore the provision of feedback that encourages and promotes learning (Stobart, 2006). feedback → learning

Feedback is a metaphor based on systems engineering. It involves using information about the current state of a system to regulate and make adjustments to that system. The ancient technology of water clocks (see Figure 4.5) exploits the concept. Water passes through a gap of a fixed size at a constant rate and this fact can be used to tell the time. If water drips through a hole in the bottom of one bowl into a second bowl, the amount of water collected there shows how much time has passed. However, if the level of water in the top bowl goes up or down, the drips will flow at different speeds and the clock will become inaccurate. For the clock to work well, the water in the top bowl must be kept at a constant level.

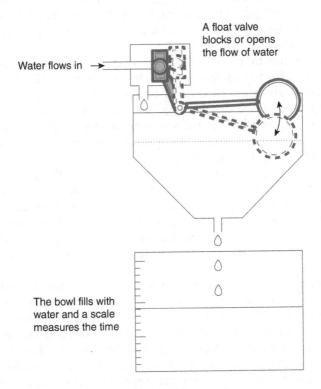

Figure 4.5 The ancient water clock: a simple feedback system

One way to solve the problem would be to employ a person to watch the system and add water when needed. But that would be very inefficient. Instead, our ancestors worked out an ingenious alternative. They put a float valve into the top bowl. If the top bowl is filled with water, the float rises and the valve blocks the inlet pipe. As the water level falls because of the dripping water, the float sinks down and the inlet pipe is unblocked, letting water through to fill the bowl. In this way, the water level is held more or less constant. The system regulates itself because information about the current state of the system is automatically used – fed back – to change the state of the system – to open or close the inlet pipe as necessary.

In a similar way, accurate information about current performance in the classroom obtained through assessment can be fed back to the teacher and learners. If learning is found to be proceeding smoothly, the class carries on as planned. If the assessment reveals that all is not going well, carefully chosen feedback can be used to trigger modifications that will keep learning moving forward efficiently – repeating, practising or revising if necessary; exploring and extending where opportunities arise. Less time is wasted because learners are not left to struggle with material they do not understand and are not held up by studying material that is already known. If no information is obtained, or if the information is of poor quality, feedback cannot be effective.

The information that teachers look for and the amount and kinds of feedback they can offer to their students to help them improve their performance will depend in large measure on their beliefs about language learning, what they accept as evidence that learning has occurred, and what they believe are the steps required to help students to make progress (Leung, 2010). The validity of a formative assessment approach is therefore closely tied to the theories of learning that support it.

Wiliam (2011) provided compelling evidence for the power of well-conceived feedback given to learners of all ages to improve learning generally and to narrow the performance gap between the higher achieving and lower achieving learners. However, he also cautioned that simply providing feedback gives no guarantee that beneficial consequences will follow and observed that some forms of feedback have actually been found to be counterproductive.

The failure of much of the feedback given by teachers to foster better learning may have a variety of causes. Wiggins (1998) suggested that students can often find the feedback they are given uninformative. It leaves them feeling that they 'know that they are close to or far from the goal, but they don't know what or where the goal is' (Wiggins, 1998, p. 47). It does not convey to the learners what a better performance would look like or what they need to change in their current performance to improve it. On the other hand, when potentially useful feedback is provided, it is often ignored by learners because it is provided at the wrong time: after the work has been completed. It has been observed that as soon as grades are awarded, many learners tend to ignore any comments from the teacher and so fail to benefit from them. *My life*

Table 4.4 lays out some of the features that have been found to characterise more and less effective feedback strategies. Effective feedback is given at a point when it can be used by learners. This means that learners should be given opportunities to improve their performance on the basis of the information they are given. Feedback is more likely to promote learning if the learners are challenged to think about ways in which their work has been successful (e.g., in communicating their intended message) and ways in which it has not been successful. They should then be able

Feedback is to be used

Table 4.4 Characteristics of effective feedback (based on Wiggins, 1998; Wiliam, 2011; Hill & McNamara, 2012)

Effective feedback	Unproductive feedback
prospective • looks forward to guide and encourage learners to reflect and take action to improve performance	retrospective • only looks back at completed performance, does not require action by the learner
directly related to learning goals • makes use of checklists or scales based on curriculum goals • learner understands the criteria	not related to learning goals • comments are inconsistent and unfocussed • learner does not grasp the criteria
continuous and timely • feedback is provided as an integral element of each unit • there are opportunities to improve before the unit ends	infrequent and delayed • comes only after the relevant unit is complete
specific • 'Successful use of linking words to connect sentences'	generic • 'Good organization'
frequent and continuous	infrequent
task referenced: descriptive of the performance not judgemental of the person • 'There are three grammatical errors in the second paragraph. Can you find them?'	person referenced: praise or criticism of the learner • 'Good job!' • 'Must try harder!'
corrective: targeted and achievable • requires action that is within scope of learner abilities • additional support (**scaffolding**) may be provided to simplify the task	excessive • asks too much of the learner in terms of difficulty or quantity

to use the insights gained through feedback to try again or to revise what they have produced.

This is one reason why advocates of assessment for learning suggest that the award of grades, which signal that a piece of work is finished, should be delayed for as long as possible and be open to modification through remedial work. Another reason is that instead of encouraging greater effort, consistently low grades can cause students to feel that they are poor learners and lose motivation while consistently high grades can encourage complacency and also lead to a reduction of effort (Wiliam, 2011).

What Hill and McNamara (2012) termed *person referenced* feedback – praise or criticism of learners – is not considered particularly valuable because it is uninformative about how performance should be modified to make it better. It is much more helpful to offer *task referenced* feedback that is concerned with the qualities of the learner's work. Brevity is favoured. One or two well-chosen observations will be more likely to bring about productive reflection than a lengthy essay or lecture from the teacher on everything that could be improved.

Feedback is more effective and the overall system of assessment more coherent if it can be demonstrated to relate to learning goals. In other words, it should be *explanatory* and *corrective* – making it as clear as possible to the learner how his or her work satisfies or fails to satisfy the criteria for competent performance and how it could be improved (Hill & McNamara, 2012). Feedback based on checklists or rating scales (provided that learners understand these) is therefore more useful than simple grades or scores.

Feedback that clearly indicates what learners can do to improve the quality of their work will be of most value. Models of successful performance can help learners to notice what is successful and unsuccessful about their own (although it should be made clear that models are not intended for direct imitation). Indeed, learners will be better placed to benefit from feedback if they can learn how to interpret the criteria and use them to assess the work of other learners and, eventually, to assess their own work.

Teachers can also benefit from receiving feedback from learners. If a class is struggling to understand a new concept, the teacher needs to know this so that he or she can provide more **scaffolding** – support that helps the learner to understand how to complete a task – or find another way to convey the ideas. When learners are already familiar with whatever is being taught, the teacher may be able to move quickly through the unit or bring in some more challenging material. If such issues are only picked up during an end of unit test, it may be too late to take action. Frequent informal assessment activities and interaction with learners can keep teachers in touch with how well learners are able to assimilate new information and help to highlight where any difficulties lie.

Task 4.8

Here are four comments a teacher has made on student essays. Look at the characteristics of effective feedback in Table 4.4.

What kind of feedback is being given in each case?

How could the comments be improved to provide more effective feedback?

1   *This is great work, well done!*
2   *In line 3, you made a mistake with your use of possessives. You wrote 'Marta is the best friend of mine' – the correct sentence is 'Marta is my best friend.'*
3   *Although your essay was generally good, I awarded you a B grade because you made a few basic mistakes.*
4   *Your essay was well organised with clear paragraphs and you made good use of examples to illustrate your ideas.*

Fostering beneficial consequences

It is clear that bringing about beneficial consequences is not simply a matter of designing better assessment tools. The nature of the washback associated with an assessment depends on the attitudes and practices of teachers, learners and other stakeholders as much as on the assessment itself. Feedback can only bring about more effective learning if teachers and learners engage and cooperate in the process. Positive assessment consequences rely on partnerships between those involved in developing an assessment, those using the results and other stakeholders. If, for example, the intention of the assessment developers is that an assessment will encourage learners to engage in more interactive speaking activities in the classroom, it will not be enough simply to add interactive speaking tasks to an assessment. Steps must also be taken to ensure that teachers are sympathetic with the objective and that they are trained and ready to use speaking activities. Work may also be needed to prepare learners and others (such as parents) for the change.

In addition to taking responsibility for designing and improving the assessment itself, developers will also need to work with others to realise the potential benefits and minimise the potentially damaging effects of an assessment. One approach, borrowing from the programme theory used in international development, suggested by Bennett, Kane, and Bridgeman (2011), involves developers collaborating with assessment users to prepare a 'theory of action' or logical framework. This is a document that sets out how intended changes in an educational system can be brought about. Like test specifications, the theory of action guides practice and can be refined in the light of experience. For example, Green (2014) provides a simple action plan for bringing about positive change involving the introduction of a test used in college admissions in Japan: the Test of English for Academic Purposes (TEAP). This lists the intended impacts (beneficial consequences) of the new test, the features of the test design intended to encourage these impacts and, anticipating the needs of stakeholders, actions to be taken to maximise the chances that the desired changes would come about (see Table 4.5).

Summary: the right tool for the job

As tools, language assessments are closer in nature to maps than to tape measures. Although they may differ in their precision and in the units they employ, all tape measures are designed to measure length. In contrast, maps represent and highlight different aspects of a multidimensional world according to the needs of the user. Like maps, language assessments do not and should not all measure and represent the same things. The choice of assessment techniques should reflect the kinds of decision that users wish to make and the kinds of consequences that they hope will follow. The four-quality framework of practicality, reliability, validity and beneficial consequences informs design and helps users to apply the PRICE principles (see Chapter 3), taking full account of the intended purpose for assessment.

Table 4.5 Extract from an action plan for promoting beneficial consequences (from Green, 2014, p. 34)

Intended impact	Features of test which will contribute to intended impact	Action plan
Maintain motivation of learners regardless of pass/fail decision for entering university.	Different levels and kinds of feedback developed to help test users interpret test scores and link the meaning of test scores to real-life language use situations and international language benchmarks. Test design which targets CEFR levels A2-B2 enables feedback regarding language ability to be given to learners at a range of levels including to students who may have not reached a level appropriate for studying in the academic context of university.	Provide information online to help test takers and educators understand the test results.

Just as there is no perfect map, no assessment can fully satisfy all four essential qualities and the best conceived map is useless if the traveller is unable to read it. Ultimately, users must be satisfied that an assessment is a justifiable use of resources because it is a better basis for decisions and leads to better consequences than the alternatives. At the same time, everyone involved should strive to improve on current practice.

Part II

The purpose of Part II of this book is to briefly survey techniques used in assessing the knowledge, skills and abilities involved in language use. Chapter 5 focuses on designing and scoring assessments of more *receptive* language use: reading and listening. Chapter 6 focuses on more *productive* and *interactive* language use: writing and speaking. This book does not have separate chapters on assessing grammar, vocabulary or pronunciation because these are seen as inseparable from spoken and written language use and so are covered within these two chapters. In some ways the division into productive, interactive and receptive language use is also artificial. Many situations require us to bring together these skills in order to achieve effective communication. Reflecting this, an increasing proportion of assessment tasks involve a degree of integration: e.g. reading a letter and writing a reply; or listening to a presentation and giving a written or verbal summary. On the other hand, each involves rather different processes and so represents different challenges for the language user. From this point of view, the distinction is worth keeping.

In these chapters, practices are brought to the reader's attention and links provided to appropriate resources. Illustrative examples from a range of assessments are used to demonstrate a variety of methods that can be used and to provide a basis for discussion of assessment qualities. Although the intention is to present widely accepted guidelines, the practice of building assessments inevitably favours one theoretical approach over others. In this book, the techniques are presented and evaluated from a broadly *socio-cognitive* standpoint (Weir, 2005a). This brings together a social view of language in use – recognizing that the ways in which we use language are shaped by social expectations and conventions – and psychological insights into the mental processes involved in conveying ideas and recognizing and making sense of the sounds we hear or shapes that we see on a page or screen.

The socio-cognitive framework offers guidance on the kinds of claims that developers might wish to make in constructing an assessment use argument:

Claim 1: Tasks involved in the assessment reflect the essential characteristics of tasks in the target language use domain (Weir refers to this as context validity).

Claim 2: The cognitive processes engaged by assessees in undertaking assessment tasks parallel the processes engaged by language users when they carry out tasks in the target language use domain (cognitive validity).

Claim 3: Results are consistent and free from bias (scoring validity).

Claim 4: Results of assessments are compatible with other evidence of the assessee's knowledge, skills or abilities (criterion-related validity).

Claim 5: Use of the assessment takes account of social values to maximise beneficial consequences and minimise harmful consequences (consequential validity).

Part III will introduce some alternative theories and the debates between them that have shaped the practice of language assessment over time.

5 Assessing receptive skills

The purpose of assessing reading and listening is to gain insight into how well assessees are able to use their language abilities to understand relevant written or spoken input. These will often be texts or recordings in the target language representing situations that learners might need to deal with in everyday life or as part of a language learning programme. Users may wish to know how well assessees may be able to understand similar texts in a workplace or in further study (a question of proficiency). They may want to understand the specific difficulties that learners experience when trying to read or listen in a foreign language and help them overcome these difficulties (a diagnostic, formative purpose). Or they may have any number of other reasons.

Anyone wishing to assess comprehension faces the fundamental problem that this cannot be observed directly. Simply watching someone read a report or listen to the news on the radio can tell us very little about how much they are able to understand. Assessment designers can only find evidence of a language learner's receptive language processing by getting them to do something else (in addition to reading or listening) in order to demonstrate how well they have understood. This 'something else' might involve the assessee performing actions, drawing, speaking or writing.

It follows that successful performance will depend not only on the ability to read an input text or listen to a recording with understanding (the focus of the assessment), but also on the ability to follow assessment instructions and to act, draw, write or speak as required (abilities that are usually not the focus and should therefore be viewed as **construct irrelevant** – see Chapter 4). When assessing receptive skills, the assessor is usually interested in the ability to read or listen with understanding rather than the ability to produce language or to follow instructions (although some assessments may also be concerned with how well the assessee is able to integrate these skills). It is therefore essential that all instructions are as easy as possible for assessees to grasp and that any acting, drawing, speaking, writing or other abilities required of the assessees in providing a response to the task are known to be well within their capabilities.

Personal reflection

Think about a context in which people need to learn a language (e.g., socialising with friends, conducting research or working as a waiter in a hotel with foreign guests).

What kinds of tasks will the learners carry out in this context and what reading and listening will they need to do?

What kinds of written texts, spoken interactions or recordings might they need to deal with?

If a test developer wants assessees to perform exactly the same tasks in an assessment that they might need to perform in the real world, what difficulties do you think that developer might encounter?

What other activities might a test developer ask learners to perform so that they could assess the reading and listening skills that learners need?

Obtaining the necessary evidence about reading or listening will involve:

- defining the nature of the knowledge, skills or abilities to be measured;
- choosing and specifying the kinds of texts or recordings that will be appropriate for use as input; and
- deciding on the kinds of tasks that assessees with these abilities should be able to perform when they encounter these texts or recordings.

The document *Task types* that can be accessed via the companion website for this volume at www.routledge.com/cw/rial includes a comprehensive list of task types that are commonly used to assess listening and reading skills, including knowledge of grammar and vocabulary.

Defining reading and listening abilities

Chapter 4 and the discussions of test design and validity concerns made it clear that building any assessment begins with a careful consideration of the decision that is going to be taken about the assessee and the knowledge, skills or abilities that are relevant to this decision. In proficiency assessment, designers need to know which knowledge, skills or abilities are essential in the target language use domain. In classroom formative assessment, the teacher must be aware of the knowledge, skills or abilities intended to be developed by the language programme. In all cases, designers must have an adequate understanding of the nature of the abilities they want to assess.

Types of reading

Urquhart and Weir (1998) make distinctions between types of reading along two dimensions. These are summarised in Figure 5.1.

When reading to find your way around a physical or virtual space, you may only need to pick out a few words from a mass of information. Finding your way through an airport (or large train/bus station) involves a lot of this kind of very quick, very selective reading. You pick out and follow the signs for *Departures* or *Arrivals*, ignoring the many other signs (and many other kinds of written information) around you. You may be confronted by displays with details of a hundred different flights, but you quickly pick out the airline and flight number on your ticket to find the right check-in counter or boarding gate.

A similar type of reading can be useful in other settings as well. When you search for information on the internet, you may sift through the search results to find the ones that seem to best match your needs. Readers pick out the links that interest them on a webpage; use a table of contents or index to navigate through a long textbook (to find the chapter on 'Assessing Reading' or the section that deals with 'Reliability'); flick through the pages of a newspaper to find stories that catch their attention or use their knowledge of how academic articles are organised to find the *methodology* of a research project. Khalifa and Weir (2009) classified these kinds of quick, selective and efficient reading as *expeditious reading*.

In contrast to expeditious reading, people often also engage in *careful reading*. In this kind of reading, the process is generally linear. The reader starts at the beginning and simply follows the writer's organization of the

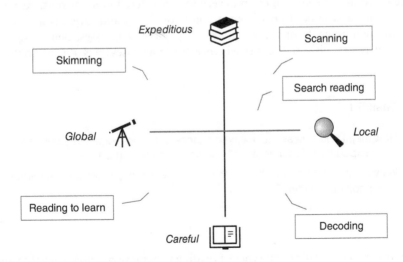

Figure 5.1 Types of reading

ideas. It is not selective: the reader tries to take in all or most of the information in the text. It is appropriate to engage in careful reading when following step-by-step instructions to carry out tasks such as operating machinery, cooking from a recipe or learning how to use computer software. When performing tasks like these for the first time, in order to avoid disaster the reader really needs both to understand each part of the text and to appreciate how all of the parts fit together. The reader attends to each new piece of information as they build up to a full understanding.

Lower-level language learners often find it difficult to reach this kind of thorough understanding of a text. They tend to be limited to the local *decoding* of words and *grammatical parsing* of each clause or sentence: picking up the meanings of the words and figuring out the relationships between them. They may be able to understand many of the individual idea units or propositions in a text, but may use so much of their mental capacity working out the meaning of each of these that they struggle to hold them all in their memory for long enough to put them together to form an overall representation of the text in their mind.

Skilled reading

Making the right choices about which type of reading to use in any given situation is important. A successful reader is able to match the appropriate type of reading to their goals and the type of text. An inexperienced cook would not be able to produce good food by just glancing once at a recipe and picking out a few words and figures. Equally, you would never get to your destination if you tried to read slowly and carefully through all of the information presented about every flight and every service offered in an airport. Readers must choose whether to read expeditiously or slowly and carefully according to the requirements of the situations they encounter. Assessment designers may therefore wish to discover whether or not an assessee is able to do this.

Task 5.1

How might you assess the ability to choose between types of reading (careful or expeditious/local or global) according to their purpose?

How could you find out whether the assessee is more successful at careful or expeditious reading?

We often combine different types of reading to achieve our goals. Khalifa and Weir (2009) made a distinction between three forms of expeditious reading: *scanning*, *search reading* and *skimming* (see Figure 5.1). In *scanning*, the reader is searching for specific words or phrases, as in the airport example. In *search reading*, the reader is looking for ideas relating to a certain topic and so has something broader than just one or two specific words or phrases in mind. In scanning, locating the key information usually marks the end of the reading process, but in search reading, finding information is usually a preliminary step. For example, in carrying out class assignments a student may want information to answer certain questions or to provide supporting arguments. The student must identify possible locations for the relevant information and evaluate which of these it is likely to be most useful to study. After finding a relevant section of the textbook through search reading, the student may then read that part of the book in depth (slowly and carefully) to learn more about the topic.

Like search reading, *skimming* or survey reading can be useful when a reader is confronted with a lot of material. Scanning and search reading have a local focus: they are concerned only with small parts of the text such as words, phrases or sentences. Skimming, in contrast, is global. The reader aims to get a quick, but effective overall understanding of a complete text: the gist. This may involve sampling a few key elements (such as chapter titles, introductory and concluding paragraphs, illustrations, opening sentences of paragraphs, etc.) to build up a general picture. Skimming allows the reader to be more efficient. Reading books or articles that are irrelevant would be a waste of time, so it can be helpful to skim them first to decide whether they are worthy of further study. Skimming can also be a useful preliminary to more careful reading. Details can be easier to assimilate when one already has an idea of the overall picture being presented. *re-reading is every good skill to have*

As well as choosing the type of reading that suits their purpose, good readers also monitor and review their comprehension. They form judgements about whether they have achieved an adequate understanding. If they are not satisfied, they may re-read sections of the text, look for additional sources of help within the text (illustrations or glossaries), or turn to external sources such as dictionaries and encyclopaedias.

Reading processes

A simplified model of comprehension processes is represented in Figure 5.2. This is based particularly on the work of Weir (2005a) and Field (2008).

When designing an assessment of reading abilities, the developers need to take into account the different types of reading that the assessees will need to carry out in the target domain. What processes, what skills and what sources of knowledge will be involved? A model of the kind presented in Figure 5.2 can help to guide decisions about the kinds of tasks that should be used.

The left-hand column (metacognitive skills) presents the ways in which readers manage the reading process. For example, a student may decide what kinds of information she wants to get from a text and sets herself the

need goal & strategy to listen/read effectively; can't do it mindlessly

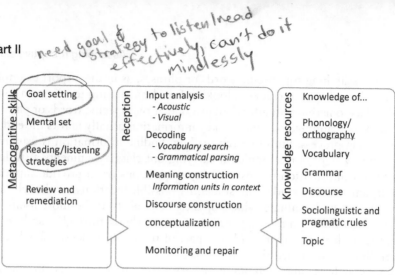

Figure 5.2 An outline model of receptive language processing

goal of extracting this. She chooses how best to read in order to obtain the information she wants in an efficient way. She thinks about what she already knows about the topic and may come up with questions that she expects the text to answer: she establishes a mental set to engage with the text. She chooses a promising source, deciding to skim through a textbook about a topic she has studied to see if the book includes information that she doesn't already know. She monitors her comprehension and finds that she isn't clear about what the writer is saying in Chapter 3. So she tries some remediation. She goes back to Chapter 3 and reads it carefully to improve her comprehension, perhaps using a dictionary or encyclopaedia as an aid: this is what Enright et al. (2000) described as *reading to learn* (see Figure 5.1).

Different choices of this kind call on different levels of the mental processing represented in the central column in Figure 5.2. In scanning, for example, the reader may only need to recognise and understand individual words or phrases: 'Passport Control' or 'Size 34: $23.95.' When reading to learn about a topic, readers will not only need to understand the meaning of words and sentences, but also build up a *conceptualization* of the overall meaning of the text, including grasping the relationships between the different ideas expressed. They may also need to be able to connect the ideas of one writer to ideas expressed by others (or by the same writer in different texts). This is particularly challenging to do because the links between the ideas of different writers are not usually explicitly presented. The reader has to fit them together in a coherent way by building up her own mental representation of the ways in which they support, oppose or develop each other (Enright et al., 2000, pp. 4–7).

Task 5.2

Look at Figure 5.2.

In what circumstances might it be important to assess processes of *vocabulary search* or *grammatical parsing*?

In what circumstances might it be important to assess the reader's *conceptualization* of the content of a text? How might you design an assessment to do this?

Types of listening

Personal reflection

What do you consider to be key differences between listening and reading in a foreign language?

What implications do these differences have for assessing comprehension?

Just as there are different types of reading, it is also possible to identify types of listening. Although it is not often feasible to control the speed of listening, it is possible to vary the level of attention paid to different inputs. People may *listen for gist, listen selectively* for specific pieces of information or *listen in depth*, attending to every detail. Successful listeners, like successful readers, are good at choosing the type of listening that suits the kinds of input they encounter and the goals they have in mind. For example, when listening to news about traffic problems, people listen selectively, attending closely only if the roads they will be using are mentioned. On the other hand, a nervous learner taking a first driving lesson would, one hopes, listen carefully to every part of the instructor's advice.

Field (2008) made the point that most assessments of 'listening' only involve a relatively narrow range of these possible listening types. Often the purpose for listening is limited to what he termed 'auditory scanning' or listening for specific details. He argued that the range should be expanded to more fully reflect the range found in target language use. Much of the listening people do outside assessments involves participation in face-to-face interaction with other people: usually listening to short utterances and having to respond very quickly to what they hear. An element of interactive listening is involved in many assessments of speaking, but may not be reflected in the scoring criteria. It is usually excluded altogether from listening assessments.

Task 5.3

Why are listening types such as selective listening and interactive listening not usually included in assessments of listening?

What kinds of tasks might be used to assess these?

Listening processes

Some cognitive psychologists have suggested that 'beyond the point of word recognition, listening and reading require essentially the same processes' (Gough, Hoover, & Peterson, 1996, p. 2). Although this view is controversial, it is clear enough that both reading and listening start from input and involve building up mental conceptualizations of a message. On this basis, both can be broadly represented by the same basic model of language reception (see Figure 5.2). On the other hand, when it comes to recognizing words and phrases in the input, the differences between spoken and written language processing are far from trivial. There are many more sources of variability in spoken than in written input, each of which may present problems for listeners. Word boundaries are not reflected in the stream of speech, and phonological effects can make it difficult for learners to recognise the individual words that are spoken. According to Field (2008, Chapter 2), in English, these effects include:

- Weak forms: function words like *a, the, and, but* sound very different and can become almost inaudible when they are not stressed – *teaching 'n' testing* compared with *teaching and testing*. Different function words like '*are*,' '*a*' and '*of*' can sound identical in continuous speech.
- Word transitions: when words occur together, sounds may be modified (assimilation) – compare the final sound in the word *met* in '*I met everybody*' /t/ and '*I met you*' /tʃ/. Or sounds may be lost (elision) – the final /t/ sound in superlatives ('*the bigges(t) car*') or /d/ sound in past tense verb forms ('*I cook(ed) dinner*') are often lost.
- Reduction: the same word or phrase may sound very different when spoken carefully and when it occurs in more casual speech. Commonly occurring phrases are often reduced and so become very difficult for learners to recognise. For example, '*do you want to*' can be pronounced as something like '*jawunna*.'

- Speaker variation: individuals speak in different ways. Each of us has a personal style of speech: a relatively loud or deep voice; a faster or slower rate of delivery; patterns of pausing and intonation; an accent. Listeners very quickly have to adjust and 'tune in' to the pattern of each new voice. This is more difficult to do and takes longer in a foreign language – one reason why assessees find it more difficult to understand recordings that involve several speakers.

The grammatical patterns found in spoken language are often rather different than those found in writing, with implications for grammatical parsing and building meaning. It is usually only written grammars that get taught in language classes (Carter & McCarthy, 2006). The lack of attention to spoken grammar in the classroom may exacerbate the problems that language learners experience when they encounter natural speech. Further variation in patterns of intonation and the placement of stress, accent, speech rate, the use of hesitation and fillers (*er, um*) and the ways in which speakers organise interactions all add to the challenges facing listeners (Hughes, 2010).

As shown by the left-hand column of the receptive language processing model presented in Figure 5.2, the listener can set goals, activate relevant knowledge and take decisions about what kinds of information to expect (establish a mental set). This leads to decisions about the kinds of messages or cues to attend to in different contexts. In an airport, a traveller might listen casually for mention of his airline or his name, but then attend closely to the message that follows any such announcement. In a lecture, a student may prepare by reading about the topic, then listen for cues such as repetition, pauses and signposting language (*first, second; the key point is*) to help to organise her notes and build her mental representation of the topic.

Difficulties experienced while listening are not always as easy for learners to remedy as they are in reading. If the student stops listening to search for a crucial word in her dictionary, the next phase of the lecture simply passes her by. Nonetheless, it is important for the listener to monitor how well or how completely the message has been understood. If the student recognises that there are gaps in her understanding, she may be able to find strategies to overcome these (comparing notes with other students, following up with the lecturer, reading more about the topic, etc.).

Choosing and adapting texts or recordings for use as input

Finding input texts or recordings that represent an appropriate level of difficulty or challenge for assessees must be a key consideration for the developer. A compromise must usually be struck between situational authenticity (Bachman & Palmer, 1996) – the extent to which the input resembles the kind of language that occurs naturally in the target language use domain – and the knowledge resources that assessees can be expected to bring to the task (Buck, 2001).

Task 5.4

Record any story from today's news media in your country.

What aspects of the story might make it difficult or inaccessible for language learners from another country?

How many of the difficulties you have identified are related to grammar, vocabulary or spoken language features and how many are cultural or connected with local knowledge?

How could you make the story easier for assessees to understand?

What effect would these changes have on the claims you could make about the knowledge, skills or abilities of an assessee who read and understood the text?

English language reading materials have been systematically graded for difficulty since the 1920s: originally to guide teachers in choosing suitable texts for school children learning to read in their first language. Many different readability formulas, such as the *Flesch Reading Ease* index, have been developed to provide quick indications of how challenging a text might be for children to read. These are generally based on easily measurable characteristics such as the average length of the words and sentences in a text. In most languages, longer words and longer sentences are associated with greater difficulty in comprehension. Longer words tend to be rarer and less familiar to learners. Longer sentences tend to be more complex and are more difficult to process. It is possible to obtain *Flesch Reading Ease* and similar readability estimates for English and many other languages with word processing software or by using online calculators.

Unfortunately, although they are easy to calculate, indices based on word length and sentence lengths, such as *Flesch Reading Ease*, do not really capture all of the causes of comprehension problems. Difficult, arcane words may be very short (*arcane* is shorter than *difficult*, but not as widely known). Long explicit sentences can be easier for learners to understand than short elliptical sentences. A much wider range of characteristics needs to be considered when specifying input texts that will mirror the kinds of input that learners will encounter in real world settings. Green (2012a) suggests a wide range of measurable features that might help to predict text difficulty; but for the most part assessment designers and item writers rely on their own judgement in estimating the difficulty of input material. This is also the case for listening. There are no simple formulas for estimating the difficulty of the recordings to parallel readability indices such as *Flesch Reading Ease* and the range of characteristics that need to be balanced in making judgements about difficulty is even greater. In addition to the nature of the grammar and vocabulary used, features of spoken language, such as rate of delivery and patterns of intonation, also affect difficulty (Buck, 2001).

Specifications

In building operational assessments, the selection of texts or recordings will be guided by the specifications and by their potential as sources for generating tasks and items (Alderson et al., 1995, p. 43). Designers and writers are faced with a choice. Is it best to:

* craft new material to use as input;
* adapt found source material to match the specifications;
* try to find material that can be used unaltered in the assessment?

In Chapter 4, we looked at tools such as Bachman and Palmer's (2010) task characteristics framework that are designed to help match the features of assessment tasks to the kinds of tasks that language learners typically carry out in the real world and so guide the development of appropriate specifications. Alderson (2000) and Buck (2001) discussed how the Bachman and Palmer framework could be applied in assessing reading and listening abilities. Read (2000) and Purpura (2004) applied the framework to assessments of vocabulary and grammar.

Recent work by Bejar, Douglas, Jamieson, Nissan, and Turner (2000) and Weir (2005a), among others, has gone a step further in bringing together the contexts within which language tasks are undertaken and the different cognitive processes that are involved in carrying them out. Khalifa and Weir (2009) set out how cognitive processes are reflected in the texts employed as input for the tests of reading in the Cambridge English language examinations. Studies using questionnaires, verbal reports by test takers and eye tracking tools have been used to explore how purpose and context shape the reading and listening process in tests and target language use domains, and how closely these processes resemble each other in the different contexts of the test and the target language use domain (see, for example, Green, Unaldi & Weir, 2010).

For most purposes, it is said to be preferable to use texts and recordings that have been obtained from sources in the real-world contexts that the assessment is intended to reflect. For general access to the public sphere, these might include newspapers, magazines, web pages and news broadcasts; for the workplace, they might include business reports, purchase orders, instructional videos, etc. important that it's general

In practice, there may need to be a trade-off between what is desirable from a theoretical standpoint and practical constraints on the kinds of text or recording that can be found for use in the assessment. Material taken directly from a target language use domain, even when very carefully chosen, is inevitably less likely to match detailed specifications than material especially written or scripted for the assessment. However, invented texts are much more likely to differ significantly from the material that learners might encounter in real world language use. The greater the differences, the more doubts are raised about whether the ability to 'listen to a public service announcement' or 'read a business letter' in an assessment sufficiently reflects the ability to do these things in real world settings.

Trade-offs in choosing and adapting material

Much of the reading that language learners will need to do outside the classroom may take the form of published or publicly accessible texts: public information, employment-related instructions and reports, and email communications. In contrast, much of the listening that language learners carry out will involve spontaneous, unscripted speech that is not as easy to find in a recorded form. Where unrehearsed, unedited recordings of spontaneous conversation are available, they may not be easy to follow because they tend to include many references to knowledge shared by the participants, but not by outsiders. In other words, the recording may be authentic, but the lack of involvement on the part of the assessee is not.

Recordings that are generally available, such as news broadcasts, lectures, interviews, dramas or public announcements, are rarely entirely impromptu, but include rehearsed, semi-scripted or even fully scripted speech. Scripted and other pre-prepared forms of speech inevitably sound quite dissimilar to impromptu, unscripted speech. Actors are trained to dramatise and highlight meanings in a script. This means that rehearsed, directed and edited broadcasts have rather different characteristics than everyday conversation.

If suitable recordings cannot be found for use as input to listening assessments, an alternative is to make recordings that (as far as possible) simulate real world language use (Alderson, 2000; Buck, 2001; Davidson & Lynch, 2002). Buck (2001, Chapter 6) recommended a range of strategies for obtaining speech with naturalistic features, while exercising a reasonable degree of control over the content. These could include scenarios in which performers improvise a transaction or conversation based on an outline rather than a script; or interviews with proficient speakers of the target language where the questions follow a set pattern. Where the need for stricter control makes the use of scripts unavoidable, Buck (2001) suggested that these should be based on recordings of genuine speech, adapted as required, then re-recorded by actors.

Writers naturally have more scope for adapting written than spoken material. Words can be inconspicuously removed from or added to a written text in a way that is not possible with audio or video recordings. Changes that writers may wish to make to a found text in preparing assessments include reshaping it to better match the text characteristics laid down in the specifications and adjusting it to better accommodate the questions or tasks that they intend to set.

For example, to meet the specifications, writers may wish to make cuts or add sentences to adjust the length of an input text, or to take an extract from a longer text. If they do this, they might also feel that they need to take out any reference to the parts of the text that have been removed. Sometimes they might change allusions to people, places or events to make the text equally accessible to assessees who lack certain kinds of background knowledge. They might also wish to take out content that could offend or upset some assessees, such as mention of fatal illnesses or potentially offensive points of view. Upsetting material might interfere with an assessee's ability to perform at their best.

When preparing tasks, writers may find that they need to revise and reorganise a text to produce the number of items called for in the specifications. They may shift ideas from one location in the text to another, remove repeated ideas, try to eliminate ambiguities or change the wording and structure of sentences to get rid of obvious hints (see Green & Hawkey, 2012, for an example of how test writers reshape texts). But, as noted previously, whenever a text is edited to suit the needs of the assessment, this inevitably raises questions about how well the revised version will reflect real world language use.

Writers of assessments are unable to control the many sources of variation in the flow of sound in the way that they can control the appearance of words printed on a page. As a result, adapting spoken material is generally more awkward than adapting written texts. Although the availability of audio and video editing software now makes it relatively easy to make minor cuts to recordings, to add pauses and to slightly modify the overall speech rate, if any changes are made to the wording it will generally be necessary to re-record material using actors (and not all teachers make effective actors).

Scripting assessments of listening

Brindley, Hood, McNaught, and Wigglesworth (1997) provided an example of the kinds of dilemmas that face designers of listening assessments. They developed a proficiency test to assess the English of immigrants to Australia and their intention was to use authentic recordings taken from the target language use domain of daily life in Australia. However, some recordings proved to be too long, others 'contained either too much or too little information, or would have required extensive contextualisation.' Some texts 'had to be edited when it was found, for example, that the items followed one another too closely and thus placed an overly demanding processing burden on candidates or that a text contained specific cultural references which would be difficult for some candidates to interpret'

(Brindley et al., 1997, pp. 40–41). Ultimately, the recordings employed in the test were either invented or adapted from broadcast material and re-recorded using actors.

The use of scripts remains very popular even though their value is contested and recorded material is now relatively easy to source. This is because they have a key advantage: they allow the designer to exert much greater control over the content of a recording. It is certainly easier to produce near-equivalent forms of an assessment task when making scripted recordings. Moreover, the level of the learners must play an important part in decisions about the kinds of recording that can be used. When assessing the achievements of learners at lower levels of ability, the main concern may not be what learners would realistically manage to understand in the real world outside the classroom. The focus may instead be on what learners are able to understand when the range of language is constrained, controlling some of the features of naturalistic speech that can cause them difficulty (such as the speech rate, false starts, reduction and the use of fillers). Scripts make this easier to do. However, heavy reliance on scripted material will deny learners opportunities to become accustomed to the features of more natural speech. Designers will need to carefully balance these considerations according to the purpose of the assessment.

The internet has provided item writers with a previously unimaginable wealth of potential input material in all modes from which to choose. However, for the present, there is no doubt that finding suitable sources for use in tests of comprehension remains a subtle and challenging activity. Increasing use of integrated multimedia resources can only add to the complexity of the challenge and it seems likely that we will continue to see an expansion of research, building on Ockey and Wagner (2018) and others, into the complex impacts upon comprehension of different combinations of textual, graphic and auditory input.

Assessing grammar and vocabulary

It can be seen from the receptive language processing model outlined in Figure 5.2 (and from the productive model in Figure 6.1 in the next chapter) that grammar and vocabulary (together with other building blocks such as phonology and orthography) are fundamental to all language use. Assessments that focus on knowledge of words and phrases, the formal properties of language and the ways in which manipulating these affects basic propositional meaning (i.e., traditional grammar and vocabulary tests) cover an important but restricted proportion of language processing. Without knowledge of grammar and vocabulary, language learners will not be able to communicate.

Assessments of grammar and vocabulary knowledge can therefore be understood as assessments of a restricted range of the processes involved in receptive, interactive and productive language use. There are many reasons why this may be worth assessing. One important reason is that problems in accessing the vocabulary or grammar of a text or recording could be the major source of difficulty in comprehension. Such assessments may therefore have a diagnostic value, revealing what learners may need to learn. For beginning-level learners, knowledge of words and grammatical patterns may be the key to understanding very simple texts.

Another reason is their potential for practicality and reliability. Large numbers of items covering a wide range of language points can be administered in a relatively short time. Scoring can also be made very straightforward, even automated. If items are subject to suitable quality control processes (see Chapters 3 and 4), the results are likely to be very reliable. In other words, such assessments provide quite effective measurement, but only of a limited aspect of general language ability. If too much weight is given to the results, the potential for negative washback is clear. Teachers and learners may concentrate on grammar and vocabulary and study only disjointed fragments of language, overlooking knowledge of discourse, pragmatic and socio-linguistic features.

Traditionally, such assessments have been administered mainly in the written mode. This is largely a matter of convenience as tasks are easier to prepare, administer and score on paper than through recordings. However, there are good reasons for assessing spoken as well as written word and phrase recognition and production, and we have seen that there are differences between spoken and written grammar that suggest the need for spoken grammar assessment. New technology offers increasing scope for assessing spoken grammar and vocabulary (as well as phonology).

Commentaries on types of tasks that can be used for assessing grammar and vocabulary knowledge are provided in the document *Task types* on the companion website for this book. For those wishing to investigate these areas in more depth, Read (2000) covers the assessment of vocabulary and Purpura (2004) covers grammar.

Preparing items for assessing reading and listening

From text to task

When educators discuss the assessment of reading and listening abilities, they are not usually referring to tasks that involve decoding words or unconnected sentences. They are talking about the comprehension of longer written texts and recordings of spoken language.

When comprehension is being assessed, the responses ought to come from an understanding of the text or recording (and should require the assessee to use the targeted processes). If the focus is on reading expeditiously, it should not be possible to obtain the correct answers by reading slowly and carefully through the whole text: assessees should be given only limited time to access the text. If slow, careful reading is the focus, sufficient time should be allowed for assessees to read in this way.

The purpose for reading a text or listening to a recording in an assessment should reflect the purpose a reader would naturally have for reading similar texts in the world beyond the classroom. Item writers should be encouraged to approach a text or recording from the point of view of a reader or listener in the real world. A first step in designing and preparing suitable tasks is to read the text or listen to the recording and note the key message or messages that a reader or listener would naturally take from the input. This is revealing about the processing involved; helps in targeting the ideas that learners would most need to understand; and informs decisions about the task types and response formats that will be most suitable.

Weir (1993) and Field (2008) have provided lists of types of input and the reasons people have for reading or listening to them. Listening to a telephone message, for example, suggests listening in depth to capture the details, but listening to announcements implies more selective listening. Listening to lectures would usually involve identifying main points and connections between ideas. Assessments should take these differences into account.

Handbooks for assessment development such as Hughes (2003), Alderson (2000) and Buck (2001) provide guidance on preparing assessments of reading and listening skills. The generic guidelines presented here draw on those sources among others and may be adapted for use in instructions to item writers and for reviewing assessment material.

Guidelines for preparing tasks

Receptive skills inputs should:

- allow you to produce (at least) the number of questions you need – i.e., be long enough, including enough ideas, facts, opinions:
  - for detailed comprehension: have enough specific details (description);
  - for summarizing: have a clear outline and enough distinct main ideas (exposition);
  - for skimming: have overt and accessible ideas/opinions (e.g., clear topic sentences, key words);
  - for inferences: include information that can be put together to support unambiguous inferences;
- be at the right level of difficulty for the assessees:
  - grammar and vocabulary of the text or recording should be level appropriate;
  - vocabulary that is likely to be unknown should be kept to a minimum (removed or reworded if necessary) and should not be tested;

- be of a type that will be familiar and equally accessible to every assessee:
  - suitable for the age group, experiences and cultural background of all assessees;
  - not cover sensitive topics such as war, death, serious disease, politics or religion that may disturb or offend some assessees;
- not be taken from textbooks or other educational materials that any of the assessees may have seen before.

Changes to sources should be kept to a minimum, especially for assessments targeting higher-level learners, but might include:

- cutting down the length and editing to maintain coherence;
- editing potentially offensive, overly technical or culturally inaccessible content;
- rewording or explaining technical or culture-specific terms;
- clarifying ambiguous wording or phrasing;
- changing the title and subtitle or opening lines to clarify the content;
- editing to avoid word matching (between questions and options).

Questions should:

- be meaningful: cover information that a reader/listener in the real world would need to extract;
- generally follow the order of the information in the text/recording (unless, as in scan reading, this would contradict the intention of the item);
- (in listening) allow sufficient run-in time before the questions for listeners to tune into the voice or voices and sufficient time between questions to allow listeners to respond and refocus their attention;
- include all the information needed to find the answer;
- be positively worded (especially avoid double negatives: *which food mentioned in the text is not unpleasant?* – these can be very confusing);
- make it clear whether they relate to facts or opinions and to explicitly stated or implicit information;
- employ simpler language than the text/recording: test understanding of the text not of the questions;
- (in listening) be based on the recording as it is heard, not on the written transcript.

Expected **answers** should:

- be unambiguous: directly stated or very clearly implied in the text/recording;

- not be recoverable from the text/recording simply by matching words from the question or options (unless that is the ability being assessed);
- not be answerable without the text/recording (i.e., from general knowledge, common sense or knowledge of grammar and vocabulary);
- not depend on, be linked to or be given away by answers to other questions;
- not come from the same part of the text/recording as any other question;
- not assume or depend on culturally specific knowledge.

Answer choices (in selected response tests) should:

- all offer logical, grammatically possible answers to the question;
- all have some support from the text;
- all appear similar (i.e., related in content, sentence structure and length);
- each be unique (avoid repeated elements: *she likes carrots and beans/ she likes carrots and cabbages/she likes carrots and radishes*).

Answer choices should NOT:

- rule each other out or seem to offer binary choices: (a) *the river is wide/*(b) *the river is narrow/*(c) *the river is pretty* (*wide* and *narrow* are opposites, suggesting one of them will be the correct answer);
- incorporate other options: (a) '*Hector enjoys tennis*'/(b) '*Hector enjoys football*'/(c) '*Hector enjoys sport*' (if option a or b is correct, so is c and if c is correct, so are a and b);
- include absolutes such as '*all the cars in Algeria are blue,*' '*everybody in Bolivia likes baseball*' (these are generally incorrect options);
- include qualifiers of quantity or frequency, such as '*cars in Canada are often blue,*' '*some people in France like football*' (these are often correct options).

Note that in assessing listening abilities, it may be better, where possible, to avoid using written selected response items altogether. Written responses require the assessee to combine reading with listening skills. This can be very demanding and rather unrealistic: although we may sometimes take notes as we listen, we do not usually listen in order to select from a set of written choices.

[handwritten margin note: Important note for assessing listening]

Task instructions should:

- be as brief as possible;
- explain what skills are being tested;

- explain the amount of time that should be spent on each task or test part;
- explain how many points will be awarded for each question or task;
- be expressed in the simplest possible language (even if written in the assessees' first language);
- make it completely clear what assessees have to do;
- be familiar to assessees (potential assessees should have the chance to practice similar items in advance);
- 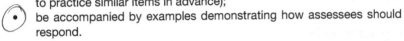 be accompanied by examples demonstrating how assessees should respond.

Test developers must make decisions about how best to obtain evidence of ability. In other words, they need to identify the most appropriate techniques to match the purpose of the assessment. Assessment tasks may be designed to tap into different levels of language processing and to reflect realistic language use. The focus may be on individual words – as in a test of vocabulary – or on grammatical knowledge and parsing – as in traditional tests of grammar. Different tasks can be designed to test the ability to recover individual ideas stated or inferred in the input, or to relate the ideas to each other and build up representations of a text as a whole.

The temptations of testing only grammar and vocabulary

A problem (or perhaps a temptation) for assessment developers is that knowledge of grammar and vocabulary and comprehension of detail are more straightforward and practical to assess than inferences, main ideas and relationships between ideas. A short text (or recording) can generate large numbers of items that focus on retrieving explicitly stated information, but the same text will only have one main idea or theme. It is also relatively easy to test for directly stated facts, but surprisingly difficult, as Hughes (2003) observes, to find out whether an assessee can recognise whether or not a text is intended to be humorous.

The document *Task types* in the Resources section of the website for this volume (www.routledge.com/cw/rial) presents a range of choices in task design. These are intended to reflect current practice rather than provide an exhaustive typology. Some of the task types presented are clearly better suited to either reading or listening, but there is so much common ground that it would be superfluous to present separate tables for each skill. The tables are divided according to response format (selected, constructed, extended and personal response) and task type. This reflects the fact that task types can be combined with response formats to give a wide variety of configurations. Suggestions are offered concerning which aspects of reading and listening might be assessed by each task type. However, the relationship between task type and language processing is not straightforward and there is no guarantee that use of a certain task type with a certain population of assessees will ensure that a particular process is being assessed. This is something that needs to be established on a case-by-case basis.

Trying out material

As described in Chapter 4, writing items is only the beginning of a quality control process that involves reviewing and trying out the material. Spaan (2007) used a listening test item to illustrate the process of revision on the basis of comments from reviewers and the experience of piloting.

Task 5.5

Review this item from a listening test. What knowledge, skill or ability is being assessed? Do you think the item will provide good evidence of the learners' abilities? Why (not)?

Listen to each question and choose the best answer from the answer choices.

Audio: *I'm working on this report. Can you look it over for me?*

Printed responses:

(a) OK, I'll look at it.
(b) I'll overlook that.
(c) Wait till it's finished.

Spaan, M. (2007). Evolution of a test item.
Language Assessment Quarterly, 4(3), 279–293.
Retrieved from www.informaworld.com

A number of problems emerged from the piloting of this item and the statistical analysis of the results. Note that information about the statistics used to investigate the quality of assessment material is available in the document 'Statistical Tools' on the website (www.routledge.com/cw/rial). First, the item proved to be rather easier than intended for the assessees. Second, the item did not **discriminate** effectively between relatively high-ability and low-ability assessees (people who did well on the test, as a whole, were not much more likely to get this item correct than people who performed poorly overall).

The reviewers concluded that one factor that might have led assessees to the correct answer and so made the question rather easy was the repetition of the word 'look' in the key (option *a*). This is something that makes the answer easily guessable: an assessee recognizing the word 'look' from the recording might be able to find the answer without fully understanding either the recording or the options. At the same time, the recording included a question, indicated by the inverted word order and the rising intonation on the word 'over.' Only option (a) is obviously the answer to a question.

(TC)

Task 5.6

Here is the item following the editing process.

What changes have been made? Why do you think these changes were decided on?

How do you think the changes have improved or reduced the quality of the item?

Audio: *I've been working on this annual report, and I'd like to know if I'm on the right track.*

Printed responses:

(a) Let me see what you've done.
(b) Let me check when we're there.
(c) Let me know when you're finished.

Spaan, M. (2007). Evolution of a test item. *Language Assessment Quarterly, 4*(3), 279–293. Retrieved from www.informaworld.com

---

Changes made to the wording of the recording were intended to remove the obvious word matching (*look* appearing in the text and the correct response) and to add difficulty by making the question implicit, using idiomatic language: '*I'd like to know if I'm on the right track.*' At the same time, it was pointed out by one of the reviewers that option (c), which was only selected by a handful of assessees, might have been implausible not only because it did not seem to answer a question, but also because it may not be very clear from the progressive form of the verb ('*I'm working*') that the report was still incomplete. The '*report*' was made an '*annual report*' to strengthen the image of a lengthy, but unfinished document, making (c) more plausible.

Changes were also made to the answer options. Use of a *Let me + verb + 'wh'* pattern in all three options plays down the role of grammatical structure in arriving at the answer. Recognizing choice (a) as the key now seems to require the assessee to recognise that '*on the right track*' implies the speaker wants the report checked before it is finished. Assessees attracted by choice (b) have probably misunderstood '*on the right track*' to refer to a train journey, while option (c) will attract those who have misunderstood that the speaker only wants the report looked at after it is completed.

Naturally, the changes described by Spaan (2007) are not the only alterations that could be made and further improvements might be suggested. For example, it seems plausible that option (c), if spoken in a dismissive tone, could be the response of an unhelpful colleague, refusing the speaker's request for guidance. It may therefore be better to include the word 'OK' at the beginning of each option to exclude this possibility. Once the reviewers are satisfied with the changes, an item reviewed in this way should be piloted again to check that it is now working as intended.

(TC)

Task 5.7

More serious criticisms of this item type have been made. Critics may question whether an item that involves reading 24 words and listening to just 21 really assesses listening rather than reading skills.

How do you think the test developer might respond to this criticism? Do you think the item provides a fair assessment of listening abilities? What evidence could you use to support or reject your view?

If you agree with the criticisms, how might you revise the item to make it more clearly an assessment of listening ability?

[handwritten margin notes: ≠ not reading / 24 different words only / 24 total - / some are same]

Useful insights into the qualities of any assessment material can be gained by asking assessees about the experience of responding. In the classroom, discussions about how learners arrived at their answers can be much more revealing of their state of knowledge than the answer alone (see 'Score reporting and feedback'). This can lead to improvements in the material (if it is revealed that learners misunderstood the item or instructions) or to improvements in learning (if the discussion leads to improved understanding).

Scoring performance

Quality control procedures for scoring selected response and short answer item formats were outlined in Chapter 3. Approaches to scoring more extensive responses will be dealt with in Chapter 6.

Score reporting and feedback

Immediately after taking a test, most people want to know their scores or grades and to learn which answers they got right or wrong. For various reasons, including the logistics of scoring a test and the need for security, external standardised tests cannot generally provide this level of feedback. Scores are often reported at least a few days after the test event (although computer-based assessment has done much to improve the speed of scoring and reporting) and answers to individual items may never be revealed.

Efforts have been made to make test results more informative than simple numbers. Increasingly, external test scores are now accompanied by brief explanations for users of what scores mean in terms of what learners can do with the language. Some tests report profile scores, showing how well test takers have performed on different test components covering different skills: one score for reading, another for listening. Sometimes, even more detail is provided and scores may be reported for sub-skills, such as reading for detail and reading for main ideas or for specific grammar points. Unfortunately, tests are not usually long enough to provide reliable diagnostic information at this level of granularity and it may not be clear how the assessees are expected to use this kind of data.

In the classroom, there are opportunities to provide more immediate feedback. Teachers have traditionally awarded grades and revealed the correct answers to completed exercises; but advocates of assessment for learning have questioned the value of both – or at least of providing them too quickly. Chapter 4 outlined some of the arguments made for avoiding or delaying the reporting of grades and providing more descriptive than evaluative commentary.

Rather than immediately revealing the correct answers, it can be more informative and motivating to challenge learners to reflect on and justify their responses. For selected response and short answer questions, Wiliam (2011) recommended giving learners individual voting cards (cards marked 'a,' 'b,' 'c' or 'd') or mini whiteboards on which they write their answers. This means that the teacher can quickly monitor how many learners have chosen each option. Learners can then be picked at random to explain their answers. Having learners explain answers can help the teacher to better understand the learners' level of comprehension; it can help the learner giving the explanation to clarify their own thinking; and it can help other learners to reflect on their answers and improve their understanding.

With more extended responses, groups of assessees may work together to produce collective responses. Again, individual learners may be called on at random to justify the answers. This means that all of the learners in the group must be ready to give an explanation and so cannot just rely on stronger members of the group. The insights gained by the teacher from this kind of assessment can be recorded and used to inform decisions about the next steps in the teaching and learning process.

Teachers have different beliefs about how learners develop reading and listening abilities in another language. Their beliefs will inform the kinds of insights they look for and the kind of feedback they offer. These issues are beyond the scope of this book, but Urquhart and Weir (1998), Grabe and Stoller (2019) and Koda (2005) for reading, and Field (2008) and Rost (2013) for listening offer helpful accounts of how listening and reading abilities develop.

Standard setting

Personal reflection

What does it mean to 'pass' a language assessment?

Think about a test with which you are familiar.

How would you decide how many points or what level of performance should be required for a passing grade?

Feedback is of central importance in formative assessment, but assessments designed for summative and proficiency purposes may offer only limited information to assessees. They prioritise other things. Ultimately, assessment users need to know what score (or grade, band, level, etc.) on an assessment represents sufficient ability for the purposes they have in mind. They need to know the appropriate **performance standard** or **cut score**.

When deciding on a suitable cut score, one must be confident that the assessment in question is valid for the intended purpose. It would not be appropriate to interpret a high score on an interview assessment, for example, to mean that an assessee would be able to read and interpret a complex text such as a legal contract. As part of the validity argument, **content standards**, developed in similar ways to assessment design statements (see Chapter 4), can be used to inform test design or to guide the selection of appropriate assessments that match an employer's needs or the content of a curriculum.

Assuming that relevant content is assessed, attention can be given to performance standards. In some cases, there is a single cut score, representing a passing score on the assessment. Sometimes more than one cut score is set and results are reported in terms of a number of grades or bands – an adequate score for someone working as an administrator, an adequate score for an international manager, an adequate score for a technical writer and so forth.

In some circumstances, users are invited to set their own local standards according to their requirements. For example, universities may choose to set different scores on tests of languages for academic purposes as entry requirements according to the levels of support available for international students and the subject being studied. In some academic subjects, such as physics, language plays a relatively minor supporting role. In others, such as law, detailed and critical interpretation is central and these require highly developed language abilities. The IELTS test, designed to assess the English language abilities of international students, reports scores as 'bands' on a nine-point scale. For students who intend to study through the medium of English, it is recommended that an overall band of 6.5 may be acceptable for studying physics, while studying on a more 'linguistically demanding' course such as law requires a minimum band of 7.5. An academically qualified learner with a band of 6.5 would be accepted onto a physics course but would require additional English language study before beginning a course in law.

Alternative methods for setting standards

Providers of proficiency tests may offer sets of test materials and sample performances to help institutions in **standard setting** or arriving at suitable local cut scores. A variety of methods have been suggested for setting appropriate and defensible standards for achievement or proficiency. A distinction can be made between *assessment-centred* methods and *assessee-centred* methods.

In assessee-centred methods, experts who are qualified to make judgements about standards are invited to join a panel. The panellists might include language teachers, applied linguists and, for proficiency tests, experts in the target language use domain – such as doctors for a test of medical language use.

The panel's first task is to identify and define groups of assessees. In the *contrasting groups method*, two groups are identified: one consists of learners who are judged to be sufficiently competent. For proficiency assessments, these may be people who have already demonstrated that they have enough ability to carry out their work. In summative assessments they may be judged to have mastered a certain level of the curriculum or to satisfy the demands of an external framework, such as the Common European Framework of

Reference for Languages (CEFR) (Council of Europe, 2001) or government mandated educational standards. The other group consists of assessees who are considered by the panel to fall below this threshold. The assessment is administered to the two groups and their scores are calculated.

It is expected that the competent learners will generally achieve high scores and the others will achieve low scores on the assessment. The range of scores for the two groups will probably overlap, but the recommended cut score is placed at the point on the scale at which most of the competent learners would satisfy the standard (obtain a score higher than the cut score) and most of the less than competent learners would not. According to the risks involved in accepting less than competent assessees, the cut score could be adjusted up or down to ensure that most or all of the less than competent assessees would fail or that most of the competent assessees would pass.

In the *borderline group method*, only one group is identified. This group is made up of assessees who are judged to be just on the borderline between adequate and less than adequate ability. If there are multiple cut scores, a borderline group must be identified for each. Again, the learners take the assessment. The recommended cut score is the median score for the group: the point at which half the group would score above and half the group would score below the standard.

Assessment-centred methods also involve panels of expert judges, but instead of judging learners' abilities, they make judgements about the difficulty of assessment material. In the *Angoff method*, which dates back to the 1970s, the panellists are asked to keep in mind a *minimally competent* learner – one who they judge would just satisfy the relevant requirements of the workplace or curriculum. They then estimate the probability that this learner would succeed in answering each item correctly. So, for example, a judge might decide that a minimally competent learner would have a 60 percent chance of responding correctly to Item 1 on a test, but only a 25 percent chance of responding correctly to Item 2. The panellists' estimates are added up and averaged to produce their recommended cut score.

The Angoff method has been criticised, not least because judgements about the probability that an imaginary assessee will respond correctly to an item are very difficult to make. Many alternatives have been put forward. The *bookmark method* is one that has been widely used. This can only be implemented after the assessment has been administered. Each test item appears on a page. The pages are ordered in the form of a booklet according to how well the assessees performed. The easiest item appears on page 1, the most difficult is on the final page. An item that 90 percent of the assessees answered correctly would appear ahead of one that 85 percent answered correctly, and so on. The booklet containing the ordered items is then presented to the panel. The judges go through this booklet and judge whether a minimally competent assessee would have a reasonably high probability (usually defined as two-thirds or higher) of answering each item correctly. When they reach a point in the booklet at which they feel the assessee would not have this level of success, they place a bookmark in the booklet. The location of the bookmark indicates how many points they think a minimally competent assessee would score. The panellists may discuss their judgements and go through several rounds of the exercise. If an acceptable degree of consensus is reached, the panellists' judgements are averaged to produce the recommended cut score.

Standard setting is not an exact science. Different panels using different methods may come up with a variety of recommendations for cut scores. This means it is especially important to carefully document and justify the procedures used. The standards arrived at will be most convincing if the panellists are satisfied that they have arrived at a fair decision, if they are generally in agreement with each other, and if very similar results are obtained by another standard setting panel that has used alternative methods.

(TC)

Task 5.8

Here are two reading tasks, or **testlets**.

First, look at the items. Can you answer any of them without reading the text? How were you able to guess the answers?

Now look at the texts. Which text would learners find more difficult? Why?

What are the main points of each text?

Assuming they have an adequate level of English language ability, how suitable would these texts be for groups such as:

- ten-year-old school children;
- first-year university students;
- business people;
- adult migrants in an English-speaking country?

What kinds of publication do you think these texts were originally taken from?

Do you think they are genuine (unaltered from the source text) or adapted for use in the test? How can you tell?

What kinds of knowledge, skill or ability are needed to respond to the items?

Reading Task 1 from Cambridge Assessment English: *Preliminary English Test (PET)* (www.cambridgeenglish. org). Note that this is an extract from an old version of the test, which is now known as *B1 Preliminary.*

Read the text 'Exploring the Arctic' and then decide if each sentence is correct or incorrect.

11 This trip is for people who like peace and quiet.

12 Many different activities are organised on board.

13 The voyage begins in Scotland.

14 The ship follows a fixed route.

15 There are different types of accommodation.

Exploring the Arctic

The Arctic is one of the few places in the world untouched by pollution where you can see nature at its wildest and most beautiful. Join our ship the *Northern Star* from 2 to 18 July, for a 17-day voyage to the Arctic. During the voyage you are able to relax and get away from it all. There are no parties or film-shows to attend, quizzes to enter, or entertainers to watch. However, we do have specialists on board who are willing to answer any of your questions about the Arctic and who will talk about the animals and birds that you see on the trip.

After setting off from Scotland, we go north along the coast of Norway to Bear Island. Along the way you'll see thousands of seabirds and wonderful scenery, with rivers of ice and huge cliffs. You will have the chance to see reindeer, polar bears, and other Arctic animals. Although we have a timetable, experience has shown that we may have to change our direction a little, depending on the weather and on which animals appear.

The *Northern Star* is a very special ship and our past voyages have been very popular. Our cabins all have the same excellent facilities, which include a private bathroom and refrigerator. Our chefs are happy to prepare any food for people on special diets. Choose just what you want to eat from the wide variety available from the dining room buffet. There is a library, shop, clinic and plenty of space for relaxation. If you need some exercise, why not go jogging every morning around the decks, or do some swimming in the indoor pool.

Prices include economy class air travel and 16 nights on board the *Northern Star*, all meals and excursions and all lectures.

Day 1   Board the *Northern Star*.

Days 2–7 We sail slowly north along the coast of Norway, stopping at places of interest.

...

Figure 5.3 Exploring the Arctic (sample reading test material)

Reading Task 2

Read the text 'Feral children and the Wild Boy of Aveyron.'

Seven sentences have been removed from the text.

Choose from the sentences (A – J) the **one** which fits each gap (1–7). There are **two** extra sentences which you do not need to use.

An example (0) has been done for you.

___

Feral children and the Wild Boy of Aveyron

Human history has echoed with curious tales of wild, hairy beasts emerging from forests on all fours – feral children. This is the story of Victor, known as 'the Wild Boy of Aveyron.'

Victor, the wild boy of Aveyron, is known to many people from Truffaut's famous film about him. This, for many people, will be the first time they have been exposed to the story of a wild child. **(0) A** ... Victor was observed on several occasions by local residents, eventually captured by farm workers and taken to the village square to be publicly displayed.

As often happens with wild children, Victor was unhappy about being caught and soon managed to escape, only to be caught again a year or so later. **(1)** . . . Subsequently, he came into contact with humans more frequently, as he began to beg food from households and farm houses in the area. But he still lived on his own in the forest, where people would occasionally see him, running and crying out like a wolf.

Victor's wild life ended about two years after he was first found, in the depths of the cold winter of 1799/1800. **(2)** . . . He was seen digging for the potatoes he'd learned to love during his short contact with humans, and once again captured. This was his last moment of freedom – he would never again know the hard life of the forests.

Victor was around 12 when he was discovered. He apparently survived in the forest for at least two years, probably considerably longer, with no other human company. **(3)** . . . However, we have no certain knowledge about his early days.

Victor's final capture was very timely. A controversial issue of debate at that time was the idea – put forward by Rousseau – that a 'child of nature' should be pure, and unaffected by the effects of society. **(4)** . . . One luminary after another examined him, and by all of these, Victor was recognised as being generally insolent and unhelpful; more like a savage creature than an innocent soul.

Victor demonstrated characteristics common to many wild children. Although when discovered he was still wearing the remains of a shirt around his neck, he seemed not to like clothes and would tear them off if made to wear them. He seemed able to endure extremes of temperature with no ill effect, and would grab and gobble his food like an animal. **(5)** . . . These included a complete lack of curiosity regarding other people. He would spend hours squatting in a corner rather than spend time with other human beings.

Victor's cause was eventually taken up by Dr Jean Itard, who spent five years of his life attempting to teach Victor human behaviour. Itard did have some notable successes in his endeavours to humanise Victor, although much that he wanted to achieve was left undone. **(6)** . . . Thus he was unable to explain who he was, how it was he was all alone in the woods for so long, or why he had a vicious scar on the back of his neck.

Victor seems to have survived on his own, but other wild children are said to have been brought up by wild animals. **(7)** . . . If we are to believe reported stories of wild children, it appears that these children disappear into the forests when very young. They are often carried off, we are told, by animal mothers who have lost their own young – and reappear a few years later when their behaviour attracts attention.

A He was found roaming alone in the woods of Lacaune in southern France at the end of the eighteenth century.

B In particular, the boy was never able to use any conventional means of communication.

C This time, he lasted a week in the house of a kindly lady who fed and clothed him, before he escaped yet again.

D However, this turned out not to be the case.

E More usually, these children can be found living in groups in cities or large towns.

F By now, he had travelled some 100 kilometres away, to the area around Saint Sernin.

G Scientists felt this may have been because of a childhood accident or illness.

H He'd possibly been abandoned at the age of six by a father who couldn't cope with his learning difficulties.

I He also exhibited signs that we now associate with some developmental disorders in children.

J Whether this is even physically possible is still debated today.

(TC)

Task 5.9

Look at the following two tasks from tests of listening.

Refer to the table of listening task types on the website (www.routledge.com/cw/rial: task types). What types of tasks are these?

Use the 'Guidelines for preparing tasks: receptive skills' to review the two tasks.

What groups of learners would each task be suited to?

What kinds of knowledge, skill or ability are needed to respond to each task?

Search language test providers websites to find more listening tasks. Review them in the same way. How do they compare to these two?

Listening Task 1 from the Versant Pro – Writing Test (www.VersantTest.com)

Versant Pro

Please type each sentence exactly as you hear it. You will have 25 seconds for each sentence. Pay attention to spelling and punctuation. Click "Next" when you are finished. After 25 seconds, your work will be saved automatically.

Example

You hear:

"Can you work on Monday?"

You type:

"Can you work on Monday?"

Listening Task 2 from the Password Listening Test (www.englishlanguagetesting.co.uk)

Screen 1:

Section 3

Listen to this introduction to a lecture about rainforests

Click play (▶) when you are ready to start.

Screen 2:

Section 3

Now listen again. When will the speaker mention the weather in rainforests?

▶	at the beginning of the lecture
▶	in the middle of the lecture
▶	quite late in the lecture
▶	not at all

Script (the test taker hears, but does not see, this)

[+ denotes a short pause, ++ a longer pause]

today's lecture is about the rainforests of the world + we're going to look at the kinds of vegetation + trees, bushes, grass + that you'll find in a rainforest ++ and then we'll go on to explore the fascinating world of the cloud canopy at the top of tall trees + and the kinds of animal and bird life that you can find there + but let's start by asking what a rain forest is and what kind of climate produces one.

6 Assessing productive and interactive skills

Personal reflection

Think about a context in which people need to learn a language. This time you might think about a different context from the one you considered in Chapter 5 (e.g., living in the country as a migrant, visiting as a tourist, steering a ship, working as a nurse, etc.).

What kinds of speaking and writing tasks will the learners often need to perform in this context?

What kinds of written texts will they need to produce? Will they need to interact face to face or over the telephone with other people? Will they need to give prepared speeches or make announcements?

What kinds of knowledge, skill or ability do you think might be important in each case?

What tasks might you be able to use to assess each of these?

As with the receptive skills, obtaining the necessary evidence about speaking and writing will involve:

- defining the nature of the knowledge, skills or abilities that should be measured;
- identifying the kinds of tasks that assessees should be able to perform and the language abilities needed to perform these tasks in the real world;
- choosing and specifying ways of getting assessees to produce the kinds of language that will allow judgements to be made about their abilities.

The document titled *Task types*, accessed via the companion website for this volume at www.routledge.com/cw/rial, includes a comprehensive list of task types commonly used to assess speaking and writing skills.

Defining productive and interactive language abilities

As Cutler (2005) observed, productive language processing in many respects mirrors receptive processing. In production, the speaker or writer begins with a message to be conveyed, and the process of production involves putting the message into an appropriate physical form: speech or writing (or sign language – although that is beyond the scope of this book). The listener or reader, in contrast, begins with uncertainty about the message and must 'unscramble' the visual or auditory signal to build (or recover) the message (see Figure 6.1). As with the receptive models of reading and listening, there is a good deal of shared ground between process models of speech and writing, so the following paragraphs will consider both together.

In these models, a speaker or writer (the addresser), like the reader or listener, has in mind certain goals for communication. These are usually conceived in terms of a message that he or she wishes to convey to one or more listeners or readers (the addressees). Drawing on a mental store of vocabulary and on knowledge of grammar and discourse, the addresser encodes the message, puts it into linguistic form (speech or writing) and transmits it to the addressee in the form of an auditory or visual signal. The addressee then recovers the message through the kinds of receptive processes described in Chapter 5. The addresser needs to make decisions on how best to formulate the message to convey it to the intended addressee in a way that will realise his or her goals. This will involve utilizing what the addresser knows about the topic, about the addressee, about the context in which the communication occurs, and about the types or genres of speech or writing that are suited to the context.

A distinction, not always reflected in process models, can be made between production and more interactive language use (Council of Europe, 2001).

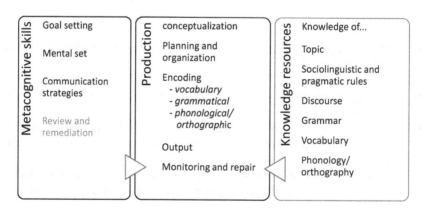

Figure 6.1 A simplified model of language production (after Levelt, 1989; Chenoweth & Hayes, 2001)

Interaction implies the kind of spontaneous exchange found in conversation, while production implies planned and rehearsed monologues – lectures or presentations – or written texts such as reports, essays and manuals. Production and interaction are perhaps best regarded as the two extremes of a continuum: even the most spontaneous conversations include brief planning pauses and do allow the participants some time to consider what they will say. It can also be argued that every text is, in some sense, a contribution to an on-going social 'conversation' or interactive exchange of ideas.

The productive end of the continuum generally implies more formal written varieties of language, although the distinction does not map directly onto spoken and written forms. Instant (written) messaging has many of the features of conversation, while contributions to dialogues can be planned, rehearsed and even scripted – think of formal business or political meetings, legal proceedings, religious ceremonies. Assessment designers need to pay heed to the kinds of productive and interactive language use that are relevant to the decisions their assessments will inform.

The productive–interactive division parallels another between the kind of language that we use at home or with friends and the more formal, careful language we use for more 'official' educational or professional purposes. Cummins (1979) labelled these as *BICS* (Basic Interpersonal Communication Skills) and *CALP* (Cognitive Academic Language Proficiency). Most native speakers of a language are proficient in BICS, but CALP is only achieved through education.

Bearing in mind the physical, linguistic and social context, the addresser mentally shapes and organises the message that he or she intends to convey. Organization is important both at the level of the individual sentence or speech unit – giving grammatical shape to the emerging linguistic message – and at the level of the text or unfolding interaction. At the more local sentence or speech unit level, it may, for example, involve provisional decisions about which information is *given* or already known to the addressee and which is unknown, or *new*. New information will usually be given prominence – in English this might involve stressing the words that refer to new information and positioning them towards the end of a sentence. Given information that relates to knowledge shared by the addresser and the addressee is often omitted, especially in casual speech (Halliday & Hasan, 1976).

Bygate (1987) distinguished between two general types of speech (although his distinction applies equally to writing): *factually oriented* talk and *evaluative* talk. Factual talk has the purpose of conveying information and covers a range of rhetorical functions, including description, narration, instruction and comparison: '*this is a book about a father and his three daughters.*' Evaluative talk is generally more demanding as it involves expressing a stance towards the content: '*this is a very moving story because it touches on family relationships.*' It covers functions such as explanation, justification and prediction. Brown and Yule (1983) suggested a somewhat different division between *interactional* language which functions primarily to build and maintain social relationships (think of greetings and chatting with friends) and *transactional* language which conveys information.

At the textual level, writers pay attention to the sequencing of ideas and to the conventions of the type of writing they are engaged in. Readers expect to find certain kinds of information expressed and ordered in established ways in a business report and this will be rather different from what they expect to find in a newspaper or in an informal email. Just as written texts tend to be organised in familiar ways, so *speech events* (Hymes, 1974) – such as booking a hotel room over the telephone, having conversations with friends or family, or participating in an employment interview – tend to follow common patterns of interaction. A greeting is typically answered with a greeting, a question by an answer, an offer by acceptance or refusal. Each turn in the conversation fulfils a social function and these functions combine in predictable ways to make up speech events. Learners need to gain awareness of how communicative language functions are typically realised in different contexts and of the sequences that are followed in familiar speech events in the target language.

In writing (or in the prepared speech of presentations and lectures), there is usually greater opportunity to plan. Longer planning time allows for more grammatically complex language involving features such as subordinate clauses. Because they are not usually under pressure to contribute to an on-going interaction, writers generally have greater scope than speakers to organise their sentences – and their paragraphs and texts – before committing to them. Textual organization may be given a preliminary physical shape through notes or outlines, or it may simply be held in the addresser's memory.

In contrast, the burden of organising and developing spoken interaction is shared between the participants and depends on their ability to take turns, recognizing when it is appropriate for them to speak and their awareness of the kinds of contribution they are expected to make as the interaction progresses.

With limited planning time, spoken interaction is often grammatically relatively simple and its vocabulary relatively vague. People do not generally talk to each other in well-formed sentences of the kind found in language textbooks (this is why some applied linguistics refer to 'speech units' or 'utterances' in spoken interaction rather than 'sentences'). Spoken grammar tends to involve more coordination: strings of speech units connected by (and often beginning with) *and* or *then*.

Like grammar, the vocabulary of spoken interaction is also constrained by the limitations on planning time. Equally, communication is facilitated when speakers are together and are able to use their shared knowledge of objects around them. Reflecting these facts, Luoma (2004) points out that the vocabulary of spoken interaction tends to be relatively generic (*'book'* rather than '*historical novel*' or '*monograph*'; '*give*' *rather than* '*donate*,' '*impart*' or '*allocate*') and vague ('*round thing*,' '*powdery stuff*'). Informal speech is often marked by references to the immediate physical environment. For example, the instructions conveyed in writing '*position the document holder to the right of the viewer, between the keyboard and the monitor*' might more simply be conveyed in interactive speech by '*put that thing over here.*'

In written production, the addresser is usually more distant from the addressee both physically (people do not usually write to each other face to face) and socially (the writer and reader may never meet and may know little or nothing about each other). This places more of a burden on the language to convey the message as there is much less scope for referring to shared knowledge. Visual features such as punctuation and typeface do offer some additional paralinguistic information, but cannot convey as much as the pauses, intonational patterns, shifts of pitch and volume, gestures and facial expressions that support face-to-face interaction.

The step of physically producing spoken or written output presents evident challenges for the language learner. Writing can involve grappling with an unfamiliar script, punctuation conventions and spelling. Speech involves articulating the different sounds of the foreign language, along with stress patterns, systems of intonation and pitch. These issues all have the potential to obscure the learner's intended message and impede communication. Features that can be indicative of the level of difficulty a speaker has in articulating their message in a foreign language are outlined in Table 6.1.

Table 6.1 Features of more and less proficient speech (based on Luoma, 2004; Tonkyn & Wilson, 2004; Hughes, 2010)

Less proficient speech	More proficient speech
Shorter and less complex speech units	Longer and more complex (e.g. more embedded) speech units
More errors per speech unit	Fewer errors per speech unit
Less and more limited use of cohesive markers (and, but etc.)	More (and more varied) use of cohesive markers
Limited to use of common words	Use of more sophisticated and idiomatic vocabulary
Pauses linked to language search	Pauses linked to content search
Pauses within grammatical units	Pauses between grammatical units
More silent pause time	Less silent pause time
Shorter stretches of speech between noticeable pauses	Longer stretches of speech between noticeable pauses
Speed of delivery noticeably below typical native speaker rates	Speed of delivery not noticeably below typical native speaker rates

Because they provide observable evidence of language processing, features of this kind are often reflected in rating scales used to assess performance.

Once the linguistic message has been articulated, both speakers and writers have opportunities to monitor and, if necessary, revise what they have said or written. Writers have the chance to do this before sharing their texts with others. Speakers engaging in interaction have much more limited time for their self-monitoring, but are more likely to receive immediate feedback (perhaps by noticing their own slips, or from questions or confused facial expressions from their conversational partners) indicating that communication has failed and that they need to reformulate the message. Monitoring and revision can occur at the local levels of spelling, pronunciation, punctuation and grammar. They may involve organization of the overall utterance or text, levels of formality, text structure, stylistic elegance and the effects on the audience. In the course of composing a text or participating in interaction, addressers may modify or even abandon their original goals.

Learners are often categorised according to how they monitor and revise their speech. Some prioritise local accuracy. As a result, they tend to speak relatively hesitantly, concentrating on grammatical formulation and pausing frequently to plan or to correct themselves. Others prioritise fluency, sacrificing a degree of accuracy to maintain the flow of speech. Both strategies have benefits and costs for the learner and can cause strain on the addressee. Assessment designers need to decide how best to take account of such choices when scoring performance (Fulcher, 2003).

A longstanding criticism of process models of language is that they tend to focus rather narrowly on how messages are transmitted between individuals without paying sufficient attention to the social constraints and conventions that govern when it is appropriate to speak (or write) and the impact of these upon meaning. By focusing on the individual mechanisms of language processing, they downplay the shared nature of communication. As Luoma (2004) expressed it, they are concerned with *speech*, the product of the individual, rather than with *talk* as a shared social activity. He and Young (1998) argued that social nature of talk raises questions about the validity of interactive speaking tests. Scores are awarded to the individual assessee, but talk is a product of shared interaction.

A further challenge for assessment designers is that the meaning of any sentence or speech unit is not universal, but can be radically modified by context. An utterance such as '*Good evening, madam,*' even if spoken with identical intonation, has a very different implication when it is said by a hotel receptionist greeting a guest at 6 p.m. than when it is said by a mother to rebuke her teenage daughter for waking up late in the morning. It can be imagined that the expected response would also be quite different in each case. Each utterance conveys something about the relationship between the participants. The receptionist indicates to the guest that he is ready to engage in a transaction, but could also do this by saying '*Next*' or '*Yes?*' or '*Hi there.*' Or he could choose to say nothing at all and simply wait for the guest to approach the desk and open the interaction. In each case, something different would be conveyed about the kind of relationship the receptionist expects to establish with the guest. The impacts of these kinds of choices upon the addressee are culturally loaded and often very difficult for language learners to gauge.

(TC)

Task 6.1

Jakobson (1960) suggested that every utterance, however banal, has several levels of meaning. It conveys something about the identity of the addresser, their feelings or opinions, their relationship with the addressee, and their place in the world more generally.

An advertising slogan such as '*Go to work on an egg!*' illustrates the point. This single sentence has meanings connected with the addressee – it attracts our attention and casts us in the role of productive, hard-working consumers. It has meanings connected with the message itself and how it is expressed – the clever word play of the pun on the literal, metaphorical and idiomatic implications of '*go to work on*': compare '*I went to work on a bike,*' '*I went to work on an empty stomach,*' '*The cops went to work on the suspect.*'

It has meanings connected with the qualities of the product as a healthy and energy-giving food. A message is conveyed about the quality of the advertising agency as a skilled communicator, establishing rapport by sharing a witty idea with the addressee, and as a competent agency, appealing to other businesses. And there is the unstated message that we should buy and consume eggs.

This call to buy eggs may be the central message, but it is conveyed largely by the nature of the genre, not by the propositional meaning of the sentence. We understand this meaning because we know from the context rather than from the linguistic content that the sentence is an advertising slogan.

How would you assess a language learner's understanding of the meaning of this slogan?

How (and why) might you assess a language learner on their ability to produce an effective advertising slogan?

Fulcher (2003) and Luoma (2004) cited 'rules' of speech put forward by Grice (1975) and by Leech (1983) to explain how we signal to each other which meanings are intended. Grice proposed that such decisions are facilitated by what he termed the cooperative principle of conversation. In interpreting speech (or writing), he suggested that we have in mind four conversational maxims or rules of thumb which include the following:

1   the maxim of quality: say only what you know to be true;
2   the maxim of quantity: give all the information that the addressee needs (but not more);
3   the maxim of relation: be relevant (to the topic or setting);
4   the maxim of manner: be unambiguous, brief, clear and orderly.

If the addressee perceives that all four maxims are being followed, he or she will tend to take what the addresser says at face value: the most obvious explicit meaning is the intended meaning. Through what Grice termed *implicature*, violation or 'flouting' of the maxims implies that something else is intended. In the example of the mother rebuking her daughter by saying '*Good evening, madam,*' the mother violates the maxims of quality and relevance because both participants are aware that it is morning, not evening (quality) and that formal greetings are not appropriate to the context (manner). These violations of the maxims signal to the daughter that her mother is being sarcastic.

Leech (1983), who was concerned with the rules that govern politeness, also put forward conversational maxims. These cover issues such as tact, generosity and agreement. The agreement principle, for example, states: 'minimise the expression of disagreement between self and other; maximise the expression of agreement between self and other.' This maxim explains why an utterance such as '*Yes. You are so right*' is interpreted as being more polite than '*No. You're completely wrong*' (even if the first of these would flout Grice's maxim of quality). Of course, people do disagree; but in order to maintain politeness they often try to mitigate the effect by being indirect or by apologising: '*I'm sorry, but I don't really follow your point*' or '*I'm afraid I'm going to have to disagree with you.*'

Personal reflection

Pragmatic considerations such as politeness and implicature present difficulties for assessment designers. Although they are certainly very important to communication and should play a part in its assessment, they are not as stable as grammatical rules and can be quite idiosyncratic. Some people are more ready to perceive violations of politeness than others. If an addressee takes offence when a non-native speaker of English asks: '*Could I borrow your book?*' instead of '*I was just wondering if you have the book and I could borrow it?,'* as in Fulcher's (2003) example, is this because the speaker is being rude or because the addressee is being over-sensitive?

Another problem is that these issues may be as much a matter of culture as they are of language. Native speakers of English in India do not necessarily share the same politeness conventions as native speakers of English in New Zealand or in Jamaica. A 25-year-old may not recognise the same politeness conventions as his 75-year-old neighbour.

Regional and global languages such as English pose particular problems as so much interaction is between non-native speakers. Should American politeness conventions apply when an Iranian is negotiating with a Chinese and a Brazilian? If not, what politeness conventions would you expect the three negotiators to follow?

In what circumstances do you think it might be important to assess politeness?

Purposes for assessment

People learn languages for a wide variety of reasons and these reasons have implications for the kinds of writing and speaking they may need to do in a foreign language. As with assessing receptive skills, the designer must first consider the purpose of the assessment. What is it that the users of the results need to know about the assessee's abilities? In proficiency assessment, a user might wish to know whether an assessee has the language skills necessary to write a technical report as an engineer, give an effective presentation on an academic topic as a teacher, or haggle over the price of a car as a consumer.

In formative classroom assessment, a teacher may wish to know what difficulties learners have in articulating certain sounds, how well learners are able to follow the conventions of a standard business letter, or whether they can control the degree of formality of a piece of writing. Each purpose might require a different balance of knowledge, skills and abilities and so suggest a different kind of assessment task. In developing assessments for different purposes and for different populations of learners, it is essential to consider how the nature of the writing and speaking that learners do will affect the kinds of linguistic knowledge they will draw on and the cognitive processes they will engage.

Assessment design

The challenges facing assessment designers who wish to assess speaking and writing abilities are rather different from those involved in assessing reading and listening. First, it *is* possible to observe people speaking and to look at their writing. On this basis, Hughes (2003, p. 75) argues that 'the best way to test people's writing ability is to get them to write' and in similar vein, He and Young (1998, p. 1) suggest that to assess a learner's speaking abilities, assessors have to 'get him or her to speak.' Unfortunately for the designer, this cannot not be quite as straightforward as turning to an assessee and issuing the command 'Speak!' or 'Write!'

While it is possible to assess some aspects of writing and speaking through grammar and vocabulary exercises and pronunciation drills, these can only give a very limited and incomplete picture in relation to the range of knowledge and abilities involved in language production and interaction outlined previously. It is now well established in language assessment that meaningful interpretations of writing ability or speaking ability can only really be supported through the use of **performance assessment**. In a performance assessment, the assessee carries out a task involving an extended response (see Example 6.1). Performance is evaluated according to a set process – usually employing a **rating scale**, sometimes referred to as a **scoring rubric**.

Example 6.1   Speaking task

You are a purchasing agent for a wholesale catering business which sells eggs to restaurants.

You need at least 240 large eggs every month, but you could buy up to 50 more as your business is expanding.

The current price of a dozen eggs is typically 97 cents, but your director has told you that you must find a lower price.

Delivery should be made within two days.

Call three suppliers of eggs. Negotiate a discount.

Place your order with the cheapest supplier who can meet your needs.

Extended performances are inevitably less predictable than responses to multiple choice items and the assessment designer has much less control over the response. This limits the reliability of any resulting scores and threatens their interpretation. There are steps that designers can take to impose control, such as standardizing the tasks. In Example 6.1, genuine suppliers could be replaced by recorded questions or by actors, each with a partly scripted role to play, so that every assessee faces a similar challenge. However, as with adaptations of input for listening and reading, attempts to control the task inevitably threaten authenticity. Actors may not respond in the same ways as real suppliers and may not respond in the same way to each individual assessee. Recordings can be used to standardise the input, but cannot be engaged in a negotiation. Even where tasks are standardised, there may be aspects of the specific task selected – the topic of an essay, the personality or vocal characteristics of an interviewer, the familiarity of the assessee with the task type – that affect individual assessees in different ways.

Strong and weak performance assessment

When it comes to rating the performance of the assessee, McNamara (1996) made a distinction between a strong and a weak sense of performance assessment. In the strong sense of the term, the focus is on the completion of the given task – did the assessee accomplish what was required? In Example 6.1, if the assessee obtained a good price and successfully placed the order, she would pass the test, even if her language ability seemed poor. In contrast, in the weaker sense of performance assessment, the task is a really a pretext for eliciting an extended sample of spoken or written language. Rating focuses more on the language used than on fulfilment of the task. In the example, the assessee who called uncooperative suppliers and failed to negotiate a price within her budget might, because she demonstrated superior language abilities, outscore other assessees who obtained a lower price.

The choice between stronger and weaker approaches to rating performance should take into account the assessees, the purpose of the test and its relationship to the real life situation the test is intended to reflect. Consider the essay assignment in Example 6.2 comparing and contrasting the work of two writers.

Example 6.2   Writing task

Write an essay comparing and contrasting the views of Freud and Jung on the function of dreams.

In a language class, the teacher may have assigned this task (Example 6.2) in order to find out whether students are able to organise an essay of comparison. The focus would be on organization and cohesion. Formative feedback would focus on these issues and any misrepresentation of the theories of the two authors in the students' essays might not be taken into account. The students' knowledge of psychological theories would not be part of the construct and differences in performance attributable to different levels of knowledge of the work of Freud and Jung would be considered as construct irrelevant. In fact, it would probably be sensible to provide the assessees with information about the two writers to make sure that all would all have the background knowledge needed to write the essay.

On the other hand, if the task was part of an assessment for prospective teaching assistants working in the psychology department, understanding of the psychological theories and the quality of the arguments would probably be given much greater importance. It might be considered as part of the construct of the assessment. In practice, rating scales used in tests of languages for specific purposes often include a 'task fulfilment' criterion that reflects the 'strong' interpretation, but greater weight is generally given to other 'weak' linguistic criteria (Douglas, 2000).

Speaking tasks

Controlled tasks with a focus on knowledge of grammar, vocabulary and phonology are relevant to receptive, productive and interactive language use. Some tasks described in the tables on the website (https://routledgetextbooks.com/textbooks/_author/rial/) accompanying Chapter 5 for listening and reading might also be interpreted as assessments of enabling skills for speaking and writing. Gap fill, ordering, intrusion and read-aloud item types, for example, are sometimes interpreted as indicators of productive abilities. Partial dictation based on short dialogues or 'conversational cloze' has been found to be a good predictor of speaking abilities (Brown, 1983). Assessments of grammar and vocabulary tend to be reasonable predictors of more general proficiency – hence their widespread use in placement tests (Green, 2012b). However, the value of these tasks is seen most clearly at the beginning stages of language learning where assessees often struggle to build simple sentences and may not be capable of producing meaningful responses to more open-ended tasks.

In assessments of more extended writing skills, key choices facing the designer include the types of writing that the assessee will be required to produce (report, email, notice, etc.) and their social purposes or rhetorical functions (to inform, evaluate, persuade, entertain, etc.). There are questions to be resolved about suitable topics and how much support to give to the writer in the form of information about the topic, language in the input that can be used in composing the response, and access to resources such as dictionaries or the internet. And there are issues around how much writing should be required: how much is needed for an adequate response that engages the processes that are of interest? How much can the assessees reasonably be expected to produce? How much would be sufficient to reflect writing in the target language use domain? Thought also needs to be given to the time that should be allowed for writing, planning, reviewing and revising. Similar considerations are important in assessments of extended (productive) speaking.

Input and interaction

For assessments of writing skills, the choice of response format generally lies between paper-based and computer-based options. Input might take the form of a written or visual prompt, or a combination of the two. In assessments of speaking, input is more often presented orally.

In the classic oral interview (see Figure 6.2), an examiner poses questions to the assessee either face to face, via a video-link or over the telephone. In effect, the examiner fills the role played in most tests by the question paper. However, individual assessees will encounter different examiners with different personalities and questioning styles.

The specific questions posed by the examiner and the manner in which they are put can affect the kind of performance that is elicited. It is therefore important to control questioning in a systematic way. In large-scale tests, attempts have been made to standardise examiner behaviour through training, by scripting or partially scripting their role, and by specifying other contextual features, such as what the interviewer should wear and where he or she should sit in relation to the assessee. This is intended to ensure that every assessee has a comparable experience (see Fulcher, 2003, Chapter 6).

An alternative to the face-to-face interview (or one conducted via video-link or telephone) is to replace the examiner with a recording (see Figure 6.3), but this brings its own problems. Recordings cannot interact realistically with the assessee, so turn taking and conversation management cannot be assessed. Some people feel very awkward talking to machines and may not perform at their best in these circumstances. Conversely, others may feel more relaxed talking to a machine than to an examiner.

The interview format itself has come under criticism because the interaction it gives rise to tends to be very one sided. The interviewer asks all the questions and controls the interaction while the assessee is just required to answer. This does not closely resemble everyday conversations, discussions

Figure 6.2 Interaction in the oral proficiency interview (OPI)

Figure 6.3 Interaction in the semi-direct or computer-based oral proficiency interview (SOPI/COPI)

or transactions, where the participants have a more balanced relationship and share in directing the interaction. Some features of conversation that may be of interest to the assessment user play little or no part in an interview (Johnson, 2001).

A possible remedy is to employ paired or group speaking assessments (see Figure 6.4). In this format, assessees are asked to interact with one another, or participate in a three-way interaction with the examiner, to discuss a topic or solve a problem. Swain (2001) outlined the arguments in favour of paired speaking tests. They elicit a wider variety of talk from the assessees who do generally initiate and take turns in the interaction. They have the potential for positive washback, encouraging interactive classroom activities, and they are more practical than individual interviews as more assessees can be tested by fewer assessors.

On the other hand, assessees cannot all be trained and controlled in the same way as examiners: assessees may have a very different experience according to the language level, personality and other characteristics of their partner. As He and Young (1998) and others have argued, scoring any interactive assessment of speaking is especially problematic because the outcome is always a product of both (or all) participants involved, not just the person being assessed.

Unfortunately, no assessment task is entirely satisfactory. Each format has its own weaknesses. Rather than searching for one ideal task type, the assessment designer is better advised to include a reasonable variety in any test or classroom assessment system so that the failings of one format do not extend to the overall system.

The tables provided on the website (https://routledgetextbooks.com/ textbooks/_author/rial/ under Resources > Task types) outline a number of broad categories of task, each of which is open to a good deal of variation. Some of the attractions and pitfalls of each are described. These tables are only intended to be expressive of the variety of options open to the assessment designer. Ultimately, the range of task types is only limited by the imagination of the designer.

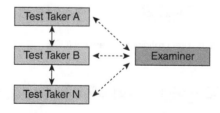

Figure 6.4 Interaction in the paired/group speaking assessment

Task review

As in Chapter 5, I suggest some generic guidelines for use in reviewing test material. Again, these may not apply in every context for assessment, but could be adapted and extended for use in item writer guidelines and quality review.

Guidelines for preparing tasks: Productive skills

Are the task instructions:

- clear enough to assessees on what exactly they will need to do;
- presented in simple language (or images) that all assessees understand;
- clearly presented on the page or screen in a way that attracts attention;
- presented in a standard and consistent way across tasks?

Are expectations clear to assessees in terms of:

- the addressee (e.g., writing to a friend or to an employer);
- type of writing or speaking required: text/speech type and function;
- time available for planning;
- time available for writing or speaking;
- number of words required;
- scoring focus (criteria);
- weighting of criteria?

Are expectations realistic in terms of:

- the kinds of language elicited;
- language functions (e.g., do assessees actually need to narrate/ describe/apologise/explain, etc. as intended in the task design);
- interaction (e.g., does the task actually involve the kinds of interaction between assessees intended in the task design);
- organization (e.g., do successful assessees organise their presentations in the way intended in the task design)?

Is there a clear focus?

- Avoid giving assessees too much freedom in deciding what kind of response to give: this results in each assessee carrying out a different task using different kinds of language.

Are tasks familiar to assessees?

- Are the tasks similar to those that assessees carry out in the real world?
- Have assessees carried out similar activities in class before?

Are tasks realistic for assessees?

- Can assessees at this level be expected to produce the type of text or speech event required?
- Will assessees at this level be able to produce the length of output required in the time available?
- Can the task realistically be accomplished adequately in the time or number of words specified?
- Does adequately accomplishing the task require as much time or as many words as is specified?

Do the topics:

- fall within the assessees' life experience or world knowledge;
- avoid sensitive issues (e.g., war, death, serious disease, politics, religion);
- avoid consistently favouring one group of assessees over another (e.g., consist of three tasks focused on sports)?

Trying out material

With more open-ended and extended performance assessments, it is particularly helpful to obtain evidence of the kinds of response that a task prompt actually generates (Association of Language Testers in Europe/Council of Europe, 2011). A first step is for writers to attempt the task themselves and for colleagues to do the same. This can also help the scoring process because these responses can be used as benchmarks for expert performance to assist scorers. However, all assessment material should be tried out with groups of learners who are as similar as possible to the assessees who will take the operational assessment.

In addition to analysing responses to see that the assessees were able to produce the kinds of language intended, the designers have the opportunity to find out from the assessees and examiners whether they experienced any difficulties in following the tasks or identified any other potential problems with the material.

A complicating factor in face-to-face assessments of speaking is that the assessor actually delivers the assessment. Assessor training and monitoring must therefore also be part of the quality control process. Are assessors able to adhere to their instructions? What impact do these instructions have upon the kind of performance that is elicited? In formative assessment, what techniques for supporting or scaffolding learner performance are most effective? What follow-up activities might be used to challenge learners to extend their learning? The material and procedures should be reviewed and accepted, revised or rejected as appropriate.

Scoring performance

Impression scoring

Chapter 5 showed how selected response formats, such as multiple choice or matching, are designed for ease of scoring. With these item types, scorers can relatively easily be replaced by machines, which will tend to be more accurate and less demanding. On the other hand, because they restrict the range of responses, selected response formats are uninformative about how well learners are able to use language for social purposes. Performance tests can provide better evidence of this, but scoring them requires skill and judgement on the part of the scorers or **raters**, as judges of extended performance are often known.

One apparently straightforward approach to awarding scores to a performance is impression scoring. The rater awards a score out of an arbitrary total to reflect the quality of the performance. Percentages are a popular option, perhaps because they give a reassuring (but spurious) air of statistical precision. Raters find impression marking easy to understand and apply. Unfortunately, as Edgeworth demonstrated over 100 years ago (see Chapter 4), individual raters can have worryingly incompatible ideas about the standards of performance represented by different scores. More rigorous alternatives are needed.

Error counts

In Chapter 4, it was noted that it is not possible to have valid and useful assessments without a reasonable level of reliability. It would therefore seem better to replace fuzzy subjective judgements with something more concrete. At one time, error counting seemed to promise a more objective basis for scoring. Instead of giving scores to reward performance, this scoring process involves deducting points for each error or each sentence containing an error. However, this does not really solve the problem of reliability. First, some errors are obviously more serious than others, yet judgements about the relative seriousness of errors would reintroduce the subjectivity that error counting was intended to eliminate. Second, error counting is limited to mechanical accuracy: it takes no account of how well a text is constructed beyond the sentence level, or of how well an overall message is communicated. Third, error counting rewards very cautious language use. Responses made up of simple sentences could outscore those made up of more ambitious language. This was not the kind of washback that assessment designers wanted to promote.

Task 6.2

Look at these two sentences from student essays:

Eggs are one of the only foods contained natural occurring vitamin D.
Eggs is naturally foods that vitamin D is contain.

Both sentences contain errors, although most judges would agree that the first communicates more successfully. In some error counting systems, both would lead to deduction of one point. In others, errors would be judged for seriousness, reintroducing subjectivity.
    Now try counting the errors in each. How many can you find? Would other judges agree with you?

Checklists

The key advantage of using checklists to score spoken or written performance is that they direct attention to aspects of performance that are considered by the designers to be important. In other words, they communicate the assessment construct to the raters. They are straightforward to use and interpret as they involve a series of yes/no decisions. Their simplicity makes them particularly suitable for use in peer- and self-assessment where learners assess each other's performance or review their own work. Learner understanding of success criteria can be increased if learners are included in the design process. They can discuss model responses and identify features that seem to characterise good performance. These features may then be brought together to form a checklist (see Table 6.2). Completed checklists can provide immediate diagnostic feedback to the assessee, showing areas of success and areas in need of improvement.

    The simplicity of checklists can also be considered a weakness. Successful communication is not readily reducible to yes/no choices and aggregating the checks to arrive at a score may, like error counting, misrepresent the relative communicative effectiveness of assessees.

Rating scales

The most widely adopted strategy for scoring performance on assessments of writing or speaking is to use rating scales. These are also known by various other names such as scoring rubrics and marking schemes.

    Rating scales combine the advantage of checklists – defining aspects of performance to be attended to – with the advantages of impression scoring – scores that reflect different degrees of success (Table 6.3).

Table 6.2 A basic checklist for assessing short interview tasks

☑   Speaks intelligibly

☒   Opens and closes the conversation appropriately

☑   Has sufficient vocabulary to answer basic personal questions (age, job, family)

☑   Produces simple personal questions accurately enough to be understood

Table 6.3 A simple rating scale

weak	adequate	good	
1	2	**3**	Speaks intelligibly
1	2	3	Opens and closes the conversation appropriately
1	**2**	3	Has sufficient vocabulary to answer basic personal questions (age, job, family)
1	**2**	3	Produces simple personal questions accurately enough to be understood

Checklists can easily be converted to simple rating scales by replacing each checkbox with a numeric scale (see Tables 6.2 and 6.3). They more usually consist of graded descriptions intended to characterise different levels of performance. The descriptions guide the rater in making a decision about which level described on the scale best matches the sample of language being assessed (scale levels are sometimes also referred to as grades, bands or points). The development of a scale and the descriptors used to define them is of critical importance for the validity of the assessment. As McNamara (1996) noted, the scale used in assessing performance tasks represents, either implicitly or explicitly, the theoretical foundation upon which the test is built.

As with task types, there are a number of choices open to the designer in creating scales that fit the purpose of a specific assessment. Weigle (2002, p. 109) reviewed rating scales used to score writing assessments and found two features that could be used to distinguish between different types. These apply equally well to scales used to assess speaking.

Task specific versus generic scales

First, scales may be task specific (designed to partner a single writing or speaking prompt) or generic (designed to work in relation to a class of tasks of a certain type). The 'class of tasks' could imply the range of tasks included on one test, the range of tasks that might be undertaken in a language programme, or a very wide range of tasks, including tasks undertaken in different languages. This is the case for the ACTFL Proficiency Guidelines (American Council for the Teaching of Foreign Languages, 1999) or the scales included in the Common European Framework of Reference for Languages (CEFR) (Council of Europe, 2001).

An advantage of the task-specific approach is that the scales can communicate the features of a successful response very clearly and in some detail to the rater and to learners, perhaps helping to guide learners on how to improve performance. However, task-specific scales have two serious shortcomings. First, every time a new prompt is devised – an essay about music replacing an essay about sports, for example – a new scale is also required. This makes task-specific scales expensive and impractical to develop. Second, it is difficult to see what such scales can tell us about more general abilities than the ability to carry out the one specific task to which they relate. In proficiency assessment, they might show an employer that an assessee is good at one very clearly delineated function, but may not provide enough information about how well they will perform other aspects of the job. At a formative level, although they provide a basis for feedback to the assessees, they are less helpful than more generic scales in suggesting how learners might perform better on different tasks in the future. For these reasons, most operational scales are more generic in nature.

Holistic versus analytic scales

Weigle's (2002) second distinction is between scales that are used to award a single score (**holistic scales**) and those that are used to award multiple scores to a single script (or spoken performance) (**analytic scales**). In holistic rating, the rater consults a set of graded descriptions such as those in Table 6.4 and considers how far the performance satisfies the stated criteria. He or she decides either which level best describes the performance (the 'best fit'), or at which level the performance fully satisfies all of the stated criteria. **Primary trait** scales are holistic scales that have been designed to accompany a specific task and reflect features of writing or speaking that are believed to be particularly pertinent to that task.

Analytic scales, in contrast, require the rater to award a number of different scores across a range of categories or **criteria**. For example, the scales in Table 6.5 include the following criteria: *Range, Accuracy, Fluency, Interaction* and *Coherence*. Separate scores are awarded to a performance on each of the criteria. These may then be added together to give an overall score. Analytic scales that have been designed for use with a specific task are known as **multiple trait** scales.

Notice that the holistic – analytic distinction is more a distinction between scoring processes than between scales. The TOEFL scale has implicit criteria

Table 6.4 A holistic scale: TOEFL iBT® Independent Writing scale

Score	Task description
5	An essay at this level largely accomplishes all of the following: • Effectively addresses the topic and task • Is well organised and well developed, using clearly appropriate explanations, exemplifications and/or details • Displays unity, progression and coherence • Displays consistent facility in the use of language, demonstrating syntactic variety, appropriate word choice and idiomaticity, though it may have minor lexical or grammatical errors
4	An essay at this level largely accomplishes all of the following: • Addresses the topic and task well, though some points may not be fully elaborated • Is generally well organised and well developed, using appropriate and sufficient explanations, exemplifications and/or details • Displays unity, progression and coherence, though it may contain occasional redundancy, digression, or unclear connections • Displays facility in the use of language, demonstrating syntactic variety and range of vocabulary, though it will probably have occasional noticeable minor errors in structure, word form or use of idiomatic language that do not interfere with meaning
3	An essay at this level is marked by one or more of the following: • Addresses the topic and task using somewhat developed explanations, exemplifications and/or details • Displays unity, progression and coherence, though connection of ideas may be occasionally obscured • May demonstrate inconsistent facility in sentence formation and word choice that may result in lack of clarity and occasionally obscure meaning • May display accurate but limited range of syntactic structures and vocabulary
2	An essay at this level may reveal one or more of the following weaknesses: • Limited development in response to the topic and task • Inadequate organization or connection of ideas • Inappropriate or insufficient exemplifications, explanations or details to support or illustrate generalizations in response to the task • A noticeably inappropriate choice of words or word forms • An accumulation of errors in sentence structure and/or usage
1	An essay at this level is seriously flawed by one or more of the following weaknesses: • Serious disorganization or underdevelopment • Little or no detail, or irrelevant specifics, or questionable responsiveness to the task • Serious and frequent errors in sentence structure or usage
0	An essay at this level merely copies words from the topic, rejects the topic, or is otherwise not connected to the topic, is written in a foreign language, consists of keystroke characters, or is blank.

Table 6.5 Qualitative aspects of spoken language use (from the Common European Framework of Reference for Languages (CEFR), Council of Europe, 2001, pp. 28–29)

	RANGE	ACCURACY	FLUENCY	INTERACTION	COHERENCE
C2	Shows great flexibility reformulating ideas in differing linguistic forms to convey finer shades of meaning precisely, to give emphasis, to differentiate and to eliminate ambiguity. Also has a good command of idiomatic expressions and colloquialisms.	Maintains consistent grammatical control of complex language, even while attention is otherwise engaged (e.g. in forward planning, in monitoring others' reactions).	Can express him/herself spontaneously at length with a natural colloquial flow, avoiding or backtracking around any difficulty so smoothly that the interlocutor is hardly aware of it.	Can interact with ease and skill, picking up and using non-verbal and intonational cues apparently effortlessly. Can interweave his/her contribution into the joint discourse with fully natural turn taking, referencing, allusion making etc.	Can create coherent and cohesive discourse making full and appropriate use of a variety of organizational patterns and a wide range of connectors and other cohesive devices.
C1	Has a good command of a broad range of language allowing him/her to select a formulation to express him/herself clearly in an appropriate style on a wide range of general, academic, professional or leisure topics without having to restrict what he/she wants to say.	Consistently maintains a high degree of grammatical accuracy; errors are rare, difficult to spot and generally corrected when they do occur.	Can express him/herself fluently and spontaneously, almost effortlessly. Only a conceptually difficult subject can hinder a natural, smooth flow of language.	Can select a suitable phrase from a readily available range of discourse functions to preface his remarks in order to get or to keep the floor and to relate his/her own contributions skilfully to those of other speakers.	Can produce clear, smoothly flowing, well-structured speech, showing controlled use of organizational patterns, connectors and cohesive devices.
B2	Has a sufficient range of language to be able to give clear descriptions, express viewpoints on most general topics, without much conspicuous searching for words, using some complex sentence forms to do so.	Shows a relatively high degree of grammatical control. Does not make errors which cause misunderstanding, and can correct most of his/her mistakes.	Can produce stretches of language with a fairly even tempo; although he/she can be hesitant as he or she searches for patterns and expressions, there are few noticeably long pauses.	Can initiate discourse, take his/her turn when appropriate and end conversation when he/she needs to, though he/she may not always do this elegantly. Can help the discussion along on familiar ground confirming comprehension, inviting others in, etc.	Can use a limited number of cohesive devices to link his/her utterances into clear, coherent discourse, though there may be some 'jumpiness' in a long contribution.

	RANGE	ACCURACY	FLUENCY	INTERACTION	COHERENCE
B1	Has enough language to get by, with sufficient vocabulary to express him/herself with some hesitation and circum-locutions on topics such as family, hobbies and interests, work, travel, and current events.	Uses reasonably accurately a repertoire of frequently used 'routines' and patterns associated with more predictable situations.	Can keep going comprehensibly, even though pausing for grammatical and lexical planning and repair is very evident, especially in longer stretches of free production.	Can initiate, maintain and close simple face-to-face conversation on topics that are familiar or of personal interest. Can repeat back part of what someone has said to confirm mutual understanding.	Can link a series of shorter, discrete simple elements into a connected, linear sequence of points.
A2	Uses basic sentence patterns with memorised phrases, groups of a few words and formulae in order to communicate limited information in simple everyday situations.	Uses some simple structures correctly, but still systematically makes basic mistakes.	Can make him/herself understood in very short utterances, even though pauses, false starts and reformulation are very evident.	Can answer questions and respond to simple statements. Can indicate when he/she is following but is rarely able to understand enough to keep conversation going of his/her own accord.	Can link groups of words with simple connectors like 'and,' 'but' and 'because.'
A1	Has a very basic repertoire of words and simple phrases related to personal details and particular concrete situations.	Shows only limited control of a few simple grammatical structures and sentence patterns in a memorised repertoire.	Can manage very short, isolated, mainly pre-packaged utterances, with much pausing to search for expressions, to articulate less familiar words, and to repair communication.	Can ask and answer questions about personal details. Can interact in a simple way but communication is totally dependent on repetition, rephrasing and repair.	Can link words or groups of words with very basic linear connectors like 'and' or 'then.'

From the Common European Framework of Reference for Languages: Learning, Teaching, Assessment developed by the Language Policy Division of the Council of Europe (Strasbourg) © 2001 Council of Europe, Language Policy Division that we could give labels for use in analytic scoring, such as 'organization and development' or 'sentence structure and usage.' Equally, the CEFR scale could be used in holistic scoring: raters could consult all the criteria but award a single overall CEFR level.

Analytic scales allow for differential **weighting** to be applied across categories. If the assessment construct suggests that one feature should be given more attention than others, the criteria that reflect this feature can be more heavily weighted and so contribute more to the overall score. For example, if a scale has three criteria and five levels, the score for the category of primary interest – *Fluency*, for example – might be doubled to give ten marks, while other categories – *Accuracy* and *Pronunciation* – might each carry only five marks. The total score would be reported out of 20, but half of the available points would be contributed from the fluency scale.

Differences between holistic and analytic scale formats are summarised in Table 6.6. Whether holistic or analytic scales are chosen, when assessees undertake a series of tasks as part of a test, a separate score should be awarded for each task. Ideally, different raters should award scores to each. In other words, if a writing test involves an essay and a letter, each should be scored by different raters. If a speaking test includes a presentation, an interview and a discussion, the recording should be split and the parts sent to different raters to score. This will substantially improve the reliability of the final result as the assessee will be given multiple opportunities to show what they are able to do and the impact of each rater's tendency towards harshness or leniency of judgement is balanced by the others.'

Table 6.6 Comparison between holistic and analytic scoring approaches

Holistic scoring	Analytic scoring
straightforward and intuitive	more time consuming for raters
reflects a natural tendency to make holistic judgements of learners' language abilities	not clear that raters are really able to differentiate between several different criteria: four or five may the maximum manageable number
raters may interpret the scale selectively, focussing only on features that they value or that they find easy to understand	helpful as a training tool to encourage raters to focus on the variety of features highlighted by the scale developers – these represent the intended test construct
not clear how the overall score is arrived at – if the assessee is strong on one criterion, but weak on another, this is not revealed by the score	differential performance across criteria can be captured in a score profile
less reliable as only one score is awarded	more reliable as multiple observations are collected
less informative – fails to identify strengths and weaknesses	more informative – potential for useful feedback to teaching and learning

Behaviour or ability?

In addition to the holistic/analytic distinction, scales can also be categorised according to whether they are more 'real world' and 'behavioural' in orientation or whether they are more 'ability/interaction' and 'normative' (Bachman, 1990; Council of Europe, 2001). Real world behavioural scales focus on specific task types (e.g., describing a picture, purchasing a ticket, engaging in a discussion, etc.) and tend to describe the kinds of language behaviour that learners display when carrying out these tasks. Ability/interaction scales focus on the test taker and describe the abilities or competences (e.g., grammatical competence, pragmatic competence, etc.) believed to underlie and support language use. Ability-oriented scales represent language use in terms of degree or frequency in relation to theoretical categories, while those in the behavioural tradition offer more concrete descriptions of the observable behaviours associated with a level of performance (see Table 6.7).

Sometimes more ability-oriented scales are **nested** within more behaviourally oriented level definitions. The Graded Examinations in Spoken English (GESE) developed by Trinity College, London, for example, include tests or grades targeting 12 distinct levels of speaking ability. Each grade of the suite represents a different level of challenge for the test taker.

There is one overall scale that covers all 12 grades and identifies the behavioural 'communicative skills' identified with each. For example, at the lowest level (Grade 1) these include 'Give very short answers to simple questions and requests for information.' At Grade 12, among a much wider range of skills, the assessee will 'initiate the discussion and actively seek ways in which to engage the examiner in a meaningful exchange of ideas and opinions.' However, assessees at both levels are rated against the same more ability-focused four-band scale. At Band B, for example, 'the candidate's contributions are generally effective, comprehensible appropriate and adequately fulfil the task,' but at D, contributions 'are very limited, lack comprehensibility and appropriacy and, although there is some attempt at the task, this is not fulfilled, even with support' (Trinity College, London, 2010).

In the metaphor of the high jump suggested by Pollitt (1991), the grade of the examination contributes to the interpretation of each score. The task 'bar' is set at a level appropriate to the target level of the test and the interpretation of the scale is adjusted accordingly. Just as it would mean something very different to say that an athlete has 'comfortably' cleared the bar at 1.5 metres (not enough to win a school competition) or 'comfortably' cleared it at 2.5 metres (a new world record), so, because of the greater task difficulty and increased expectations, a Band B at Grade 6 is not the same as a B at Grade 9, even though the wording of the rating scale is the same.

Nested systems are popular in schools, where expectations may be lower when students are in their third year than when they are in their fifth, but the same grading system operates across years. However, nested scales may

Table 6.7 Differences between ability and behaviour-focused scales

Focus	Ability/interaction/normative	Behavioural/real world
Examples of scales	Cohen and Olshtain (1993), ETS Test of Spoken English (TSE) and Test of Written English (TWE)	American Council for the Teaching of Foreign Languages (ACTFL, 1999), NATO STANAG 6001 Scales used with the Common European Framework of Reference (Council of Europe, 2001) and the Canadian Language Benchmarks (Pawlikowska-Smith, 2000)
Example descriptors	Uses linguistic forms that are fully appropriate for expressing the intended speech act. | Some use of inappropriate linguistic forms for expressing the speech act. | Continuous use of inappropriate linguistic forms for expressing the speech act (Cohen & Olshtain, 1993). Demonstrates syntactic variety and appropriate word choice. | Demonstrates adequate but possibly inconsistent facility with syntax and usage. | Serious and frequent errors in sentence structure and/or usage (Test of Written English, ETS, 1990).	Can follow specialised lectures and presentations employing a high degree of colloquialism, regional usage or unfamiliar terminology. | Can understand the main points of radio news bulletins and simpler recorded material about familiar subjects delivered relatively slowly and clearly (Council of Europe, 2001). Advanced-Mid speakers can handle successfully and with relative ease the linguistic challenges presented by a complication or unexpected turn of events that occurs within the context of a routine situation or communicative task with which they are otherwise familiar. Communicative strategies such as circumlocution or rephrasing are often employed for this purpose (ACTFL, 1999).

convey a dispiriting message to learners who improve their language skills as they progress through the school, but find that they drop from an A to a B or C grade. Such results are difficult to interpret for feedback purposes as they provide relatively little information on what exactly learners could do to improve.

Approaches to developing rating scales

Personal reflection

If you were asked to produce a rating scale for scoring how well a learner can hold a casual conversation in English, what steps would you include in your development plan?

How would you judge whether or not use of your rating scale had led to accurate scores?

Taking up a distinction made by North (2000), Fulcher (2003) categorised recent methods of scale development within two general approaches: *intuitive* and *empirical*. Intuitive rating scale development is carried out by appointed experts (language teachers, applied linguists or language testers), working either individually or in a group. These experts prepare rating scales according to their intuitions, established practice, a teaching syllabus, a needs analysis or some combination of these. The resulting scale may be refined over time according to experience or new developments in the field.

There is no direct correlation between the use of intuition or empirical data in scale development and the ability or behavioural orientation of the scale, Intuitively developed scales include both more ability-oriented scales such as the scale for sociolinguistic ability proposed by Cohen and Olshtain (1993) and more behaviourally/real-world oriented scales such as the Foreign Service Institute scales or their successors, the Interagency Language Roundtable American Council for the Teaching of Foreign Languages (ACTFL) and NATO STANAG 6001 scales.

Fulcher (2003) was critical of traditional intuitive approaches to development. He argued that they lack any persuasive evidence for the assertions they make about differences between assessees. He contrasted this with what he called *empirical methods*, which are more directly based on evidence. He described three alternative empirical approaches.

The first of these, *empirically derived, binary-choice, boundary-definition (EBB) scales* were introduced by Upshur and Turner (1995). Performances (written scripts or recordings of speaking test tasks) are divided by expert judges into two categories: stronger and weaker performances. The judges state their reasons for deciding which performance should go into which category. The two sets of performances are each then further subdivided into 'stronger' and 'weaker' categories. Again, reasons are stated. The justifications made for each division are used in preparing a series of yes/no questions that can be followed in rating. Each choice is simple and concisely worded and narrows down the range of scores

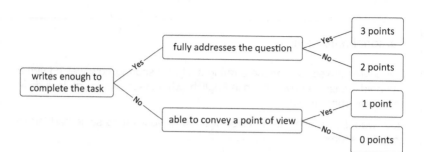

Figure 6.5 Example of a simple four-level EBB scale for essay writing

that can be used to describe the performance (see Figure 6.5). The rater goes through the yes/no questions step by step until he or she arrives at a final score.

The second empirical approach involves *scaling descriptors*. Large numbers of descriptions of performance are collected from rating scales or other sources. These are broken down into their constituent parts so that the developer has a large collection of isolated statements such as 'makes frequent errors with simple grammatical structures' or 'can give directions to places around town.' Groups of expert judges first decide whether these descriptions are meaningful in classifying learners. If they are not, they are edited to make them more meaningful or they are rejected. The experts then rank the statements according to difficulty. They may also classify them according to the aspect of language being described. Statements of similar difficulty are grouped into sets to form a level and the level descriptions are arranged into a scale. The resulting scales are taken to reflect a consensus view of the characteristics of different levels of language ability. This is, in outline, the approach that was taken to building the scales associated with the Common European Framework of Reference for Languages (CEFR) (Council of Europe, 2001; North, 2000).

Fulcher, Davidson, and Kemp (2011, p. 9) objected to such quantitative 'scaling descriptors' approaches, arguing that 'Measurement-driven scales suffer from descriptional inadequacy. They are not sensitive to the communicative context or the interactional complexities of language use.' Both the ordering of descriptors into levels and the categories used have been questioned because they seem inconsistent with second language acquisition research (Green, 2012a). Areas of concern include the trade-off discussed previously between accuracy and range. As learners expand their repertoire of language, or as they become more fluent, they often lose a degree of accuracy. As a result, learner language does not necessarily or consistently become more accurate in the way some scales seem to suggest. However, defenders of quantitative scales point out that they are concerned with broad characterizations of functional language ability, while second language acquisition research tends to focus on discrete elements of language form (North, 2000). Although learners become less accurate in their use of certain structures, their overall ability to communicate may nonetheless improve.

It has also been argued that scales sometimes misrepresent the nature of language in use. As noted in the overview of speaking abilities, highly competent interactions between skilled speakers of a language are rarely consistently 'complex' (CEFR, C2: grammatical accuracy scale) with a 'high degree of grammatical accuracy' (CEFR, C1: grammatical accuracy scale), displaying 'a very broad lexical repertoire' (CEFR, C2: vocabulary range scale), but are often quite simple syntactically and may involve a rather restricted range of vocabulary (Hughes, 2010).

Such concerns have led other developers to take a third, more qualitative, empirical approach: *data-driven* scale development (Fulcher, 1987). This involves the systematic analysis of performances by learners (from the population who will take the assessment) on the relevant tasks. Key features that help to discriminate between learners are identified from these sample learner performances. These features are then incorporated into descriptions that can be used to build rating scales. Unfortunately, according to Fulcher et al. (2011), a major shortcoming of this method is that it tends to generate very detailed level descriptors that raters find too complex and time consuming to be practical for routine use.

Although there has certainly been a major shift towards more data-driven scale construction and validation, the value of expert judgement and the wealth of knowledge which experts can bring to the development process should not be discounted. The best methods for rating scale development are said to take advantage of the strengths of a range of intuitive, quantitative and qualitative approaches. The CEFR (Council of Europe, 2001, p. 207) advocated 'a complementary and cumulative process' that brings together all three.

Rater training

A well-written scale helps to define the test construct for the raters so that they are guided to features they should attend to in a performance. This can enhance levels of agreement. However, it is not enough simply to provide raters with scales. It is well established that interpretations of any linguistic description, however complete and clearly written, will vary. This means that raters have to be trained to use scales effectively and consistently. Quality control procedures are needed to ensure that this happens.

Before a rating session, or at fixed times during a school year, **rater training** can be carried out. Raters look at and discuss a set of previously scored performances to help them understand the scale. In order to ensure that their judgements are consistent with the consensus interpretation of the scales, they then rate some performances. If their judgements consistently match the consensus view, they are accepted as raters. If not, they are rejected or have to undertake further training. As the effect of training can be transient, raters have to be monitored over time to ensure that they remain consistent, perhaps by requiring them periodically to score additional performances that have already been assigned scores or by comparing their judgements with those of other raters.

Where scores have serious consequences for the assessee, it is essential that the results should not depend on the views of a single rater, even if that rater is an experienced expert. It is good practice to obtain scores from at least two raters who are given no opportunity to consult or to see each other's scores. If they are in agreement, that suggests that the score is accurate. Where there are minor differences – one level on a nine-level scale, for example, an average is often taken as the final score. If more substantial disagreements occur, a third independent rating should be obtained. The two closest scores may be averaged to give the final score. Again, if one rater often seems to be out of step in his or her judgements, he or she may be rejected or given further training.

Task 6.3

Many testing organizations now provide recordings of assessees taking their speaking tests.

Search the internet and find three examples of assessees taking the same test. If the scores are provided, do not look at them yet.

Use the scales in Table 6.5 to award scores to each performance.

Which of the criteria – Range, Accuracy, Fluency, Interaction, Coherence – did you find it easiest to judge? Why?

Which score category did you award first?

Did you feel there were other features of the performance that were important but that were not included on the scales?

If you found details of the scores awarded by the testing organization, do they agree with your judgements concerning the rank order of the three performances?

Using computers to score performance

As computer technology advances, automated scoring of more open-ended performances is becoming an increasingly practical alternative to human ratings for large scale test providers. Automated essay scoring has already been in use for many years and with advances in speech recognition, automatic scoring of tests of speaking is also becoming increasingly popular.

Automated scoring systems usually depend on first obtaining large numbers of human ratings. These are used to 'train' the machines by building statistical models of what responses at different score levels 'look like.' Text analysis software has been developed that can count features of a text such as word and sentence lengths, the frequency of occurrence of different words, phrases and grammatical structures, relationships between parts of a text and so on. Given enough samples of assessee writing (or speech captured through automated speech recognition tools), the machine comes to associate certain patterns of features with scores at different levels.

For example, if the first essay the system is given to analyse has 18 words per sentence and is scored as A, but the second has 16 words per sentence and is scored B, the machine would then predict that words per sentence might be a useful feature in telling the difference between an A and a B level essay. According to this hypothesis, the next essay, which has 18 words per sentence, should score A. If the prediction is right, the model is strengthened; if it is wrong, the machine makes adjustments and reduces the importance given to sentence length. Of course, no automated scoring system could actually rely on just one or two features and some take account of hundreds or even thousands of features. Once the machine has developed a model that works well on the samples it has been given, it can then be used to score performances that have not previously been rated by humans.

At present, automated scorers have to be retrained every time a new prompt is used. The levels of investment required and the number of samples needed for training put them beyond the means of most organizations. Outside a few large testing agencies, until more generic automated scoring systems can be developed, human judges working with rating scales will probably remain the standard means of obtaining consistent scores on performance tests.

Scales can be developed through a wide range of methodologies. Best practice in development will bring together theoretical insights, evidence of the language elicited by test tasks and the practical needs of assessors. Validity arguments supporting the use of rating scales in the assessment of spoken language will need to show not only that the descriptors reflect theories of spoken language use and the nature of the language actually elicited by the testing procedures, but also that raters are interpreting the scales in the ways intended.

Personal reflection

Look at the table of task types on the website (https://routledgetextbooks. com/textbooks/_author/rial/).

If you work as a teacher, what kind of short answer tests would suit your students' needs? Why?

What kinds of extended response tasks would be suitable? Why?

What kind of marking of written and spoken performance seems to best suit the teaching or testing situation *you* are in? Why is this suitable?

Would you ever use error counts or impression marking? Under what circumstances?

Consider a group of language learners that you know; suggest some descriptors that would be suitable to include in rating scales to assess their writing or speaking. Draft a rating scale using these.

Compare your rating scale with examples you can find on the internet from other assessment systems. What differences do you notice?

Score reporting and feedback

Reporting to different audiences

As with assessments of reading and listening, outcomes may be reported in the form of numeric scores or grades expressing assessors' judgements of assessee performance on a task or series of tasks in relation to other learners or in relation to rating scale criteria. Scores from different assessment components are often aggregated to give one overall score for a test or period of study. Profile scores may also be provided at the level of skills (a score for speaking and a score for writing), elements (scores for accuracy, fluency, organization, task completion, etc.) or tasks (C for the essay, B for the letter writing, A for the oral presentation, etc.).

Descriptive reporting of speaking and writing performance is more straightforward than with reading and listening as the assessor is able to observe directly how the assessee responds to the assessment tasks. Often, rating scales employed by assessors also function to convey the meaning of the scores to users of the results. Alderson (1991) raised the objection that the kinds of scales employed by trained assessors may be too technical or detailed to communicate effectively to non-specialists. He recommended the use of adapted **user-oriented scales** for this purpose.

Feedback

Their retrospective standpoint, delayed feedback, reductive scoring and limited sampling limits the diagnostic and formative potential of external tests (Stobart, 2008). Classroom assessment, in contrast, can take a future-oriented standpoint: 'How close is the assessee to being able to carry out this kind of task?' 'What does he or she need to learn in order to accomplish it?' Feedback can be immediate and targeted. Grading and scoring can be delayed and shifted to the background, with more attention given to more informative, descriptive commentaries and teacher – student conferencing. A wider and perhaps more representative range of task types can be exploited when the constraints of standardization and time limitations are relaxed.

One way in which language teachers have always provided feedback to learners is through error correction. Sinclair and Coulthard (1975) observed that much classroom interaction follows what they call an I-R-F pattern. The I stands for initiation – the teacher asks a question or calls on a student to speak: '*What colour eyes does Jane have?*' R is for response – a student answers the question: '*Mmm. She has blue eyes.*' F is feedback – the teacher accepts or corrects the learner's response, often with an evaluative comment: positive ('*Good. Yes, she has blue eyes.*') or negative ('*No, she has brown eyes.*').

This kind of feedback is certainly immediate, but research has suggested that it is not often taken up by the learner and used to modify performance: it does not actually fulfil the primary function of feedback: promoting effective learning. During the 1970s and 1980s, some researchers inferred from this that there is no benefit in trying to correct learner language and that explicit correction might even impede natural, unconscious processes of language acquisition (Krashen & Terrell, 1983, Chapter 7). However, more recently, it has been found that error correction and a 'focus on form' (Long & Robinson, 1998) can, indeed, be beneficial. The reason why so much feedback is ignored by learners may be that it is not informative enough. If the correct answer is simply provided, there is no thinking for the learners to do and little opportunity to learn.

Ways that have been suggested to encourage reflective thinking include allowing time for learners to self-correct and increasing **wait time** for learners (the time between putting a question and expecting a response; Walsh, 2011). Especially in the beginning stages of learning, learners may need a good deal of time to formulate a response to teacher questions. Teachers may, perhaps incorrectly, interpret silence as error. They are naturally reluctant to spend a long time waiting for an answer from an individual learner as this can be uncomfortable for the learners and slow the pace of a lesson. However, if questions are put to the whole class, time for formulation allowed for all and then learners chosen at random to respond (William, 2011, suggests a lottery system involving student names written on sticks), then all learners may be engaged in first formulating a response and then suggesting alternative answers. This provides more information for the teacher than traditional individual questioning because it provides evidence about more members of the class.

Meddings and Thornbury (2009) recommend a five-point strategy for the treatment of the successful or unsuccessful use of linguistic forms in the classroom that reflects current thinking. It includes *retrieval, repetition, recasting, reporting* and *recycling*. Retrieval involves taking note of what a learner has said or written and implies flagging this unit of language for attention. This may be done by a teacher, by other learners or by the learner who produced it. Reporting and repetition (orally or in writing) focus the attention of learners on what was said or written, inviting them to think about it and what it communicates (or is intended to communicate). Learners may report back to the class things that have been said or written by other students, or the teacher may select them and write them on the board for general consideration.

Recasting involves rephrasing learner language in a form that is more like the target language. This does not have to suggest that there is a single 'correct' way to express the speaker or writer's ideas, but suggests alternatives that are more target like. These alternatives can be suggested by other learners who may take collective decisions about which they think are the most appropriate. Or an alternative may be suggested by the teacher: 'This is how I would express your idea.' The more the teacher involves other learners in making judgements about correctness and effectiveness, the more the teacher is likely to learn about the students' level of understanding and ability to use the forms in question.

Recycling involves finding opportunities to use what has been learned in new contexts. This could be further tasks that involve using the kinds of grammatical or discourse patterns that have been the focus. The objective of these kinds of teaching strategies is to encourage learners to attend to the formal characteristics of the language, thinking about how to express different concepts and to achieve different communicative purposes.

Assisting learners to complete tasks by intervening with structured support, rather than providing the correct answer, is referred to as scaffolding (see Chapter 4). This involves modifying the difficulty of a task so that the learner is able to complete it. For example, if, in an interview, a learner is unable to respond to a question (*What is your home town like?*), the teacher might try rephrasing or reducing the scope of the question (*Where is your home town?*). If the learner is still unable to answer, the teacher might provide a series of binary choices (*Is your home town large or small? Is your home town near the sea?*). The extent of support could range from suggesting one or two words to modelling an answer. Once the learner has managed to complete the task with support, the assistance can be progressively withdrawn until the learner is able to carry out the task without it.

On one level, this can be seen as a helpful teaching technique as the process should aid the learner in improving his or her ability to carry out this kind of task. However, it can also be seen as a very powerful assessment technique because it reveals to the assessor not only whether or not the learner is currently able to carry out the task, but also how close they are to being able to carry it out independently.

Standard setting

The standard setting methods described in Chapter 5 were developed with objectively scored multiple choice tests in mind. In setting standards for performance assessments and for assessments involving a variety of task types, including portfolios, a holistic approach such as the **body of work** method may be more appropriate. This can be considered an assessee-centred method like the borderline and contrasting groups methods described in Chapter 5; but instead of first classifying learners as minimally competent or borderline and then having them take the assessment, samples of assessee performances on the assessment covering the full range of score levels are collected in advance and then presented to the panel of expert judges.

The judges view performances by specific assessees on all of the tasks involved in the assessment and then each panellist comes to a conclusion about whether or not they consider the assessee to be minimally competent. The panellists repeat the same procedure with the responses of other assessees at different score levels. Several rounds of discussion may be held in which panellists are given feedback on how far their decisions agree with those of other panellists. Statistical tools such as *logistic regression* may then be used to identify cut scores that most efficiently classify the assessees into competent and non-competent groups. Multiple cut scores can be set in the same way to represent different levels of proficiency.

Task 6.4

Here are two writing tasks taken from international tests of English. Review them using the box 'Guidelines for preparing tasks: productive skills.'

What knowledge, skills or abilities are tested by each task?

Writing Task 1 from Versant Pro – Writing (www.VersantTest.com)

Part D: Passage Reconstruction

Screen 1.

You will have 30 seconds to read a paragraph. After 30 seconds, the passage will disappear from the screen. Then you will have 90 seconds to reconstruct the passage. Show that you understood the passage by rewriting it in your own words. Your answer will be scored for clear and accurate content, not word-for-word memorization. After 90 seconds, your work will be saved automatically.

Example:

You read;

Mike went for ten job interviews. At the last interview, he finally received a job offer.

You type:

Mike had ten job interviews. He got an offer after the last interview.

Screen 2.

You read;

Corey is a taxi driver. It is his dream job because he loves driving cars. He started the job ten years ago and has been saving up money since then. Soon, he will use this money to start his own taxi company.

You type:

Versant Pro Writing Test™ 2009 NCS Pearson, Inc. Reproduced with permission. All rights reserved.

Writing Task 2 from the Pearson Test of English General: Level 3

SECTION 7

Read the web article and complete the notes. Write no more than three words in each gap from the article.

Portfolio careers: creating a career out of several part-time jobs

If you have a portfolio career. you have several part-time jobs instead of one traditional full-time job. These might include part-time, temporary and freelance employment with different employers: when combined, the jobs are the equivalent of a full-time position. A portfolio career offers more flexibility. Freedom and variety than conventional employment, but involves some risk as well as requiring a high level of organizational skills.

If you opt for a portfolio career, it will usually be built around core skills or interests. For example, someone whose background is in education may teach part-time, write textbooks and examination materials, mark exams at certain times of the year, and perhaps train other teachers.

Most employment experts believe that James Hardy, an American management guru, was responsible for the sudden increase in the popularity of portfolio careers in the early 1990s. He suggested that individuals could gain more control over their working lives by having several small jobs rather than one big one.

Many people believe that another factor in the increasing status of portfolio careers is Harold Rivers' recent book How to Succeed in a Workplace without jobs. He suggests that the lack of job security today means that we are all temporary workers. There are many reasons to consider a portfolio career: to gain better work/life balance; to experience variety and use a range of skills; to control your own work life and to seek new challenges.

One survey of portfolio careerists shows that the majority (around 65%) were satisfied with their success in establishing a new type of career. They mainly put their success down to their ability to network. But, establishing a portfolio career isn't easy for many. It can be difficult to balance the demands of different jobs and find employers willing to take you on a part-time basis. There's also the possibility of isolation if you work from home, a possible drop in earnings and the risk of being out of work for periods of time.

Example. A portfolio career consists of _several part-time jobs_ rather than a full-time job.

40 A portfolio career can include different kinds of _____.
41 A portfolio career would suit someone who is able to _____ themselves well.
42 Key _____ will usually be at the centre of a portfolio career.
43 James Hardy thought portfolio careers gave individuals more _____ in relation to their professional lives.
44 Portfolio careers have also gained status because there is not much _____ nowadays.
45 Most successful portfolio careerists believe that this is because they can _____ well.
46 If you have a portfolio career, possible risks include temporary unemployment, feeling alone and less _____.

(7 marks)

SECTION 8

Use the information in Section 7 to help you write your answer.

47 You have read the article about portfolio careers. Write an email giving advice to a friend who is considering changing to a portfolio career. Write about 90–120 words and include the following information:

- the advantages of a portfolio career
- the disadvantages of a portfolio career
- how you think your friend could succeed

Write your answer here. Do not write outside the box.

(10 marks)

From Pearson Test of English General Practice Test 1: Written Test Level 3 Upper Intermediate © Pearson Education Ltd (2011).

Task 6.5

Speaking tasks

Here are three speaking tasks.

Describe them in terms of Bachman and Palmer's (2010) task characteristics framework on p. 38. What are the main differences between them?

What kinds of response would you expect assesses to give to each?

*Speaking Task 1 from **Cambridge Assessment***
***English:** Cambridge Young Learners 'Movers'*
(www.cambridgeenglish.org)

> The examiner tells the child the name of the story and describes the
> first picture – e.g., 'Fred is sad. He can't play football. His ball is very
> old. His mum's saying, "Take the dog to the park."' The examiner then
> asks the child to continue telling the story.

Figure 6.6 Speaking Task 1 from Cambridge Young Learners sample papers: *Movers. Volume 2.* © UCLES 2013. Reproduced with permission. All rights reserved.

*Speaking Task 2 from the Versant Aviation English Test
(www.VersantTest.com)*

Part F: Corrections and Confirmations.

In this task you will hear a radiotelephony exchange between two speakers, Speaker 1 and Speaker 2. The speakers are a pilot and an air traffic controller, but not necessarily in that order. Speaker 1 speaks first, then Speaker 2 responds next. After you hear the exchange, imagine that you are Speaker 1. Your task is to continue the dialog and reply to Speaker 2's response. If Speaker 2's response includes wrong information, correct that information. If Speaker 2's response includes a question or request, respond appropriately. For each question, you will see a call sign for your information.

Example: East Global Air 295

(Speaker 1) "East Global Air 295, contact Atlanta Radar 122.15."

(Speaker 2) "Atlanta Radar 121.5, East Global Air 295."

After you hear this exchange, you could say: "East Global Air 295, negative, contact Radar 122.15." OR another possible answer is: "East Global Air 295, I say a 22.15."

1   Charlie Romeo 4013
2   GABCJ
3   Coastal Wing 927

Versant Aviation English Test™ 2008 © NCS Pearson, Inc. Reproduced with permission. All rights reserved.

*Speaking Task 3 from Cambridge Assessment
English:* Cambridge English Business
English Certificates Handbook for Teachers
(www.cambridgeenglish.org)

This is an example of a test that uses an *interlocutor frame* or partial script to control what the examiner says to the assessee. The words spoken by the examiner are shaded.

PART 2   6 minutes (8 minutes for groups of three)

Now, in this part of the test, I'm going to give each of you a choice of three different topics. I'd like you to select one of the topics and give a short presentation on it for about a minute. You will have a minute to prepare this and you can make notes if you want. After you have finished your talk, your partner will ask you a question.

All right? Here are your topics. Please don't write anything in the booklets.

[Hand each candidate a Part 2 booklet (open at appropriate task) and a pencil and paper for notes.]

🕐 *60 seconds*

Now, *B*, which topic have you chosen, A, B or C?
Would you like to talk about what you think is important when *[interlocutor states candidate's chosen topic]*?

A, please listen carefully to *B*'s talk, and then ask him/her a question about it.

🕐 *about 60 seconds*

Thank you. Now, *A*, please ask *B* a question about his/her talk.

Now, *A*, which topic have you chosen, A, B or C?
Would you like to talk about what you think is important when *[interlocutor states candidate's chosen topic]*?

B, please listen carefully to *A*'s talk, and then ask him/her a question about it.

🕐 *about 60 seconds*

Thank you. Now, *B*, please ask *A* a question about his/her talk.

Thank you.

Can I have the booklets, please?

[Retrieve Part 2 booklets, pencils and paper.]

Figure 6.7 Speaking Task 3 from Cambridge English Business English Certificates Handbook for Teachers, pages 78–79 © UCLES 2012. Reproduced by permission. All rights reserved.

2

A: What is important when...?

Selecting staff for promotion

- Attitude to work
- Current performance
-
-

Back up
questions

Is the employee's **attitude to work** the most important thing to consider? (Why/Why not?)

Why is it important to consider an employee's **current performance**?

Select from the following additional prompts (if the above have already been covered):

How important is it to consider **ambition**? (Why?/Why not?)

How important is it for the candidate to have **skills appropriate** for the new post? (Why?)

2

B: What is important when...?

Considering a career change

- Further study or training
- Opportunities for future promotion
-
-

Back up
questions

Why is it important to consider **further study or training**?

Is it important to consider **opportunities for further promotion**? (Why/Why not?)

Select from the following additional prompts (if the above have already been covered):

How important is it to consider **financial rewards**? (Why?)

Is it important to consider **flexible working arrangements** when considering a career change? (Why/Why not?)

2

C: What is important when...?

Planning an advertising campaign

- Market research
- Selecting appropriate medium
-
-

Back up
questions

How important is it to carry out **market research**? (Why?)

Is selecting the **appropriate medium** the most important thing? (Why/Why not?)

Select from the following additional prompts (if the above have already been covered):

How important is it to **budget effectively**? (Why?)

Why is it essential for the advertising campaign to **support the image** of the product?

Figure 6.7 (Continued)

Part III

The practices introduced in Parts I and II are informed by theoretical insights into language, learning and assessment. Part III of the book turns the spotlight onto these informing theoretical ideas. It is intended both to extend understanding of the issues touched on in Parts I and II and as a starting point for further exploration of the language assessment literature for those who wish to go deeper.

Language assessment, like language teaching, has a long history and has inherited its concerns from a variety of academic disciplines – linguistics, psychology, education, sociology – and from different cultures – the US, Europe and a broad range of other local traditions. Inevitably, these strands have sometimes been at variance with each other. There have been conflicting views of the nature of language, of how assessment should be conducted and of the proper role of assessment in educational systems (the current debate between advocates of standardised testing and socio-cultural theorists being one manifestation of this).

Readers will be introduced to some of the issues that have occupied language assessment researchers and shaped the practice of language assessment professionals. These include:

- developments in allied fields;
- shifting goals for language education;
- the proper relationship between assessment and teaching;
- the nature of communicative competence and language proficiency;
- technological change;
- ethical and critical approaches.

The final section considers the future for language assessment. The promise of new means of delivering assessments, of monitoring learning and of measuring aspects of learner language is balanced by the challenges raised by new perspectives on language. These new perspectives include an emphasis on the social rather than individual nature of discourse and questions over whether native speaker norms can provide appropriate benchmarks for judging learner language.

7 Multiplication and division: trends in language assessment

Personal reflection

In your view, who should take the main responsibility for assessing learners' language abilities:

- language learners themselves;
- teachers;
- specialist assessment organizations or agencies;
- employers?

What should each of these groups know about the qualities of language assessments?

How do you think language assessment may have changed over the past 100 years?

What do you think might have changed in relation to . . .

- Who takes language assessments and why?
- The techniques used to assess language abilities?

Introduction

In the spring of 1961, a conference was held in Washington, DC to discuss options for a new test of English for international students coming to study at American universities. As the delegates settled back in their chairs, John Carroll, a leading psychologist and linguist, began the opening address with the words: 'Language testing has a long history, and much experience and wisdom have accumulated . . . [it] has reached such a stage of professionalization that a whole book on the subject is about to appear' (Carroll, 1961, p. 313).

Today, we can point to shelves of books that appear each year on language assessment. There are online resources university courses, regular international conferences, academic journals and national, regional and global professional associations dedicated to the subject. Numbers of test takers for the largest language tests can now be counted in millions rather than the few thousands seen at that time. Looking back at the idea of a profession represented by as little as the promise of one 'whole book' may prompt a wry smile. In fact, Carroll's paper and the book he referred to – Lado's *Language Testing* (1961) – are now widely seen as laying the foundations for the era of greater professionalism that was to follow.

The growth of a profession

The influence of Carroll's paper and Lado's *Language Testing* would be far-reaching, but the development and global spread of the profession was slow. The teaching of language testing as a branch of applied linguistics was pioneered in a few places over the course of the 1960s, notably by Alan Davies and Elisabeth Ingram at the University of Edinburgh. It was only in 1984, however, that the first academic journal dedicated to language assessment, also titled *Language Testing*, was launched. The International Language Testing Association (ILTA), the global association for language testing and assessment practitioners and scholars, was set up in 1992.

The early focus was very much on the practice of formal testing and it was only really from the 1990s that research and guidance concerning other forms of classroom-based language assessment by teachers and learners would begin to be published in any quantity in international journals. In spite of the shifts in perspective over the intervening decades, the topics raised by Lado and Carroll remain relevant. Many of the same questions that exercised language testers in 1961 are still widely discussed today.

The issues that have attracted the most attention over the intervening years have generally been technical questions concerning *what* it is that is being assessed (i.e., what is 'language proficiency' or 'language ability') and *how* better to assess it. Davies (2008a), describing the changes in textbooks used to teach about language testing and assessment since those early days, called these matters of 'skills and knowledge.' Skills include appropriate testing and analysis techniques: item writing, test delivery systems and statistical test analysis. Knowledge covers theories for language description and measurement and may involve exploring different models of language learning and approaches to language teaching, as well as language assessment.

More recently, language assessment researchers, reflecting the growing role of sociology in applied linguistics, have become increasingly interested in questions of values. There is greater interest in the *who* and *why* of assessment: the people involved and their reasons for using assessments. Davies called these concerns 'principles.' He placed in this category debates concerning the use of language tests as policy tools, their fairness and effects on society. They involve the responsibilities of language assessors, the ethical choices they make and the impact of their work. Who are the people or agencies that commission and use language assessments? For what purposes do they use these assessments? What uses of assessment can be supported on ethical grounds? What effects do the use and misuse of assessment have on educational systems? What other social consequences result when tests and assessments are introduced?

Origins

The use of the word 'testing' rather than 'assessment' in the title of Lado's book is worth noting because it reflects the early focus of attention. In the work of Lado and his colleagues, testing implied a psychological (and predominantly American) understanding of educational assessment as a branch of scientific measurement: **psychometrics**. The objective of psychometrics was to bring to psychological phenomena the advantages associated with being able to define and measure physical properties like temperature and distance. The term 'test' was used to distinguish a new approach to assessment that had come to the fore in the USA in the 1920s and 1930s from the examinations that preceded it.

An early examination in English as foreign language: the University of Cambridge certificate of proficiency in English (CPE)

Task 7.1

A traditional examination: the University of Cambridge Certificate of Proficiency in English

Here are some extracts from a traditional English language examination given over 100 years ago: the University of Cambridge Certificate of Proficiency in English (CPE) (June 1913). The test as a whole took over 13 hours to administer including a three-hour paper on English literature and a two-and-a-half-hour paper on translation.

How are these items different from the items on any more recent tests you are familiar with?

What criticisms would you make of the test?

Translation into French

My grandfather's recollections of Culloden were merely those of an observant boy of fourteen, who had witnessed the battle from a distance. The day, he has told me, was drizzly and thick: and on reaching the brow of the Hill of Cromarty, where he found many of his townsfolk already assembled, he could scarce see the opposite land.

Grammar

1   Give the past tense and past participle of each of the following verbs, dividing them into strong and weak; add explanations: *tell*, *wake*, *buy*, *eat*, *lay*, *lie*, etc.
5   Correct or justify **four** of the following sentences, giving your reasons:

   (a) I hope you are determined to seriously improve.
   (b) Comparing Shakespeare with Aeschylus, the former is by no means inferior to the latter. . . .

English essay

(*Two hours*)

Write an essay on **one** of the following subjects:

(a)   the effect of political movements upon nineteenth century literature in England;
(b)   English Pre-Raffaellitism;
(c)   Elizabethan travel and discovery;
(d)   the Indian mutiny;
(e)   the development of local self-government;
(f)   Matthew Arnold.

The widespread use of written examinations, like mass public education and the teaching of modern languages, was largely a nineteenth-century innovation, although it drew heavily on the traditions of spoken examinations used in European universities and on the written Chinese civil service examinations, which dated back over a thousand years. Examinations typically posed a small number of questions, each requiring lengthy responses. The questions were set and marked by teachers or subject specialists. They often offered assessees some choice about which questions they wished to answer. An example of the content of examination in modern languages can be seen in the Cambridge CPE (Table 7.1). Examinations were designed to establish whether an assessee knew what the examiner thought they should know at one point in time. Scores were expressed as numbers (usually percentages or marks out of some other number) but usually involved the examiner's subjective judgement of the quality of the response. They indicated (but did not claim to *measure*) the extent to which the assessee had mastered the knowledge or skills valued by the examiner. There was no expectation that an assessee's results on one examination should be related to their results on any other.

Tests were an early twentieth-century development that promised something far more powerful. In contrast to the old examinations, they were based on a shared, scientifically grounded understanding of the ability being assessed and a measurement scale representing increasing levels of that ability. They could be administered periodically to monitor rates of progress and to make comparisons between learners, between schools or between the education systems in different states or countries. Educational testing emerged alongside public health initiatives such as the testing of vision and hearing and the monitoring of child development. Just as a child's height and weight could be measured to check whether they were developing normally, their foreign language abilities could be measured periodically to establish whether they were progressing in line with expectations.

Table 7.1 The format of the 1913 version of the Certificate of Proficiency in English (Weir, 2003)

	Paper	Time (hours)
Written	Translation into French or German	2.0 hrs
	Translation into English & Grammar	2.5 hrs
	English Essay	2.0 hrs
	English Literature	3.0 hrs
	English Phonetics	1.5 hrs
Oral	Dictation	0.5 hrs
	Reading Aloud & Conversation	0.5 hrs

Tests looked rather different to the examinations of the time. They included a large number of very short, unrelated questions, set by measurement specialists, requiring very brief responses. Conditions for administration were strictly controlled and test takers were not given any choice about which questions to answer. Multiple choice and similar question types were favoured because scoring could be made entirely objective. It required no judgement on the part of the scorer, who would simply match the response to the answer key provided. Tests could therefore be very quickly and reliably scored by untrained clerical staff or by the newly available electrographic machines. The first commercially available Test Scoring Machine, invented by a high school physics teacher, was introduced as the IBM 805 in 1936 and demonstrated its value in the large-scale testing of army recruits during World War II (Fulcher, 2010). The applied linguists who became language testers were generally enthusiastic critics of examinations and supporters of testing.

By the 1960s, traditional examinations were still dominant in most education systems around the world and examiners were often hostile to psychometric ideas. Even so, the distinctions between tests and examinations were not as clear-cut as they had once been. Practices associated with psychometrics were becoming increasingly influential. By then, many traditional examinations included some test-like questions and employed statistical techniques in analysing and evaluating results.

What to assess? Constructs

Personal reflection

How would you define language ability? What different component abilities does it involve?

How far can the ability to use a language transfer from one context (e.g. interacting with friends) to another (e.g. a nurse interacting with other medical professionals)?

How far is 'business language' the same as 'academic language' or 'social chat'? In what ways are they similar or different?

How long do you think it would require to adequately assess someone's language abilities?

Developers of language assessments look for established theories to guide them in deciding what to target in their tests. Chapter 4 introduced the idea that all assessments involve **constructs** and showed the need to define, describe and justify what is assessed. This had always been important for examiners, but it was crucial for testers, who wanted their tests to include a representative sample of the knowledge, skills or abilities involved in language use. Unfortunately, like other constructs that psychologists have tried to measure (such as intelligence, critical thinking or social development), there has been a great deal of disagreement about the existence and nature of language ability or language abilities, and views have shifted over time.

Different theoretical accounts of language and different theories of measurement have come in and out of favour in different parts of the world. Such changes and disagreements are problematic for testing, which depends on consistent, standard practices. Perhaps, for example, at the beginning of a learner's career, tests were mostly concerned with knowledge of written grammatical forms and there was no testing of spoken forms. Five years later, when the learner came to the end of the course, changing ideas about language education meant that the focus had shifted to the ability to pronounce sounds. In circumstances like these, the attempt to track progress through testing would be bound to fail as the results on the final test would cover different knowledge, skills or abilities from the test given five years earlier.

Conflicting and shifting views of language education

A practical handbook in language assessment for teachers written in the late 1960s reflected the three objectives of traditional language programmes in formal schooling that predominated for most of the last century: 'to enjoy the literature written in the target language, to appreciate the culture of the target country and especially to converse freely with its people' (Valette, 1967, p. 4).

There was, perhaps inevitably, a certain tension between these goals. The older ideal of language education, in formal schooling at least, was for learners to develop an appreciation of the finest in the foreign literature and culture. This aim was gradually displaced in many Ministries of Education and other policy-making bodies by the more utilitarian, vocational view that knowledge of foreign languages is a basic skill that has economic value: readying workers to participate in international markets. Learners themselves often wish to acquire a language not so much to access the cultural highlights and modes of thought as to help them to travel, to build a new life in a foreign country, to access technical information, to do business, or to participate in a religion.

Shifting priorities in language education and developments in linguistic theory have inevitably influenced ideas about the constructs that language assessments should measure. In summarizing trends, Spolsky (1977)

Table 7.2 Phases (or tendencies) in language assessment

Language testing	Language teaching	Favoured techniques
1 **Pre-scientific/ traditional**	Grammar translation	Translation, grammar exercises, essays.
2 **Psychometric-structuralist**	Audiolingualism	Multiple choice tests of grammar, vocabulary, phonetic discrimination, reading and listening comprehension. Focus on discrete linguistic components.
3 **Psycholinguistic-sociolinguistic**	Natural approach	Cloze, dictation. Focus on integrated language use.
4 **Communicative**	Communicative/ task-based approach	Assessment tasks intended to reflect 'real-life' language use. Focus on language use in social contexts.
5 **Formative testing**	Behavioural objectives and mastery learning approaches	Tests that are sensitive to instruction and inform remediation. Focus on the products of learning.
6 **Assessment for learning**	Constructivism and socio-cultural approaches	Interactionist/supported assessment, teacher conferencing, portfolio assessment, self and peer assessment. Focus on the process of learning.

described four overlapping phases (1 to 4 in Table 7.2), each associated with different conceptions of construct. I have added two further categories (5 and 6) because they are more closely associated with classroom-based assessment by teachers, while Spolsky was concerned with more formal testing, generally at the institutional level or above.

Since the 1980s, as more attention has been given to the history of language assessment, it has become clearer that it is rarely possible to fit operational assessments neatly into any one of these phases. On the other hand, Spolsky's distinctions do point towards key influences and broad historical developments within a more complex reality. Language assessment has been shaped by a wide range of influences, including practicality, political expediency and established customs, as well as developments in allied disciplines. Global trends including the growth in international trade, mass migration, tourism and the advent of mobile technology and the internet have brought new reasons for learning and using languages, and naturally assessment has also been affected by these broader social changes.

Lado and language habits

Both language examinations and language tests had, as Carroll observed in his speech, existed long before the 1960s. The important innovation that Carroll, Lado and their colleagues introduced was the combination of psychometric thinking about testing with insights from contemporary linguistics that had previously had a more limited influence on language education and its assessment. The systematic attention they gave to linguistic theory as the basis for construct definition marked the point at which language assessment began to emerge as a distinct field of inquiry.

Lado's ideas about constructs were grounded in the dominant linguistic theory in the US at the time, associated with Leonard Bloomfield's standard textbook, *Language* (1933). Influenced by behaviourist psychology, Bloomfield believed that learning a language was largely a matter of imprinting sounds, words and sentence patterns in the mind through habit formation: 'the thousands of morphemes and tagmemes [grammatical units] of the foreign language can be mastered only by constant repetition. . . . Every form that is introduced should be repeated many times' (Bloomfield, 1933, p. 506). In classroom assessment, the emphasis was on accuracy. Accurate language should be rewarded with enthusiastic praise because this was believed to reinforce good habits. Incorrect forms should be quickly put right and the learner asked to imitate and repeat the correct form. The hardest habits to imprint would be those that involved forms that were very different than those found in the learner's native language.

Skills and components

In Lado's linguistic model, sometimes known as a **skills/components** model, language was made up of linguistic components and the 'total skills' of listening, speaking, reading and writing (see Carroll's interpretation of this model in Table 7.3). The linguistic components included pronunciation (sound segments, intonation and stress), grammatical structure (syntax and morphology), the lexicon and another element not as widely included in psychometric language tests and so excluded from Carroll's similar schematic in Table 7.3: 'cultural meanings.'

Lado recommended **discrete-point** testing in which each of the components is tested separately. However, he also acknowledged that components would always occur in combination in language use, which involves the 'total' skills of listening, speaking, reading and writing and that tests of these might also have value in some circumstances. Valette's (1967, p. 18) recommendations on preparing texts for use in a classroom test of listening comprehension show how a discrete-point approach to language affected

Table 7.3 Grid for measurement of language abilities

Skill	Language Aspect			
	Phonology or orthography	Morphology	Syntax	Lexicon
Auditory comprehension				
Oral production				
Reading				
Writing				

'total skills' testing: 'the teacher should, a couple of days in advance, prepare a first draft of the script . . . making sure that he has used all the structures and vocabulary used that week': the priority was not so much to capture language in use in realistic situations, but to exemplify the key linguistic components.

Lado favoured basing both teaching and assessment on *contrastive analysis* – the identification of differences between a learner's native language and the language being learned. These differences could be used to predict the problems that learners would have when taking up a new language. For example, Spanish speakers learning English find it difficult to distinguish between the 'd' sound in '*day*' and the 'th' sound in '*they*' (phonetic /d/ and /ð/) because there is no such contrast in Spanish. Spanish learners should therefore be drilled and tested on their ability to hear and reproduce words like *thirty* and *dirty*. Japanese speakers often have trouble dealing with post-modifiers and relative clauses in English (sometimes preferring incorrect patterns – 'the *doesn't work clock*' – to the relative clause – 'the clock *which doesn't work*.' Lado would argue that similar structures should be included in a test of English for Japanese speakers.

Testing with skills and components

The influence of the skills/components approach can be seen in the test of English for international students that eventually emerged from the process set in train by the 1961 conference: the *Test of English as a Foreign Language* (TOEFL®). Introduced in 1964, the TOEFL, alongside more discrete-point tests of 'structure and written expression' and vocabulary, included tests of reading comprehension and listening (see Table 7.4 and Task 7.2). All parts of the test were scored objectively: the subjectively scored elements of the traditional language examination – essays and tests of speaking – were excluded.

Table 7.4 The 1964 TOEFL (based on Spolsky, 1995)

Paper	Time limit (mins)	No. of Questions	Content
Listening	30–40 minutes	50	20 statements with paraphrasing response options, 15 brief dialogues with comprehension questions 15 questions based on 5 minute lecture
Structure and Written Expression	25 minutes	40	15 sentence correction items 25 paragraph completion items.
Reading Comprehension Vocabulary	55 minutes	50	5 texts (100–250 words each) from social science, fiction and natural science texts: 4/5 items with each Testing . . . a) specific facts, b) interpretation of facts and sentences, c) understanding the passage (inference and tone) Vocabulary: sentence completion and phrase synonyms

Task 7.2   Ⓣ Ⓒ

Psychometric language test design: the TOEFL test

Look at these sample Listening items from the TOEFL test (from 1976)

How are these items different from those included in the CPE?

Listening comprehension

In this section of the test, you will have an opportunity to demonstrate your ability to understand spoken English. There are three parts to this section, with special directions for each part.

Part A

Directions: For each problem in Part A, you will hear a short statement. The statements will be **spoken** just one time. They will not be written out for you, and you must listen carefully in order to understand what the speaker says.

When you hear a statement, read the four sentences in your test book and decide which one is closest in meaning to the statement you have heard. Then, on your answer sheet, find the number of the problem and mark your answer.

Look at Example 1.   Sample Answer
You will hear.   John dropped the letter   Ⓐ Ⓑ Ⓒ Ⓓ
                        in the mailbox.
You will read: (A) John sent the letter.
                        (B) John opened the letter.
                        (C) John lost the letter,
                        (D) John destroyed the letter.

Sentence (A), "John sent the letter." means most nearly the same as the statement "John dropped the letter in the mailbox." Therefore you should choose answer (A).

. . .

Part C

Directions: In this part of the test, you will hear a short talk and a conversation. After each, you will be asked some questions. The talks and questions will be **spoken** just one time. They will not be written out for you, so you will have to listen carefully in order to understand and remember what the speaker says.

When you hear a question, read the four possible answers in your test book and decide which one would be the best answer to the question you have heard Then, on your answer sheet, and the number of the problem and fill in (blacken) the space that corresponds to the letter of the answer you have chosen.

Listen to this sample talk.

You will hear: People who search for unusual rocks and semi-precious stones are sometimes called rock hounds. Rock hounding is becoming more and more popular as a hobby in the United States. There are over 1,600 rock hound clubs around the nation, and their membership represents only about seven percent of the people who participate in the hobby.

The state of New Mexico has devoted a unique state park to the rock hounds. People who visit the park can take samples of rocks away with them. Most parks forbid the removal of any rocks or other materials. Among the rocks found In the New Mexico park are amethysts, opals, and agates.

Now look at Example 1.
You will hear:

Sample Answer

What is the topic of the talk?   Ⓐ Ⓑ Ⓒ Ⓓ

You will read:
(A) A popular hobby.
(B) The state of New Mexico.
(C) An unusual kind of animal.
(D) New kinds of clubs to join.

The best answer to the question "What Is the topic of the talk?" is (A), "A popular hobby." Therefore you should choose answer (A).

The TOEFL® Test Directions are reprinted by permission of Educational Testing Service, the copyright owner. All other information contained within this publication is provided by Routledge. No endorsement of any kind by Educational Testing Service should be inferred.

Objections to discrete point testing

In the 20 years after 1964, the TOEFL programme expanded and thrived while the test itself remained much the same. Despite (or perhaps because of) its growing dominance, it attracted its share of criticism from teachers. Traynor (1985) voiced the concern of many that the absence of speaking and writing tasks in the test would lead to a neglect of these skills in teaching. In response to such criticism, writing (essay) and speaking tests were first offered as optional extras before being fully incorporated into the test in 2005. Traynor was also troubled that many items seemed to depend on knowledge of North American culture. Johnson et al. (2005, p. 79) reported the apprehension of the teacher in their study that multiple choice items of the kind used in the TOEFL 'trick' the unwary test taker into giving incorrect responses and that the language of the test 'does not always correspond to everyday language use.'

The theoretical underpinnings of discrete-point testing were also coming under attack. During the 1960s and 1970s, applied linguists reacted against both Bloomfield's structuralist linguistics and behaviourist learning models of the kind favoured by Lado. Evidence emerged that contrastive analysis – identifying key differences between language systems – was inadequate as a means of predicting learning problems. Learners often made errors that could not be traced to differences between languages and, in fact, learners from very different language backgrounds seemed to pass through similar stages of language development. Second, there was a growing realization that systems of linguistic description like Bloomfield's did not provide an adequate basis for language learning because they focused 'too exclusively on knowledge of the formal linguistic system for its own sake, rather than on the way such knowledge is used to achieve communication' (McNamara, 2000, p. 14). The skills/components approach to testing seemed to be more concerned with language as a system than with learners' awareness of how to use that system in their lives, putting language to use as a means of communicating with other people.

Applied linguists such as Corder (1971) and Selinker (1972) argued that it was unhelpful to view the language used by learners as being simply 'correct' or 'incorrect' as judged against the grammatical rules presented by language teachers. They argued that rather than forming language habits by repeating words and grammatical patterns, each learner developed a personal *inter-language*, shaping and refining their own (often subconscious) systems of grammatical rules as they developed their understanding of the new language. These rules did not necessarily conform either to the norms of their native language or to those of the target language.

A learner's inter-language could be more or less effective for communication even if it did not match the grammatical patterns assessed in discrete-point tests, which were based on a native speaker model. A discrete-point test of grammar might reveal whether or not a learner could apply a formal rule but could not reveal the way or ways in which that learner might attempt to express an idea in conversation or in a letter. As a diagnostic tool, such a test could only show whether or not the learner had taken up the taught patterns; it would reveal nothing about the rules that learners had formed for themselves, how far these might be from the intended target, or how effective they might be in real life communication.

Consider this discrete point item from Lado (1961, p. 161):

$$\text{The } \begin{bmatrix} boy \\ boys \end{bmatrix} \text{ strikes the car and runs.}$$

An assessee may score a point by knowing that according to the subject-verb agreement rule the answer must be *boy*. However, the same assessee might misunderstand the meaning of the sentence – perhaps thinking it means that the boy starts the car and drives away. Or they might be unable to tell the story of a boy hitting a car, based on a series

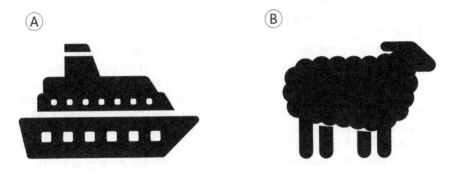

Choose the picture that matches the word you hear.

Figure 7.1 Phonetic contrast

of pictures. A second assessee might not be able to apply the subject-verb agreement rule but might nevertheless understand the meaning or tell the story effectively. A discrete-point grammar test would reward the first assessee, even though they are less effective at using the language to communicate.

It was also pointed out by critics that it was very difficult to produce tests that isolated just one component of the language system, without involving any other components. The classic **minimal pairs** test is intended to test the single component of phonetic discrimination. Figure 7.1 shows the classic example of a minimal pairs item. The assessee must distinguish between two sounds: the 'ee' sound /i:/ of sheep and the 'i' sound /ɪ/ of ship. But, as the critics pointed out, an assessee might fail to give a correct response for reasons unconnected with phonetic contrasts. Regardless of the sounds, an assessee might simply not know which word refers to the animal and which to the boat. In this case, the item would be testing vocabulary knowledge rather than phonetic discrimination.

There seemed to be limits to the kinds of information that discrete-point tests could provide. In order to gain a comprehensive and reliable picture of whether or not a test taker was able to recognise the sound contrast in the ship – sheep example, a test would need to include a wide variety of items testing recognition of the /ɪ/ and /i:/ sounds in combination with different sounds and in different positions within the word – *is: ease; bin: bean; jellied: gelid* – and within different positions in sentences or utterances – *The sheep is over there, in the water. There is picture of a ship on the wall.* While this might be feasible in classroom-based assessment, where a teacher could reasonably spend a few minutes focusing on one sound contrast, it would certainly be impractical in a proficiency test intended to provide a general picture of the assessee's abilities within the very limited time usually available for testing.

Interpreting scores from discrete-point tests also seemed problematic. It was unclear how the many component parts should be put back together again to establish something meaningful about the test takers' ability to use the language as an organic whole. This problem involved both the content of the test (What balance of components would best represent overall language proficiency? Should phonology and syntax be considered equally important?) and the meaning of the scores (What proportion of the questions on the test would the test taker need to be able answer correctly in order for users to infer that he or she knew enough language to cope with academic study or to practise as a doctor?).

When these objections were factored in, the scientific objectivity of the approach appeared to be fatally undermined. Certainly, the scoring processes were objective, but the process of compiling the test was not. There was no scientific basis for deciding how many items should be included on the test to represent each of the components. Deciding which component was actually represented by each item was also a matter for subjective judgement.

Integrative testing

Personal reflection

What does the term 'integrative testing' imply to you? How do you think this may have differed from discrete-point testing?

What kinds of task would you expect to find in an integrative language assessment?

In the other highly influential language assessment publication of 1961, Carroll agreed with Lado about the need to test 'very specific items of language knowledge and skill judiciously sampled from the usually enormous pool of possible items' (Carroll, 1961, p. 318). In other words, he also favoured a skills/components approach. But unlike Lado, he placed more emphasis on skills than on components. He was also less enthusiastic than Lado about the value of contrastive analysis. He felt that the issue for a proficiency test should be 'how well the examinee is functioning in the target language, regardless of what his native language happens to be' (Carroll, 1961, p. 319). He worried that the logic of contrastive analyses led towards the use of different tests of proficiency for learners from each language background: an obviously impractical proposition.

His solution was to recommend the use of what he called **integrative** tests. These were tests that could measure the rate and accuracy with which learners were able to bring together different aspects of language ability under realistic time constraints to produce or comprehend complete utterances or texts. Anticipating later developments in performance testing, he suggested that a starting point for tests for international students should be a detailed investigation of the kinds of language task that they might need to undertake at university and the level of performance needed to support academic success. Test developers would need to consider questions such as 'what kinds of English mastery are required for the foreign student to comprehend reading matter in the several academic disciplines?' or 'what standard of proficiency in English pronunciation is required for foreign students to be understood by American students and teachers?' (Carroll, 1961, p. 315).

Cloze tests

A paper by Carroll, Carton, and Wilds (1959) investigated a new set of techniques proposed by Wilson Taylor (1953) as a means of judging the suitability of written texts for children of different ages: **cloze** procedures. Cloze involves asking assessees to restore texts that have been partially erased. Points can be awarded either for providing precisely the word that has been erased from the source text (exact words scoring) or by providing any word that would fit in the context (semantically acceptable scoring). Carroll and his colleagues saw the potential of cloze procedures as integrative tests of language proficiency. A learner with low proficiency in a language might struggle to restore much of a text made up of relatively common words in simple sentences; a learner with high proficiency should be able to restore more missing material to texts composed of less common words in more complex sentences. Although the choice of scoring method apparently makes little difference when cloze procedures are used with native speakers, Carroll et al. (1959) saw the semantically acceptable scoring method as more appropriate for language learners.

Task 7.3

Cloze techniques

Here are some examples of word and letter cloze techniques, based on Carroll et al. (1959).

In what ways are these tasks different from the examples of discrete-point tests in Task 7.2?

What do you think might be some advantages and disadvantages of these cloze techniques?

Word cloze: write a suitable word to fill each gap (1 to 6).

Penny Baxter lay awake beside the vast sleeping bulk (1)_____ his wife. He was always wakeful on the full (2)_____. He had often wondered whether, with the light so (3)_____, men were not meant to go into their fields (4)_____ labor. He would like to slip from his bed (5)_____ perhaps cut down an oak for wood, or finish (6)_____ hoeing that Jody had left undone.

Marjorie Kinnan Rawlings (1938) *The Yearling*

Letter cloze: choose a letter to fill each gap (7 to 12). An asterisk (*) represents a space between words.

(7)_SORBING*TH	OPPED(8)_RAINI	WAS*DAMP*A(9)_
(10)_BILTY*	THE*TO(11)_	HIR(12)_*WE

Answers:

Word cloze: (1) of (2) moon (3) bright (4) and (5) and (6) the

Letter cloze: (7) B (8) * (9) T (10) A (11) U (12) T

In Taylor's (1953) work, cloze referred to the deletion of words at set intervals in a text – Carroll et al. (1959) deleted every tenth word in texts that were each 205 words long. However, it has also been used to refer to any kind of partial deletion – Carroll et al. (1959) also experimented with deleting the first, middle or last letter from sequences of 5, 7 or 11 letters (see Task 7.3) and with erasing sounds from recordings. A later variant that has been quite widely used in language tests is the *C-test*. This involves deleting the second half of every second word (Klein-Braley, 1985). However, te_ _ takers of_ _ _ report find_ _ _ this a_ annoying exper_ _ _ _ _.

Cloze procedures are based on the insight that language includes a good deal of redundancy: we can generally understand a message without attending to every word and often anticipate what we will hear or read next when listening or reading. Because elements tend to appear together with regularity, language users are able to draw on language habits to form what Oller called an *expectancy* of what is likely to come next in a text. Proficient users of English will expect to see a vowel follow certain strings of consonants such as *thr-* or *cl-*. The nonsense words '*thronk*' and '*clonk*' are plausible in English, but the words '*thrko*' and '*clnko*' are not. In filling in a gap, learners may draw on awareness of syntax and lexis. They will expect a noun to follow an adjective in certain contexts and will be aware that some words are more likely to occur together than others – '*fast food*' and '*a quick meal*' are heard much more often in English than '*quick food*' and '*a fast meal.*'

Task 7.4   (TC)

Cloze and gap-fill techniques

Pick a text from a textbook and make a cloze test by deleting every seventh word. By convention, the first and last sentence of the text is kept intact.

Make a C-test by deleting the second half of every second word, replacing each missing letter with an underscore _.

What would these tests tell you about a learner's language abilities? Would any of the items be difficult to mark? Why?

Do the items only involve linguistic knowledge, or do you need knowledge of the topic to find the correct answer?

One of the attractions of integrative tasks such as the cloze procedure for testers was that sets of passages ordered according to their difficulty for 'typical' language learners might form 'a rational scale for measuring competence in terms of the extent to which native performance in the language is achieved' (Carroll et al., 1959, p. 112). If a scale of this kind could be constructed, a new approach to reporting and interpreting scores would become possible. Carroll (1961, p. 321) suggested that scores might best be reported as probabilities – as in 'the chances are only three out of ten that an examinee with a given score level would be able to pass the freshman English course.'

Speaking tests

This line of thinking was very influential in another major testing initiative of the period on which Carroll served as a consultant: the US Foreign

Service Institute (FSI) Language Proficiency Ratings. The FSI scheme was originally developed at the time of the Cold War to measure the language abilities of US government employees. In recognition of the need for government agents to be able to interact in foreign languages, a structured oral interview was used rather than discrete-point tests of language components.

Traditional speaking tests or 'oral examinations' had continued in use, largely unchanged in format, since the previous century. Orals, as they were known, typically consisted of a reading aloud phase, after which the examiner might ask a few questions based on the text that had been read. This would be followed by a brief conversation between the examiner and assessee. In the Cambridge examinations (CPE had been joined in 1939 by the *Lower* – subsequently *First* – *Certificate in English*), the examiner would award marks to the candidate for *fluency*, *pronunciation* and *intonation*. Certain numbers of marks might be associated with a certain standard as in 'Pass $^8/_{20}$, Good $^{12}/_{20}$, Very Good $^{16}/_{20}$' (Roach, 1945, p. 7).

These speaking tests suffered from some obvious weaknesses:

- Because assessees needed to be tested individually by trained examiners, the tests were difficult and expensive to administer.
- Examiners could be inconsistent in their scoring, making the results unreliable.
- The scoring criteria were vague and did not seem to reflect linguistic theory.

The practical logistical limitations were inevitable, but perhaps overstated. Where the assessment of speaking skills was considered important enough, the investment in examiners and support systems could be made. Reliability, on the other hand, was more difficult to improve and this made testers anxious. When results were so variable, effective measurement seemed impossible. Traditional examiners were more prepared to downplay this niggle, although they did take measures to address it. Their approach to scoring both essays and orals relied on **moderation**. Experienced examiners were asked to check a sample of the marks given by junior examiners (of course, in the days before cheap, portable recording equipment, this was easier to do for essays than for oral examinations). They might also observe examiners while they conducted an oral, challenging and altering any marks that seemed too harsh or too lenient. Comparisons could be made between marks awarded for speaking and scores on other test components, or with results from the same school in previous years. Adjustments were made where individual examiners appeared overly harsh. Teachers familiar with the assessees might also be consulted. The system was hierarchical, with more experienced examiners assumed to be more accurate than novices and with the chief examiner as the ultimate authority.

Although these practices may have seemed satisfactory where small numbers of examiners were working in a familiar setting, there had long been concern that even experienced examiners varied in their interpretation of standards so that assessees could receive very different results depending on who was examining them. As secretary of the Cambridge examinations, Roach (1945) recognised that when tests were being given in over 50 different countries, it was difficult to be confident that examiners working in all these different locations were all awarding marks in the same way and on the same basis. Roach experimented with the use of recordings of performances to train examiners in understanding the scoring system. He also introduced joint examining by two examiners – one sent out from Cambridge, the other a teacher working locally – to more effectively transmit and maintain the intended standards.

The third issue, the theoretical basis for the scoring criteria, was not addressed by Roach, perhaps because he was, in any case, sceptical of the benefits of criteria, arguing that 'standards of impression marking cannot be well defined beforehand by written instructions' (Roach, 1945, p. 38). This contrasts with the approach developed for the FSI. Scoring was based on a rating scale used to focus the examiners' attention during the interview on key features of test performance derived from (Bloomfieldian) linguistic theory: *accent, comprehension, fluency, grammar* and *vocabulary* (Wilds, 1975). The outcome of the interview was a rating on a scale that could be used to assess the employee's ability in any language, ranging from 0 (no functional ability) up to 5 (equivalent to an educated native speaker).

In addition to rater training aimed at encouraging agreement on the interpretation of levels of performance, several other strategies were used to promote reliability. One was a degree of standardization in the interview procedure itself, which followed a sequence of phases intended to 'warm up' the assessee with a few straightforward questions before increasing the level of challenge to find the point on the scale at which the assessee might not be able to function effectively. This was backed up by the collection of data on the extent to which raters agreed with each other in their ratings (see *inter-rater reliability* in Chapter 4).

The mastery learning movement

Personal reflection

What makes someone a successful language learner? Are some learners naturally better at learning languages than others?

What elements might you include on a test to find out whether someone would be able to quickly learn new languages?

Using graded language tasks such as reading passages or speaking activities of increasing difficulty to establish an individual's overall proficiency in a language had obvious attractions for both teachers and testers. In language teaching it suggested a sound basis, **mastery learning**, for sequencing instruction. Learners who demonstrated they had successfully mastered one learning target by passing a qualifying test would progress to the next unit. Learners who failed to achieve the required score would be given more practice before attempting the test again. In proficiency testing it could be assumed that an assessee who was able to complete a cloze test or carry out a spoken activity at one level would also be able to successfully complete tasks at all of the levels below.

The idea of staged targets for language learning has a long history. Four hundred years ago, Comenius divided language learning into four ages, suggesting that only the child's mother tongue and Latin as (the pan-European language of the educated) needed to be learned at the highest level (Figure 7.2):

$$
\left.\begin{matrix} \textit{The first} \\ \textit{The second} \\ \textit{The third} \\ \textit{The fourth} \end{matrix}\right\} \textit{age is} \left\{\begin{matrix} \textit{babbling infancy} \\ \textit{ripening boyhood} \\ \textit{maturer youth} \\ \textit{vigorous manhood} \end{matrix}\right\} \textit{in which we learn to speak} \left\{\begin{matrix} \textit{indistinctly} \\ \textit{correctly} \\ \textit{elegantly} \\ \textit{forcibly} \end{matrix}\right\}
$$

Figure 7.2 Comenius's language learning levels from the *Great Didactic* (Comenius, 1638)

The four stages corresponded to four language courses conceived by Comenius – the *Vestibulum, Janua, Palatium* and *Thesaurus*. The innovative features of the mastery learning movement were its technical rigor, its inclusivity and the formative role given to assessment. It was not only a matter of finding out whether learners could do the thing they had been taught, but of taking appropriate action to help those who were not yet be able to do it.

Language aptitude

In traditional classrooms, all learners were expected to progress through the material at the same speed, no matter whether they already knew what was being taught or were at a complete loss to understand any of it. Selection was built into the system: those who were unable to keep up would fail the test and so fail to progress to the next stage of education. Mastery learning was inclusive: every learner was expected to succeed. For Carroll (1963), everybody had the capacity to learn, but some were equipped to do this faster than others. Learning aptitude represented this variation between learners in the rate at which they could learn. Supporters of mastery learning suggested that the differences seen in eventual *achievement* in the classroom could be reduced by increasing variation in the *teaching* (Bloom, 1968). In other words, if the content and pace of teaching could be better matched to learners' individual aptitudes, it would bring improved results and reduce the gap between the highest and lowest achieving learners.

Mastery learning brought greater variety with different learning plans for individuals or groups within a class. Learners with high levels of aptitude would be allowed to progress quickly to more challenging tasks without being held up by slower learners. Those who struggled with basic concepts would not be left behind to sit in confusion as their classmates forged ahead but could be given extra help until they could grasp the more basic material. To measure aptitude for language learning and to identify which learners were likely to make relatively rapid progress, Carroll, with Carl Sapon, developed the Modern Language Aptitude Test (MLAT) (Carroll & Sapon, 1959), which measured features such as short-term memory and the ability to associate sounds with symbols.

Behavioural objectives

In mastery learning approaches, the milestones used to chart progress along the continuum of proficiency are generally known as **behavioural objectives**. These objectives, often presented in the form of 'Can Do' statements, specify the observable behaviours that should result from successful learning. Ideally, these observable behaviours should be meaningful real-world applications of the skill being taught (Block, 1971). Carroll (1971, p. 31) argued that 'it is most essential . . . to be able to state as exactly as possible what the learning task is, particularly its objectives, in testable form. That is, a teacher must be able to determine when a student has mastered a task to a satisfactory degree.' Similar requirements have continued to inform the design of objectives in language education (see for example ACTFL, 2014).

At the end of a unit of instruction, a test can be given, closely based on the specified objective. If teaching and learning have been successful, every learner should pass the test. Given such measurability, student progress may be tracked through periodic, formative testing. Feedback based on test performance can be used to guide extra instruction – using alternative methods – for learners who do not achieve the intended objectives (Bloom, 1968). This placed a new emphasis on testing (as well as teaching) by teachers, making assessment central to the classroom educational process.

Two approaches to score interpretation

Score interpretation

The history of assessment since ancient times has involved at least two contrasting approaches to the interpretation of scores. Bachman and Palmer (2010) called these **relative** and **absolute** score interpretations.

Relative score interpretations

One approach has been to treat performance as a competition: assessees are judged in relation to each other. In individual sporting contests, only the fastest athletes or strongest throwers are awarded medals. Similarly, in the *competitive examinations* used in ancient China and taken up in nineteenth-century Europe, only a few candidates would be chosen as worthy of a place working as government officials. Any number of people could enter for the examinations, but only a fixed number could be selected. If five jobs were on offer, the highest scoring five candidates would be chosen whether the number of entries was 5 or 500. In many traditional classrooms, each week the highest scoring student would be given a reward for coming 'top of the class'; the lowest scoring student might be punished and humiliated.

In many individual competitive sports, such as archery, everyone has a set number of opportunities to shoot at the same target from precisely the same distance. Scoring is straightforward: different numbers of points are awarded for shots that hit different zones on the target. Similarly, in standardised tests, everyone is given precisely the same tasks to perform and questions are designed with objective scoring in mind. However, it's not always easy to tell from the results of such tightly controlled tasks how well the competitors would perform under more natural conditions. The learner in a class with the best control of grammar, the highest vocabulary test scores and great pronunciation is not always the one who is able to communicate most effectively with the foreign visitor.

Absolute score interpretations

An alternative approach to assessment has involved deciding whether or not the assessee is qualified to enjoy a certain status. Unlike the imperial examinations in China, in ancient Greece and Rome and in the mediaeval European universities qualifications were awarded when the assessee was pronounced by his teacher, or other competent judges, to be worthy to be called a scholar. In this kind of *qualifying examination*, there is no limit to the number of people who can pass. Modern examples of qualifying examinations that are often cited are the driving tests used in many countries. Any number of individuals may qualify as drivers, provided that they demonstrate their ability to control a car, show awareness of road conditions and display a good knowledge of the rules of the road.

Unlike competitive examinations, many qualifying examinations are **performance assessments** that involve the simulation of real-life conditions. Because the focus is on carrying out realistic, often complex and somewhat unpredictable tasks, it is not easy to standardise conditions. Traffic conditions can be trickier in certain locations or at certain times of day, and different learners will have more knowledge of an essay topic or feel more comfortable talking to an older examiner than their classmates.

In complex performance assessments, instead of everyone being asked to perform the same task, individuals may have the freedom to choose different kinds of tasks with different levels of difficulty. Even when every assessee is given the same prompt, each has to interpret what is required and so plays a part in deciding what the task involves. Judgements about the assessee's abilities will involve weighing the contribution of the qualities of each performance against the demands imposed by the task.

The psychometric approach to testing taken up by Lado (1961) was based on the measurement of differences in relation to an underlying trait (language ability) and in this respect was more compatible with the competitive model. The focus was on the individual's language ability and the intention was to find out what levels of language ability were to be expected in a particular population of people – what was 'normal' and the extent to which people differed from this norm. Tests were designed with the intention of spreading out learners as effectively as possible in order to differentiate between the more and less able. Through a process of standard setting, interpretations could then be established for different score levels. Expert judges would decide what score on the test would be sufficient to qualify an assessee for different purposes.

Mastery learning seemed to require a different approach to measurement, closer to the qualifying model. The objective was not to identify a norm for a population and then to differentiate between those who possessed more or less of the attribute. Instead, learners who seemed to have reached a certain level of functional ability would be identified. They could then be administered a test to confirm their ability to carry out relevant tasks. For example, a teacher might decide that one of her students had enough ability to pass on simple telephone messages. The learner could be given a simulation task involving passing on messages in order to confirm the teacher's view. Different tests would have to be developed to represent different uses of language, presenting different levels of challenge. Scores should be interpreted in terms of achieving a criterion of communicative success in real world language use. This approach to interpreting scores is known as **criterion-referenced** measurement.

Pragmatic tests and the unitary competence hypothesis

In his book *Language Tests at School*, John Oller (1979) suggested a more psycholinguistic approach to testing. In place of the structuralist interest in knowledge of language as a system, his main concern was with how efficiently and skilfully language could be processed in the mind of the learner. He rejected discrete-point testing, arguing that valid language tests should be both *integrative* – testing language components in combination rather than attempting to separate them out – and *pragmatic* in the sense that they should engage the test taker's awareness of meanings and contextual constraints, as well as knowledge of linguistic forms. Along with the more integrative comprehension tests, oral interviews and essays disparaged by Lado, Oller was also enthusiastic about the potential of dictation and cloze techniques as integrative task types engaging multiple elements of language – form and meaning – at the same time. Where Carroll et al. (1959) had questioned the value of cloze tests on the grounds that they seemed to require too much knowledge of contextual information beyond the sentence, Oller saw this as one of the key attractions of the technique.

Oller (1979, p. 42) gives the following example of a cloze exercise:

> In order to give correct responses, the learner must operate (1)_____ the basis of both immediate and long-range (2)_____ constraints.

The correct answer to (1), *on*, can be deduced from the immediate context. In other words, the test taker could probably supply the correct answer even if only given: '_____ the basis of.' On the other hand, (2) is more ambiguous. If the test taker is only provided with 'long-range _____ constraints,' any number of words might fit the gap: Oller suggests *missile*, *legal* and *leadership*. However, the context – a text about language assessment and cloze procedures – rules out these possibilities and suggests words such as *semantic*, *linguistic* or, the original word, *contextual*.

At the time, some applied linguists such as Stephen Krashen were suggesting that the teaching of grammatical structures, the core of most language programmes, might be misguided. Second language acquisition research had revealed interesting consistencies in the order in which certain features of languages were acquired (regardless of the order in which they were presented). This suggested that there might be parallels between the way in which babies acquire the grammar of their first language without conscious effort and the way in which adults learn a second or additional language. The mental processing capacity of the brain might impose limits on what could be learned at different stages of development. Instead of endlessly repeating certain words, phrases and structures as in behaviourist classrooms, in Krashen and Terrell's (1983) 'natural approach,' teachers should present learners with linguistic input at a level on the proficiency continuum just beyond what they were currently able to produce. The purpose of classroom assessment was therefore to discover what kinds of language learners could spontaneously produce and what kinds of text they could process.

The unitary competence hypothesis

Taking up Campbell and Fiske's (1959) multi-trait, multi-method approach to validity (that tests of distinct abilities should yield different results while tests of the same ability should give similar results – see Chapter 4), Oller noticed that the results of supposedly different test parts such as listening comprehension, oral interviews and grammar were often, in fact, very similar. In an interpretation that seemed to fit well with the evidence for common developmental sequences in language acquisition, he believed this was evidence that the different tests were all measuring essentially the same underlying ability: language proficiency. This suggestion, known as the **unitary competence hypothesis**, was briefly very influential, but lost credibility when Oller's interpretation of the statistical evidence was called into question.

Although the idea of a unitary competence was not ultimately upheld and the natural approach to language teaching failed to take hold, the integrative approach to assessment did have a lasting effect. Cloze tests, in particular, proved very attractive to test providers because they were so practical to build. Unlike the skills/components approach, there was no need to invest in expensive test development and item writer training procedures because once a text was chosen, test construction was automatic. Unlike oral interviews or essay tests, there was no need to train raters because scoring was also relatively straightforward. However, contrary to Oller's hopes, further research suggested that cloze procedures did not often assess much more than the knowledge of grammatical structures and vocabulary found in their discrete-point predecessors.

The 'promised land' of communicative testing

The approaches to language assessment described up to this point share a view of language as an abstract system, deliberately distanced from the social contexts in which it was used. However, during the 1970s, following insights from the emerging field of socio-linguistics, there was a decisive shift in perspective. Hymes (1972) was particularly influential. Campbell and Wales (1970, p. 247) summed up the key issue: 'by far the most important linguistic ability has been omitted [from current linguistic theory] – the ability to produce or understand utterances which are not so much *grammatical* but, more important, *appropriate to the context in which they are made.*'

According to the situation, we make different choices about when to speak or write and for how long, about the words and grammatical forms we use and how we arrange them. For example, many people are likely to make rather different choices about how they describe their current boss according to whether they are being interviewed for a new job or relaxing at home with their friends and family. All aspects of language are affected from the words and grammar we use to our rate of speech and our pitch, tone and accent. Sociolinguists began to explore variation in language and to look for the principles that might explain the different ways in which we communicate according to the nature of the context we are in.

This shift in perspective filtered into the world of language assessment. In October 1980, a symposium was held in Lancaster in north-west England. A small group of language assessment specialists gathered to discuss a set of influential recent papers. The symposium led directly to the publication of a book summarising the discussions (Alderson & Hughes, 1981) and to the establishment of a newsletter that would later develop into the field's first dedicated journal, *Language Testing*. Dominating the agenda were papers rejecting Oller's evidence for a unitary language competence and promoting **communicative** or **specific purposes** approaches to assessment.

Sociolinguistic influences on testing practice

Wanting to introduce a more sociolinguistic perspective to language assessment, Cooper (1968) had made a distinction between the 'linguistic competence' dealt with in the skills/components model and what he called 'contextual competence.' Contextual competence involved knowing 'what to say, with whom, and when, and where' (Cooper, 1968, p. 58) and this required its own distinct grammar, or set of rules. Although linguistic competence could be acquired independently of contextual competence, both were needed for effective communication. Cooper's distinction was taken up by Munby (1978, p. 17), who considered that 'Existing testing frameworks, concentrating as they do on linguistic competence, do not necessarily assess a person's communicative ability. Knowledge of the target language may not be sufficient for effective communication to take place in that language, and our ability to predict communicative competence depends upon the test content being based upon the specific communication requirements of the particular category of learner.'

The first paper considered at the symposium was Keith Morrow's (1979) manifesto for a communicative language testing. For Morrow, this was revolutionary and represented the ideal world or 'promised land' for testers. It would bring testing up to date and align it with the fashion for communicative teaching based on realistic interaction in the target language. The point was not to test knowledge of language systems, whether as discrete components or integrated whole, but the ability to use language functionally to carry out real world tasks: to understand and pass on ideas, to form and maintain relationships, to negotiate transactions.

Morrow was critical of Oller for failing to take account of the situations in which language is used. Believing that all uses of language reflected the same basic underlying ability, Oller (1979) had given only limited attention to issues of content, such as the kinds of text that should be employed for cloze procedures or dictations. He suggested, for example, that 'material intended for fifth grade geography students' (Oller, 1979, p. 365) might work well as a basis for cloze tests aimed at university-level students and that 'dictation at an appropriate rate, of kinds of material that learners are expected to cope with, is a promising way of investigating how well learners can handle a variety of school-related discourse processing tasks' (p. 269). He did not explore further how developers should identify these materials.

In contrast to Oller, advocates of communicative testing insisted on the **authenticity** of their test material, aiming to reproduce real life conditions in their tests (although, as Bachman, 1990, pointed out, they paid too much attention to the test content and not enough to how assessees responded to this). Where Lado (1961) had argued that tests should reflect differences between the assessees' first language and the target language, Morrow, argued that tests should reflect their social purposes for using the target language. There should be tests of the language used in workshops for engineers and tests of the language used in clinical settings for medical practitioners. Lado had used the term 'integrated skills' to refer to listening or reading (as distinct from discrete elements such as vocabulary or intonation), Brendan Carroll (1980) used the same term to refer to the integration of modalities involved in carrying out real life tasks: listening and speaking integrated in conducting a conversation or discussion; reading, listening and writing along with graphics or other supporting visual material in preparing a simulated academic assignment.

ELTS: an experiment in communicative testing

The *English Language Testing System* (ELTS) (launched in 1979), on which Brendan Carroll worked, was designed, like the TOEFL test, to assess the English language ability of international students, but took a radically different approach. In place of discrete tests of grammar and vocabulary, ELTS tested the use of reference material (in a component titled 'Study Skills'), included an integrated test of reading and writing, and offered test takers a choice of modules linked to different disciplinary areas.

The ELTS test (see Table 7.5) offered a choice between a *Non-Academic* test for vocational candidates, a *General Academic* option, or one of five modules covering broadly defined areas of study: *Life Sciences*; *Social Studies*; *Physical Sciences*; *Technology*; *Medicine*. In addition to three sections in their chosen subject area (M), each candidate was required to take two common tests in the General (G) section.

Table 7.5 The design of the ELTS test

Subject specific modules	M1 Study Skills
	M2 Writing
	M3 Individual Interview
General modules	G1 General Reading
	G2 General Listening

Within the subject-specific part of the test, the three modules (M1, M2 and M3) were linked so that test takers wrote about a topic in the Writing paper (M2) that had been introduced in the Study Skills module (M1). The Interview (M3) would also involve a topic from M1.

(TC)

Task 7.5

Look at these sample items from ELTS

How are these different from the other examples of test material you have seen so far in this chapter?

In what ways do you think these tasks more closely resemble real life language use?

Listening (G2)

SECTION 4
LISTENING TO A SEMINAR

Some students are meeting their course director for the first time to discuss their programs of studies. Two of them are asking the director questions. Imagine that you are a member of the group, and listen to the conversation.
This timetable may help you to understand the conversation.

TIMETABLE: GROUP A

INTRODUCTORY COURSE: Tuesday October 7 - Friday October 11

	TUESDAY	WEDNESDAY	THURSDAY	FRIDAY
10 a.m.	Tour of campus	University library	Computing Centre	Tour of city
12:30		LUNCH		
2 p.m.	Lecture: Room 2	Meeting with tutors; Tour of Department	Language Centre	Student Fair; Randolph Hall
6:30		DINNER		
8:00	Film show	Concert	Reception: Hunter Hall	Party: Room 17

After each part there will be a pause for you to answer questions on what you have heard. They are printed in this booklet and you may look at them as you listen. Remember, you will hear each part once only. LISTEN CAREFULLY.

That is the end of the first part of the conversation. Now answer questions 27 to 31.

27 At which of these times could a student expect to find Dr Talbot in her
   office?

   A   Monday at 9 a.m.
   B   Wednesday at 11 a.m.
   C   Thursday at 10 a.m.
   D   Thursday at 2 p.m.

. . .

31 Dr Talbot starts with the first page of the timetable because

   A   it's the most complicated.
   B   it's on the yellow sheet.
   C   it deals with the introductory course.
   D   the students ask her to.

Now you will hear the second part of the conversation.

. . .

Study Skills (M1)

SECTION 5

Bibliography

Boaden, N. (1971) Urban *Policy–Making: influence on county boroughs in England and Wales*, London, Cambridge University Press.

Butler, J.R. and Pearson, M. (1970) *Who goest home?: a study of long-stay patients in acute hospital care*, Occasional Papers on Social Administration. No. 34. London, C. Bell and Sons.

Davies, R. (1968) *Social Needs and Resources in Local Services: a study of variations in standards of provision of personal social services between local authority areas*. London, Michael Joseph.

Department of Employment and Productivity (Annual) *Family Expenditure Survey: Report*, London, HMSO.

Department of the Environment (1974) *Housing for People who are Physically Handicapped*. Circular 74/74, London HMSO.

Department of Health (1966) *Health and Welfare: The Development of Community Care*, Cmnd. 3022 London, HMSO.

Department of Health and Social Security (1972) *Digest of Health Statistics, 1971*, London. HMSO.

Engberg, E. (1968). 'Family flats with a nursing annexe.' *Lancet I*, 1106.

Harris, A. I. et al. (1971) *Handicapped and Impaired in Great Britain*. Part I. Handicapped and Impaired; the Impaired Housewife; Leisure activities of impaired persons. Part 2. Work and Housing of Impaired Persons in

Great Britain. Port 3. (1972) Income entitlement to supplementary benefit in Great Britain. London, HMSO.

'Homes for the physically handicapped,' (1969), Architects Journal 150, 365.

Hospital Advisory Service (annual) Reports, London, HMSO.

Heather, M. (1971) 'Scrooge areas' New Society, 2 December, London.

Miller, E. J. and Gwynne, G. V. (1972) A Life Apart; a report of a pilot study of residential institutions for the physically handicapped and young chronic sick, London, Tavistock Publications.

Orwell, S. (1973) 'The implementation of the Chronically Sick and Disabled Persons' Act, 1970,' London, National Fund for Research into Crippling Diseases.

Research team of Department of Clinical Epidemiology and Social Medicine, St. Thomas's Hospital Medical School (1972) 'Collaboration between health and social services; a study of the care of responauts' Community Medicine 128, No. 23. September 22.

Skeet, M. (1970) Home from Hospital; A Study of the homecare needs of recently discharged hospital patients, London. The Dan Mason Nursing Research Committee of the National Florence Nightingale Memorial Committee of Great Britain.

Skinner, F. W. (ed) (1969) Physical Viability and Community Care, Tower Hamlets Council of Social Service, Bedford Square Press of the National Council of Social Service.

Wager, R. (1972) Care of the Elderly: an exercise in coat benefit analysis commissioned by Essex County Council, London. Institute of Municipal Treasurers.

Section 5: BIBLIOGRAPHY

Read quickly through Section 5 in the Source Booklet and then answer these questions:

31 Which of the following authors gives an account of treatment for long-term patients?

   A   Butler, J R and Pearson, M
   B   Miller, E J and Gwynne, G V
   C   Skeet, M
   D   Wager, R

32 Which of the following government reports deals with analyses of figures only?

   A   Department of Health (1966)
   B   Department of Health and Social Security (1972)
   C   Department of the Environment (1974)
   D   Department of Employment and Productivity (Annual)

33 If you wanted to read about the ways in which social services provisions
vary from area to area which of the following authors would you choose?

A   Boaden, N
B   Davies, B
C   Orwell, S
D   Skinner, F W

© British Council (1987) *The English Language Testing Service Specimen Materials* booklet

Texts and task types in communicative tests were drawn as directly as possible from the target language use domain. When designing another new test of English for academic purposes, Weir (1983) took this principle even further than Brendan Carroll by using direct observation to answer the kinds of questions posed, but left unanswered, by John Carroll (1961) at the inception of the TOEFL. These included: 'What kinds of English mastery are required for the foreign student to comprehend reading matter in the several academic disciplines?' Using Munby's (1978) comprehensive framework for describing language use – the *communicative needs processor* – Weir carried out a form of *job analysis*, roaming university campuses, observing and characterizing the English language requirements of the language use tasks that international students needed to carry out on their courses. The test that he produced at the end of this process, the *Test of English for Educational Purposes* (TEEP), required assessees to listen to a lecture and take notes, read an article on the same topic, then synthesise ideas from both in a short essay. In other words, they had to carry out, within the time limits imposed by the test, a typical academic study cycle.

Communicative and specific purpose-driven approaches to language testing were greeted rather sceptically by many researchers. Just as John Carroll (1961) had been concerned that contrastive linguistic analysis implied the need for a separate test for groups of learners from different language backgrounds, Alderson (1988) worried that as no two learners had identical needs: communicative testing implied a personal language test for every learner. Preparing individualised tests was obviously not a practical proposition. Bachman (1990) argued that the communicative emphasis on successfully carrying out 'real world' tasks could not substitute for a clear definition of the knowledge, skills or abilities involved. The fact that an assessee succeeded in ordering lunch in a role play assessment would be rather meaningless unless it could be assumed that the abilities involved in doing so were really the same abilities required to order lunch in a restaurant or to carry out other similar activities. Finally, a language test, as Perren (1967) memorably expressed it, was 'a test not a tea party.' In other words, however carefully the assessment designer attempted to reconstruct real life conditions, the people involved understood that they were, in fact, participating in a test and so would not behave in the same way as in real life.

Rapprochement: communicative language ability

The Bachman model of communicative language ability (Bachman, 1990; Bachman & Palmer, 1996, 2010) built on earlier models suggested by Canale and Swain (1980) and Canale (1983), among others. The model brought together the task-focused communicative approach with the ability-focused skills/components tradition (see Chapters 5 and 6). In the model, communicative language ability involves language knowledge (see Figure 7.3) and other characteristics of the language learner, such as topic knowledge, strategic competence (planning, monitoring) and affect (motivation, anxiety). These interact with the characteristics of the task and setting (whether in a language assessment or real-life context) to engender a performance. For Bachman and Palmer (2010), the language knowledge element is made up

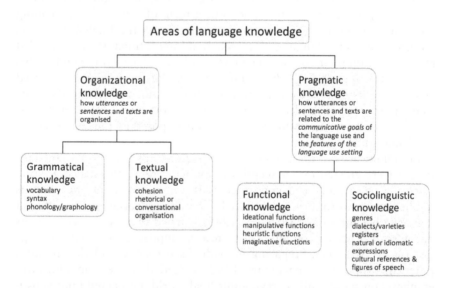

Figure 7.3 The Bachman model of language knowledge. Reproduced by permission of Oxford University Press from *Language Assessment in Practice* by Lyle Bachman and Adrian Palmer © Oxford University Press 2010, p.45.

of organizational (grammatical and textual) and pragmatic (functional and socio-linguistic) components. Organizational knowledge enables the production of well-formed texts and sentences (or speech units), while pragmatic knowledge involves producing language that is appropriate to the context and to the user's goals for communication.

The pervasive influence of the Bachman model on subsequent language testing practice is evident in revisions made to both the more communicatively oriented ELTS test and the more structurally oriented TOEFL during the 1990s. In the revision of ELTS that eventually led to the 1995 version of its successor (IELTS™ – the *International English Language Testing System*) some of its more experimental communicative aspects were jettisoned. The production of multiple versions to cater for learners from different disciplines was abandoned, along with the study skills modules and the thematic links between the reading and writing sections. The content was increasingly standardised through, for example, use of an interlocutor frame or partial script to control the part of the assessor in the speaking test.

The revisions of the TOEFL test that culminated in the launch of the (internet-based) TOEFL iBT© in 2005 involved movement in the opposite direction. The structure and written expression and vocabulary components were dropped, to be replaced by tests of writing and speaking that included greater integration with written and spoken input and simulated academic language use. The 2020 versions of the two tests (see Table 7.6) appear in many ways more like each other than their predecessors (Tables 7.4 and 7.5). Samples of current test materials can be found on their respective websites.

There has been a degree of convergence between competing approaches and it is now widely agreed among language assessment specialists that language ability involves multiple components. The Bachman and Palmer model proved to be highly influential, providing the basis for many testing projects and for the Cambridge Language Assessment series of standard textbooks on testing published between 2000 and 2005. However, it would be misleading to suggest that there is now a consensus on how language abilities should be conceptualised for assessment purposes. The Bachman model has been criticised on the grounds that it fails to explain the relative contribution made by its various components or the dynamic ways in which they might interact with each other in communication (Widdowson, 2003).

The relationship between language ability and the contexts in which language is used has been a point of contention. For Bachman and Palmer (2010, p. 34), the components of the model interacted with, but were clearly distinguished from, other 'attributes of the individual language user' (such as age, personality, etc.) and 'characteristics of the language use situation, which included, among other things, the language – written or spoken – that

Table 7.6 The TOEFL iBT and IELTS tests compared

Section	Time limit		Questions		Tasks	
Test	iBTOEFL	IELTS	iBTOEFL	IELTS	iBTOEFL	IELTS
Reading	60–80 minutes	60 minutes	36–56 items	40 items	Read 3 or 4 texts from academic texts and answer questions. Prose summary completion, table completion, and multiple choice.	Read 3 texts multiple choice, sentence or prose summary completion, short-answer questions, and matching lists or phrases.
Listening	60–90 minutes	30 minutes	40 items multiple choice, short answer, notes/summary/flow chart completion, sentence completion, labelling a diagram, and matching.	34–51 items chart completion and multiple choice.	4–6 lectures (some with classroom discussion); 2 campus-based conversations between 2–3 people; each is heard only once.	2 conversations, 2 monologues. One of each is more social and one more academic in character – discussion and lecture.
Speaking	20 minutes	11–14 minutes	6 tasks 2 independent tasks and 4 integrated tasks.	3 parts	Integrated tasks: test takers read a short passage, listen to related material, and then orally integrate the information in their own words. Independent tasks: test takers respond to familiar topic based on own experience.	Part 1: introduction and interview based on selected, familiar topics. Part 2: individual long turn in which test takers respond to a selected task card. Part 3: two-way discussion linked to the Part 2 topic.
Writing	50 minutes	60 minutes	2 tasks	2 tasks	Write essay responses based on reading and listening tasks; support an opinion in writing.	Task 1: test takers report on a diagram, table, or data Task 2: test takers write an essay on a given topic based on their own experience.

the language user is processing, the physical characteristics of the situation, and, in many cases, other language users.' McNamara (1995) and He and Young (1998) took issue with this view, arguing that in speaking tests it does not really make sense to try to measure individual abilities. Both the interviewer and the interviewee contribute to the interaction and to the nature of the language generated. Any score that is awarded must, in fact, reflect a jointly constructed performance.

In the *interactional* view favoured by Chapelle (1998) and Chalhoub-Deville (2003), the contexts in which people use language are an integral part of language ability. In other words, different contexts imply different language abilities. The 'pragmatic competence' that a learner has in university study is not the same as the 'pragmatic competence' involved in working as a hotel receptionist. It cannot, therefore, be assumed that a learner who demonstrates a certain level of pragmatic competence in one setting will be able to transfer their competence to other settings. Similar but more radical challenges to the Bachman model have come from advocates of alternative approaches to assessment in the formative tradition. These are considered in the next section.

Although most critics of the Bachman model have characterised it as overly cognitive, being concerned with individual mental processes rather than social and interactive aspects of language use, Weir, Vidakovic, and Galaczi (2013) objected that the Bachman model has very little to say about how language is processed in the mind of the user. As a result, they suggested, the model offers no clear guidance on why one language use task may be more or less demanding than another. This objection led to the development of Weir's (2005a) socio-cognitive framework, which accounts for task difficulty in terms of the demands imposed by different contextual characteristics on the assessee's cognitive resources (see Chapters 5 and 6).

The debates over the nature of language abilities raise fundamental questions about the basis for their measurement and the interpretation of the results of assessments. The intractable issue to be resolved is just how local and how general language abilities might be. If language use involves a number of distinct, but interrelated abilities, can each of these be measured separately? How meaningful and useful is it to report a single score when multiple abilities are involved? If the language abilities measured by an assessment are local to a specific context, can scores be used to inform decisions about other contexts? And what would make another context sufficiently 'parallel' for the scores to be useful? Increasingly sophisticated statistical techniques are being developed to try to pin down the complex constellations of abilities that might contribute to language use, but if abilities are highly context dependent, these efforts may be in vain.

Developments in formative assessment

By the 1960s, social and technological changes had given rise to new ways of thinking about education. It was realised that traditional patterns of

8 to 12 years of schooling, followed by a lifetime of employment in a familiar occupation, were unsustainable. Few children in industrialised countries could expect to spend their lives working in the fields or factories or following other established occupations in the way that their parents or ancestors had. Instead, even if they continued working for the same employer, they could expect to experience rapid change. Citizens would need to adapt to new industries and new forms of leisure. The concept of *permanent education* (Council of Europe, 1970) or *lifelong learning* was suggested as a response to these new needs. People of all ages should be able to access education and training at many different points in their lives in order to make the most of new opportunities. More learning would take place outside formal school systems in the workplace or at home.

Since ancient times, education had been seen as a process of mastering a more or less fixed body of knowledge. Traditional systems of qualifications – school graduation certificates, university degrees, professional examinations – still embodied this classical model. They did not offer enough flexibility to reflect the explosion in new forms of knowledge that was going on. To provide for greater flexibility, while still communicating what learners had achieved, qualifications would need to become *modular* and *learner centred*. In working towards and adding to their qualifications, individual learners would need to be able to choose different pathways, integrating knowledge, skills and abilities picked up in formal and non-formal settings. This implied that learners themselves would need to become self-regulated, making informed choices about what and how they should study: learning how to learn as well as learning about academic subjects.

Following the lead of workplace education, by the 1990s, self-assessment, peer assessment and feedback were becoming established in language classrooms. Oskarsson (1980) and Brindley (1989) were pioneers of learner-centred language assessment, promoting the use of self-assessment checklists, portfolios and learning logs. In 1998, the publication of Black and Wiliam's *Inside the Black Box* brought together evidence from over 650 studies showing that effective use of formative assessment could substantially improve the performance of school children across the curriculum. This gave a renewed impetus to learner-centred approaches in language assessment through the concept of **assessment for learning**.

Assessment for learning owes a good deal to the formative testing and mastery learning of the 1960s, but also differs from it in important ways. Poehner (2008) has pointed to a distinction that can be made between more **interventionist** and more **interactionist** approaches to assessment (not to be confused with interactional views of language ability). Mastery learning and formative testing had involved a straightforwardly interventionist approach. Learners might be given a **pre-test** – assessing how far they were already able to carry out a task. This would be carried out under controlled conditions. Teachers would look at the results and identify areas of strengths and weakness. They could then intervene to focus a unit of instruction on improving performance before administering a **post-test** to establish how much improvement had been made and whether learners were now able to carry out the task successfully.

Influenced by the work of Vygotsky (1986), and Bruner (1983), learner-centred assessment, or assessment for learning, introduced more exploratory interactionist approaches. The assessor could participate in the assessment, carrying out the tasks with the assessees collectively or individually. The rationale behind the approach is that if the assessees are able to improve on the initial performance when given hints or support, this indicates their immediate potential for learning. If the assessees fail to answer a question correctly, the assessor can step in with structured assistance or **scaffolding**. Through this process, the assessor learns and documents how much help is needed, and in what areas, to bring about improved performance. If the assessees are able to give a correct response, the assessor might ask follow-up questions to check whether they are able to apply their understanding to other similar problems, showing how well they have assimilated the concepts being assessed.

Differences between the two approaches are summarised in Table 7.7. For advocates of assessment for learning, the interactionist approach has two key advantages. First, it gives the students/assessees a real and immediate opportunity to learn. Because they receive feedback and have opportunities to correct themselves, they can learn from the experience of assessment in a way that is not possible in assessments given under traditional test conditions. Second, it is claimed, an interactionist approach to assessment not only provides better tools for teaching and learning, but is also more **revealing** than traditional tests because it can inform the user about how far each learner will have to develop in order to perform independently.

Through a process referred to as **mediation**, the teacher helps learners or assesses to tackle tasks involving the use of language that they are unable to manage without such assistance. This process reveals a **zone of proximal development**: the distance between what the learners are able to do with support from others and what they are able to do independently. This indicates where there is immediate scope for them to learn. Poehner (2008) gave an example of two learners who made an error with verb tenses while speaking. One was stopped by the teacher and was immediately able to correct herself without further help; the other was only able to give the correct form when it was modelled for her. Although both assesses made errors, the learner who needed more scaffolding was clearly much further from being able to use the appropriate forms independently. The rich understanding of a learner's state of development that can be obtained is, it is argued, potentially far more informative for users than traditional proficiency and achievement test scores.

Table 7.7 Interventionist and interactionist assessment for learning (based on Poehner, 2008; Wiliam, 2011)

	Interventionist	*Interactionist*
Questions addressed	How much has the assessee already learned? What can he/she do? What can't he/she do? How does this person's performance compare with other people's?	How does this person learn? Under what conditions and by how much can performance be improved? What are the main obstacles to a better level of performance?
Assessment focus	retrospective: products of past experiences	prospective: processes involved in learning and prospects for improvement
Assessment conditions	standardised: same for everybody	individualised: responsive to what is discovered during the assessment
Assessee performance	independent one opportunity to perform	supported repeated opportunities to perform
Role of assessor	presents tasks records responses disengaged	presents tasks identifies obstacles engaged: mediates tasks, provides feedback promotes learning
Outcomes	scores as estimate of current state of knowledge, level of skill or ability	descriptions of learning potential: identification of obstacles to learning and of what is possible with intervention of the assessor or other expert
Interpretation of results	identification of outcomes of learning, strengths/ weaknesses to inform future teaching identification of need for intervention	identification of obstacles to learning and performance suggestions on ways of helping learners to overcome these obstacles

Language testing specialists have tended to ignore the more interactionist, informal assessment that teachers carry out routinely during their classes, concentrating instead on interventionist formal periodic testing. Bachman and Damböck (2017), for example, considered that teachers were well-trained and skilled in the former and so excluded it from their handbook. Assessment for learning advocates, in contrast, are critical of teacher-training and of teaching that prioritises interventionist over interactionist assessment. They argue that teachers also need extensive support to become more skilled informal assessors. Black and Wiliam (1998), for example, suggested that because teachers in many countries lack effective training in assessment, they tend to base their practice on the examples provided by external tests. They identified a number of weaknesses commonly found in teachers' use of assessment.

Many of these weaknesses involve assessment practices that would be equally unacceptable in external testing programmes:

- Lack of collaboration and review: methods used by teachers are not shared and reviewed by colleagues, so good practices fail to spread and poor practices are not noticed and corrected.
- Construct under-representation: teacher-made assessments often focus narrowly on things that are easy to assess and neglect other areas (e.g., teachers find it easier to give grammar and vocabulary tests and may avoid assessing speaking skills because this is more challenging both to manage and to score).
- Testing as ceremonial: assessment is often treated as a bureaucratic chore or ritual with the objective of satisfying the expectations of managers or parents rather than as a way of collecting meaningful information about learners.
- Failure to use assessment information: teachers often ignore assessment records passed on by their learners' previous teachers.

Others involve practices that could be considered acceptable in some external testing, but that are not so appropriate for the language classroom:

- Normative score interpretations: an overemphasis on competition and grading that can eventually persuade lower scoring learners that they are unable to learn.
- Lack of useable feedback: marks and comments made on learners' work that do not make it clear what the learners need to do to improve.
- Speededness: teachers are often pressured to complete a given number of units of work within a set period rather than moving at a rate that is more appropriate to their learners' needs.

Among those who embrace the concept of assessment for learning, a distinction can be made between people who take a more cognitive view of language learning, which is compatible with the Bachman model and socio-cognitive approach, and those who favour a more **socio-cultural** analysis. Like the early advocates of mastery learning, the cognitivists accept the dominant model of language learning which involves stages of acquisition and growth in individual functional abilities. They see assessment for learning as a means of helping learners to progress along an imagined scale of ability from beginner to mastery. In this view, standardised testing and classroom-based assessment have the potential to complement each other within a coherent system. Unfortunately, the point by point grammar-based progression in contemporary language syllabuses rarely matches what is known about how the abilities involved in language use develop in the minds of learners.

Dynamic assessment

Some advocates of socio-cultural theory reject both the measurement metaphor of scales of ability and the view of languages as abstract systems of rules. In this vein, Poehner and Lantolf (2005) and Poehner (2008) argue in favour of a form of **dynamic assessment** which is opposed to traditional testing (or *static assessment* as they would characterise it). In this perspective, language learning does not happen in the mind of the learner, progressing along a partly predetermined pathway of individual development, but is a social process of assimilation into a specific local set of cultural practices and relationships. In contrast to the Bachman model and going well beyond the interactionalist standpoint, language use is seen to be inseparable from context. Development occurs as new forms of interaction are gradually taken up and internalised by the learner. The learner becomes an increasingly active participant in a particular community, with the teacher providing mediation between the learner and the target culture. Mediation, which characterises dynamic assessment, is contrasted with feedback. Poehner (2008) argues that feedback is focused only on successful task completion, while mediation is focused on the development of underlying abilities. However, as Leung (2007) notes, this is not a characterization of feedback that would be acknowledged by many advocates of assessment for learning.

From the socio-cultural point of view, current frameworks and scales are simply an expression of one (dominant) set of values (Leung & Lewkowicz, 2006): values that can be contested and that are subject to change. One example of shifting standards has been the place of the 'educated native speaker' in rating scales. In the FSI scales, the highest-level learners were defined as having ability 'functionally equivalent to that of a highly articulate well educated native speaker' (Lowe, 1982). Over time, the ideal of native-speaker competence as the ultimate objective of language learning has been rejected. It is recognised that non-native language users can communicate effectively without being mistaken for native speakers and may prefer to retain a distinctive identity. References to native-like performance in the highest points on proficiency scales have now generally been replaced by formulations such as 'precision, appropriateness and ease' in language use (Council of Europe, 2018). For socio-cultural theorists, assessment constructs such as levels of language learning and proficiency are not predetermined properties of the human mind, fixed in the same way as physical properties, but that they are cultural products that shift according to what is most valued at the time.

Assessment wars: teacher assessment versus external tests

Standardised testing and classroom-based assessment (especially assessment of a more interactionist nature) are clearly very different. However, these differences are not always seen to be problematic, provided that each approach is reserved for a different purpose. Many proponents of interactionist approaches to assessment are prepared to accept a need for standardised proficiency testing and are pleased to show that increased use of formative assessment in the classroom can lead to improved performance on public tests (Black & Wiliam, 1998). Equally, many advocates of standardised testing acknowledge the benefits of assessment by teachers for effective learning but might not believe that it has much value for decision-making beyond the individual classroom.

It is in the territory of summative achievement assessment or assessment *of* learning that there is greatest scope for conflict. This is an area where both teacher assessment and standardised testing may seem appropriate. More test-oriented and more learner-centred approaches are each seen to encroach on the domain of the other.

From the learner-centred point of view, when standardised tests are used – or 'dehumanizing and oppressive pseudo-assessments' as van Lier (2006, p. 29) refers to them, hinting at the emotional tone of the debate – they can come to dominate the curriculum, taking control over the content and pacing of instruction away from the teacher and encouraging teaching to become more test like (see the section on 'Washback' in Chapter 4). It may appear to teachers that that the knowledge of learners that they have built up over an extended period is discarded in favour of the limited snapshots of learners' abilities provided by tests. More formative applications of assessment are crowded out by the need to cover the content that will be tested.

On the other hand, from the psychometric point of view, classroom-based assessment involves a variability of conditions and procedures that is incompatible with the goal of objective measurement. Relying on teacher judgements for high stakes decisions seems like a regression to a time before testing: a time when unsystematic procedures and biased judgements went unchallenged.

Quality standards: shared or separate?

Some suggest that teacher assessment or classroom-based assessment, at least for summative purposes, should be judged against the same quality standards as external tests. Bachman and Damböck (2017), for example, argued that the validity of inferences made on the basis of teacher assessments should be demonstrated in similar ways, using similar techniques, as for standardised tests. Others have argued that the tools used for judging the quality of tests are not readily transferable to more complex performance assessments (Moss, 2003; Cheng & Fox, 2017). Interactionist assessments certainly cannot be reliable according to the established indices because conditions are flexible and everyone may finally give a successful response to each item. As a result, numeric scores based on the proportion of correct responses cannot be used to show which learners have been more and which less successful, even if teachers feel that they have gained powerful insights into their students' learning (Poehner, 2008).

The advantages of relying on teacher-made assessments for summative purposes include the greater variety of tasks that it is feasible for teachers to employ over a period of time; greater potential for integration between summative and formative assessment within the curriculum; insights into learning processes, as well as outcomes; potential for professional development with better understanding of assessment issues; and greater flexibility to experiment with innovative task types. One major concern is that resources may not be made available to support the significant work involved in training, building shared standards, generating materials and moderating. Because of this, results may be inconsistent. However, if sufficient investment is made, teacher assessment of learning can be reliable. Although it may not be possible or desirable to standardise teacher assessments, Harlen (2007) collected research evidence suggesting that if scoring criteria are clearly specified, training provided and teachers' work moderated, the results over an extended period are at least as reliable as those from standardised tests.

Another concern is that when teachers are asked to take on responsibility for summative assessment, this can place them in the contradictory and potentially corrupting position of being held accountable for training learners to succeed and at the same time judging whether or not they have achieved success (Brindley, 1998; Teasdale & Leung, 2000). Many of the same problems – such as narrowing of the curriculum – have been reported with high-stakes teacher assessment systems as with external tests. Such problems seem to be most acute when objectives and standards are imposed at a policy level without sufficient involvement of teachers and others affected by the decision-making process (Rea-Dickins, 2001). This has led to prescriptions for more 'democratic' systems of assessment that involve a wider range of people at the design stage and that rely on multiple sources of evidence, including both classroom-based assessment and external tests (Shohamy, 2001).

Frameworks and standards

Content standards and frameworks are often used as to lend coherence to national and international systems of language education and can provide a link between curricula, classroom-based assessment and examinations. Examples include the *Canadian Language Benchmarks* (Pawlikowska-Smith, 2000), the US TESOL *PreK-12 English Language Proficiency Standards* (TESOL, 2006), and *China's Standards of English Language Ability* (National Education Examinations Authority, 2018); but perhaps the best known internationally is the *Common European Framework of Reference for Languages* (CEFR) (Council of Europe, 2001). This is intended to aid communication between language educators working in different sectors and in different countries. Language assessments can be mapped to the overall scheme in terms of the content (what uses of language and what contexts of use does the assessment relate to?) and in terms of level. The framework partitions classroom language learning into three broad levels – A: *Basic User*; B: *Independent User*; and C: *Proficient User* – each of which can be subdivided to make finer distinctions. To aid the process of developing tests, the Council of Europe has published a *Manual for Test Development and Examining for use with the CEFR* (Council of Europe, 2009) and to help the developers to relate their assessments to the framework there is a *Manual for Relating Language Examinations to the CEFR* (Council of Europe, 2009).

The CEFR has proved popular with policymakers and others (such as publishers and test providers) seeking to communicate about standards of language ability. On the other hand, the framework has been criticised as being too vague to use as a basis for test specifications (Weir, 2005b) and its role in policymaking has been called into question (Fulcher, 2004). One concern is that it has sometimes proved too easy to ignore the horizontal or content dimension of the framework when considering levels. If, for example, it is decided on the basis of a job analysis that the level of ability in a language required for someone to work as an air traffic controller equates to B2 on the CEFR, it does not follow that anyone assessed with a B2 level will have a suitable profile of language abilities. They may be relatively weak in spoken language skills, or lack knowledge of the specialist vocabulary associated with aviation. Standard assessment use arguments must still apply. Regardless of the CEFR, the assessment content must be shown to justify the inference that the assessee has the language abilities needed for the work. The content must be relevant to the target language use domain and the assessment results must be of adequate quality to justify decision-making.

However controversial its use may sometimes be, the CEFR has certainly raised the profile of assessment issues across Europe and around the world. Its greatest contribution may be the process of reflection that it promotes. Each section of the framework concludes with an invitation: '*Users of the Framework may wish to consider and where appropriate state* . . . In relation to assessment, issues listed for consideration include, among others, '*the extent to which teachers are informed about standards (e.g. common descriptors, samples of performance); encouraged to become aware of a range of assessment techniques; and trained in techniques and interpretation*' and '*the relevance of the specifications and scales provided in the Framework to* [the users'] *context, and the way in which they might be complemented or elaborated.*' Serious engagement with such questions should serve to improve assessment practices without imposing the unitary approach that some critics fear.

Ethical and critical language assessment

The focus of attention among language assessment professionals has expanded over the past two decades from a concern with techniques to include what Davies (2008a) called the principles of assessment. One expression of this expanded concern has been an interest in the consequences of using assessment procedures, whether as part of a more inclusive definition of validity such as that put forward by Messick (1989) or as an aspect of additional qualities invoked when judging test usefulness, such as fairness or impact (see Chapter 4).

Fairness and bias

McNamara and Roever (2006) reported how these concerns led to efforts on the part of test providers to incorporate **fairness reviews** – reviews of test materials intended to eliminate any items that might be biased in favour of one group of test takers over another or that might cause offence – into test production procedures. Test results can be investigated for **differential item functioning (DIF)** – evidence that one group of assessees has performed better than another on one test item in a way that is inconsistent with their overall test performance. While fairness reviews can be integrated into the routine production of classroom-based assessment material as well as tests, DIF detection requires data from large numbers of assessees and is therefore limited to relatively large testing programmes. It is more difficult to detect the prejudices affecting teachers' grading practices. There has also been a growing interest in the practice and consequences of **accommodations** or changes made to the material or administration of a test to make it more accessible to learners with disabilities (such as Braille test versions of a reading test for blind assessees).

If DIF can be traced to construct irrelevant factors, it is evidence of unwanted **bias**. For example, McNamara and Roever (2006) recounted a study by Takala and Kaftandjieva (2000) that compared performance of male and female assessees on a 40-item vocabulary component of the Finnish Foreign Language Certificate Examination. The researchers found that males tended to perform better on items such as *grease*, *rust* and *rookie*, but females performed better on *ache*, *turn grey* and *jelly* (McNamara & Roever, 2006, p. 111). Unfortunately, DIF is often difficult to interpret. The words listed previously might seem to reflect the roles of men and women in Finnish society, but it was less clear why women were more likely to know the word *plot* and men to know the word *association*. It is often unclear how far detecting instances of DIF implies bias or unfairness. If males are more likely to know the word *rust*, should it be removed from the test, or is its DIF simply a fair reflection of the realities of language use?

Translanguaging and assessment

In the twenty-first century, people are becoming increasingly mobile, often crossing social and national borders. When this happens, they often benefit from being able to draw on knowledge of more than one language or set of cultural expectations. In interaction, they may greet each other in one language and discuss business in another. They do not compartmentalise their language resources, but often switch seamlessly between two or more languages in the course of a brief conversation; or they may discuss their ideas in one language while composing a written message in another. Such uses of multiple languages are sometimes referred to as translanguaging.

García and Wei (2014) observed that assessments of school knowledge delivered in a monolingual format (even where students are given a choice of test language) are biased against multilingual learners who may, for example, know a technical term in the language of schooling, but only be able to explain its meaning by using the language they usually speak at home. As a result, multilingual children may be unfairly excluded from opportunities that remain open to their monolingual, but no better qualified classmates.

Language education has traditionally treated languages as distinct. We give monolingual assessments of a language such as English, Chinese, or French (or of the ability to translate or interpret from one to another), but usually not of the ability to make flexible use of multiple languages – and other resources such as gesture – to communicate effectively in multilingual contexts. Indeed, if an assessee makes use of a language other than the one being assessed in the course of an assessment, they are likely to be penalised rather than rewarded.

It has been argued, from the perspective of language assessment for specific purposes, that rather than attempting to assess peoples' ability to use one language to predict how well they may perform across contexts for language use, perhaps we should attempt a more comprehensive analysis of how effective communication is achieved in those contexts, including through the use of multiple languages. In assessments based on such analyses, monolingual speakers who are unable to accommodate less proficient speakers of their language, might not score as well as flexible and creative multilinguals.

Baker and Hope (2019) described the development of a test in the context of a bilingual university in Canada where professors are expected to have a working knowledge of both French and English and are tested on their language abilities. Following a job analysis, the test addressed, 'the ability to follow meetings that occur primarily in French with some alternation in English and where production in French is not required' (p. 412). The recording used in the test involved a meeting in which, following common practice at the university, both French and English were used, although the comprehension questions addressed only the ideas that were expressed in French. Test takers were given the option of responding in either language (or in a combination of the two). The test was positively received by assessees who felt that it reflected the reality of departmental meetings.

Task 7.6

Assessment and translanguaging

What do you think might be the advantages and disadvantages of a test based on translanguaging theory?

Would you consider using multiple languages in your teaching/learning context?

Self-reflection and self-regulation

Related to the concern for fairness, there has been a growing interest in the profession of language assessment itself, its history, the identity of its members and their roles and social responsibilities. This has been reflected in the publication of histories such as Spolsky (1995), Davies (2008a, 2008b) and Weir (2013) and by guidelines on ethical questions: the International Language Testing Association's (ILTA) *Code of Ethics* (2000) and *Guidelines for Practice* (2007) are both available for download from the ILTA website at www.iltaonline.com.

The ILTA *Code of Ethics* sets out nine principles covering the responsibilities of assessment professionals towards assessees, the profession and society more generally. For example, Principle 7 states that 'Language testers in their societal roles shall strive to improve the quality of language testing, assessment and teaching services, promote the just allocation of those services and contribute to the education of society regarding language learning and language proficiency' (International Language Testing Association, 2000). The *Guidelines for Practice* outline the obligations of test designers, producers, administrators and users and the rights and responsibilities of test takers. They include, for example, requirements for designers to clearly state the intended purpose of their tests, for the accuracy of scoring to be checked and reported, and for users to be aware of the limitations of assessments and to ensure the relevance of the construct to the decisions they intend to make.

The ILTA *Code of Ethics* and *Guidelines* are not policed – there is no committee to check that they are being followed by members of the association – and there are no formal sanctions when they are breached. McNamara and Roever (2006) and others have questioned their value, criticizing their brevity and vagueness. For example, it is unclear from the ILTA *Guidelines for Practice* what steps test providers ought to take to ensure that users of results are aware of the limitations of an assessment, or what action they should take if the users ignore their guidance. The history of self-regulation in the tobacco and automotive industries and elsewhere provides many unfortunate examples of producers preferring to conceal, deny or downplay known risks. In assessment, there is undoubtedly the potential for conflict between the immediate business imperatives of test developers (such as selling more tests, generating income, satisfying important clients) and spelling out the limitations of assessment systems.

Whatever their shortcomings, documents like the *Guidelines for Practice* do at least provide language assessment professionals with guidance on ethical behaviour and can support arguments for good practice and quality management within organizations. They serve to promote the sense of language assessment as a shared, global endeavour with its own distinct identity and underline the importance of making assessments as good as they can be.

Task 7.7

A city is going to host a major international sporting event. Thousands of visitors from around the region are expected to attend. They are not expected to speak the local language, but the city authorities expect that most will be able to speak at least some English. The city government plans to employ a large number of guides to assist the visitors by giving directions, helping them with common problems, or directing them to more specialist help. Now, a year before the event, city officials have asked for your advice.

- In addition to carrying out other checks (e.g. Do they have the necessary knowledge? Do they have criminal records?), the city government plans to give people who want to work as guides an English test. They want to use the national test of English usually given to school children at the age of 16. What advice would you give?
- Once they have selected a suitable assessment, how should the city government decide the pass mark for the test? What are the risks associated with setting the pass mark too high or too low?

> • What long-term impact do you think the use of the new assessment might have on the city? Do you think the impact will be damaging or beneficial to local people?

Critical language testing

If the ILTA *Code of Ethics* and *Guidelines* represent a growing awareness of the social responsibilities of language testers, some commentators have gone much further in questioning the role of tests and assessments as instruments of coercion and social control. Shohamy (2001), reflecting the sociological direction taken by critical applied linguistics such as Pennycook (2001) and drawing on the work of social theorists such as Foucault (1975), called for a **critical language testing** that would identify and challenge the political values and assumptions reflected in assessment practices. The apparent technical objectivity of tests can conceal a political agenda, and we all need to ask searching questions about whose interests are really served when assessments are used.

As an example of the abuse of the power of language assessment, McNamara and Roever (2006) pointed to tests that are ostensibly intended to improve the employment prospects of immigrants, but that have been used to adjust the numbers of immigrants to a country or to block immigration by people from certain backgrounds.

Kim and Elder (2009) questioned the fairness of the International Civil Aviation Organization (ICAO) policy on testing the English language proficiency of pilots and air traffic controllers. The policy places the onus on non-native users to bring their English to an appropriate standard but fails to address the part sometimes played by the poor communication skills of native speakers when potentially dangerous incidents occur. Similar criticisms have been made of the use of tests of academic language ability. Learners are obliged to improve their language skills to gain entry to universities, bearing the substantial costs that are often involved. Institutions on the other hand are not required to provide more accessible courses or to provide learning materials that are adapted to the needs of language learners.

Higher, wider, deeper: some emerging trends in language assessment

The most visible changes in language assessment practice over recent years, as in many other areas of our lives, involve the increasing use of digital technology. Most large-scale international tests and many classroom-based assessments are now delivered by computer, smartphone or tablet, with test material appearing on screen and with keyboard input replacing handwriting. The effects on performance and the equivalence of results when tests are delivered by computer – perhaps in the form of recorded questions in a speaking test, or on screen in a reading test – have now been researched in some detail (see Chapelle & Douglas, 2006). Results suggest that when assessees are familiar with using new technology, the shift to a digital delivery system rarely has a substantial effect on scores.

So far, the use of computer technology to deliver assessments seems to have had a largely conservative, even regressive influence on language assessment design and administration procedures. Many current e-assessments employ outmoded techniques associated with discrete point testing. Short, selected-response items are popular with developers because they are very practical. They fit more easily onto the screen of a mobile device and can be straightforwardly scored by a machine.

In 1988, Bunderson, Inouye and Olsen predicted four generations of e-assessment. The first two involved the migration of assessment from paper to computer-based delivery systems and, taking advantage of this, the introduction of adaptive tests (described in the next paragraph). Both of these developments were already well underway in the 1980s (indeed, the earliest experiments with testing by machine had been conducted in the 1920s), but now digital delivery is becoming the norm and adaptive assessment is well-established.

Computer adaptive tests (CATs) are sensitive to the ability level of the assessee. If the assessee gives an incorrect response to the first item on a CAT, the computer will select an easier item next. If the first response is correct, the second question will be more difficult. Proceeding in this way, the computer selects material that increasingly closely matches the assessee's level of ability. CATs can be much more efficient than traditional linear tests because they can arrive at an accurate estimate of ability with relatively few items. Low-level assessees are not faced with 95 questions they cannot answer correctly in addition to the five that they can. On the other hand, the computer needs to have enough high-quality pretested material of known difficulty to cope with different patterns of responses and this makes CATs relatively expensive to produce.

Scoring speech and writing by machine

Personal reflection

Do you trust computers to make fair and accurate judgements of language learners' speaking and writing skills?

In what ways do you think computers might be better than humans at judging performance?

What effects do you think the increasing use of computers will have on the language assessments of the future?

While selected response formats are the easiest to manage, automated speech recognition and computational linguistics make it possible for machines to score written and even spoken performance, especially when responses are more guided or controlled (Xi, 2012). The results are often indistinguishable from those obtained from trained human raters (see Chapter 4). Automated essay scoring is routinely used in large-scale assessment and there are now a number of systems that can even provide learners with potentially formative corrections and feedback on the accuracy and coherence of their writing.

The use of automated assessment has often been met with a good deal of scepticism. It seems unreasonable to think that machines could be capable of judging the effectiveness of human communication. Critics have demonstrated that it is possible to obtain high scores from machines by submitting nonsensical essays that use complex sentences and sophisticated, topic-related vocabulary (Perelman, 2012), but in practice there is little evidence that assessees are able to exploit this fact. It seems to be more difficult to write high scoring nonsense than to produce a cogent, on-topic essay. It has also been suggested that feedback from automated essay scorers, although often helpful, tends to encourage a focus on surface features – grammar and vocabulary – rather than on coherence and the quality of the ideas (Vojak, Kline, Cope, McCarthey, & Kalantzis, 2011). The most productive use of automated scoring may be in combination with human teachers and raters who are able to complement the strengths of automated scoring and to support learners in using the information that the machines can provide.

While the automated scoring of essays is now widely established, it has proved more difficult for machines to evaluate extended unscripted speech, although this capability is also improving as the technology develops (Wang, Zechner, & Sun, 2018). So far, automatic speech recognition technology has proved most effective in measuring features such as hesitation and pronunciation and in evaluating the accuracy of short, predictable utterances that involve reading aloud, repeating back utterances or describing simple pictures.

New forms of e-assessment

The third and fourth generations of e-assessment, which Bunderson, Inouye and Olsen called 'continuous measurement' and 'intelligent measurement' involve a more radical shift: one that seems to be especially challenging for language education. As learning is increasingly mediated by electronic systems, every task that a learner engages with can contribute to an evolving, constantly updated model of the state of his or her knowledge, skills and abilities. Computers, unlike teachers, have the capacity to log everything that students do as they engage in a language course including when and for how long they are active and how they interact with each activity. This makes available to educators an unprecedented amount of information about how learners are proceeding in their learning.

Continuous measurement integrates the concepts of mastery learning and adaptive testing. As in an adaptive test, classroom activities are ordered according to their difficulty. As learners progress, each new activity provides an increasing level of challenge. Over the duration of a course (or sequence of courses), if learners succeed on one activity, they progress to the next, which is a little more difficult. If they fail, they can be given more practice with easier material. Because digital environments allow unobtrusive tracking of learner performance and because all the activities are mapped onto a shared scale of increasing difficulty, the learner's level is always known – effectively their 'score' is constantly updated – and traditional educational testing becomes redundant.

Intelligent measurement takes this a stage further and integrates feedback mechanisms into the assessment, emulating a human coach. It is, in dynamic assessment terms, interactionist rather than interventionist. The system not only indicates to learners whether or not they have been successful but provides targeted support when it is needed. The vision is for intelligent tutoring systems (Wenger, 1987) that share many features with video games. First, video games are immersive. They invite the player into a stimulating imaginary world. Similarly, the classroom environment can be replaced by more realistic and appealing scenarios for the learner to negotiate: scenarios that may be peopled by other learners, real teachers and virtual characters fuelled by artificial intelligence. Second, they can offer a structured progression with higher-level challenges that integrate and build on completed activities. Third, they can provide a personalised experience, offering content and proceeding at a pace that suits the abilities, inclinations and interests of each individual learner. Learners actively choose some elements (such as which characters to interact with, or interesting scenarios to participate in) and the system adjusts others (such as the level of challenge or the focus of an activity) according to their performance.

Most video games allow players repeated attempts and opportunities for practice until they are able to complete a level. Similarly, if a learner has difficulty with pronunciation, a language learning application may offer coaching on the problematic sounds; if the learner has failed to recognise certain words, these can be repeated in later activities, or presented in additional practice sessions. For such mediation to work effectively, the system has to be provided with a sophisticated estimate of the learner's abilities that includes areas of potential strength and weakness. Over time, feedback from accumulated learner data can be used to refine the system itself. As large numbers of learners engage with it, logs of their behaviour can be used to provide insights into common sources of difficulty and to suggest modifications.

Although the potential is self-evident, the current assessment functionality of language learning apps remains limited. Any system that offers learners elements of remediation and choice inevitably requires large amounts of material, which is expensive to produce. Because feedback systems for vocabulary learning and pronunciation are relatively easy to manage using established technology, apps tend to focus on these features. It is far more difficult to deal with issues of pragmatics or sociolinguistic appropriateness.

In the era of data analytics, intelligent tutoring systems are beginning to escape the confines of the controlled game environment: recording, assessing and assisting real-world language use. Language activities can be encouraged and tracked on a mobile device in the same way as is done for exercise or heart rate. Objects in the environment or words selected from automated translation services can be tagged for use in learning activities. Performance in real-world interaction can be scaffolded through augmented reality, recorded and monitored and used as a basis for feedback. Intelligent measurement thus promises to combine and enhance the benefits of assessment for learning and proficiency testing.

The end of testing?

Although the technical means already exist and many of us would welcome a world without formal tests and exam day nerves, there remain some serious challenges to be met before intelligent measurement could replace current assessment practices. One is public resistance. People may not love tests, but they do generally accept them as a fair basis for allocating resources. Any alternative is likely to be greeted with scepticism and resistance, especially if there is any suggestion that serious, high-stakes decisions should be made on the basis of performance in a 'game.' It has taken a long time for games to be accepted as tools to support learning and their use in assessment is even more controversial. Conversely, learners who are happy to experiment and receive feedback in a formative learning environment may be less comfortable with the idea that their data will also be used for summative purposes. Instead of relieving test anxiety, continuous measurement may threaten to turn every day into an anxiety-inducing exam day.

A second problem is the limitations of current theories in relation both to language learning and to measurement. With our current state of knowledge, we are not in a position to programme intelligent systems that can provide learners with appropriately sequenced activities involving authentic language use, that can pinpoint sources of difficulty and offer support to accelerate learning. Good human teachers remain, for now, far more effective than machines at providing coaching in language use.

New models of measurement

An established view of language assessment sees it as combining applied linguistics and measurement theory (Bachman, 2004). Reflecting the latter, language assessment validation research has involved the use of increasingly sophisticated computer-based analysis tools. Bachman outlines the use of statistics in describing test scores, improving test material and evaluating test use. Tools such as classical test theory, Rasch measurement, item response theory and generalizability theory are routinely used by test providers in evaluating test material and identifying the extent and possible sources of measurement error.

While classical test theory is founded on norm-referenced score interpretations, Brown and Hudson (2002) and Brown (2005) provided useful accounts of alternative statistics available for criterion-referenced testing. Other statistical tools such as factor analysis, regression analysis and structural equation modelling are regularly reported in the research literature because they provide evidence of relationships and patterns in test responses that suggest how tests or test components reflect underlying abilities. More complex performance assessments demand more complex measurement and the value of innovative techniques for analysing language assessment results is a recurrent theme in validation research.

As well as being used to investigate the outcomes of assessments, technology is increasingly being used to explore the processes involved when learners engage with assessment material. Video recordings, eye-trackers (which record where assessees focus their attention) and keystroke loggers (which record processes of writing and revision) have been used to explore how assessees tackle assessment tasks (Strömqvist, Holmqvist, Johansson, Karlsson, & Wengelin, 2006; Winke, 2013). These provide insights into cognitive processing and supplement the information available from verbal reports by assessees on how they have responded (Green, 1998).

Corpora are electronic databases that sample written or spoken language from specified contexts in a form that makes it amenable to detailed linguistic analysis. Corpora that sample defined contexts of language use (medical language, legal language, etc.) can be used in the design of tests of languages for specific purposes (Barker, 2013). On the other hand, samples taken from test performances can be used in the development of learner corpora to tell us more about the nature of the language that is actually produced in response to assessment tasks. Study of learner corpora reveals the linguistic forms that are used and the errors made by learners from different backgrounds at different levels of ability. As part of a wider programme of research called *English Profile*, Hawkins and Filipovic (2012) explored the language used by assessees at different levels of the Common European

Framework of Reference for Languages (CEFR) in completing assessment tasks. They derived from this what they term *criterial features* of learner language that distinguished most efficiently between higher- and lower-level learners.

Weir et al. (2013) reported that at its launch just three assessees took the Cambridge Certificate of Proficiency in English (and all three failed). Today millions of people take the larger national and international tests each year and the expansion shows no signs of abating. One aspect of the recent growth in numbers has been diversification in the assessments on offer. The growing numbers of assessees make it more practical to provide assessments that have a more specific focus. Tests of languages for general business or academic purposes have been joined by tests for engineers, lawyers, accountants and other professions that involve international cooperation. Reflecting changing educational policies around the globe, large numbers of younger children are now taking language assessments. This has led to the launch of new international assessments for young learners and the appearance of a specialist literature relating to this area (see, for example, McKay, 2005).

The involvement of teachers in high-stakes summative assessment has also expanded. Even traditionally examination-driven school systems such as Singapore and Hong Kong have begun to incorporate school-based assessments into their educational systems (Davison & Hamp-Lyons, 2010). With growing awareness of the social responsibilities of the language assessment profession, this has led to calls for professionals to work together to improve the assessment literacy of teachers, policy-makers and others and to provide better public information on assessment issues. The closed world of assessment expertise is being opened up to public scrutiny. In some countries, this has led increasingly to legal challenges to assessment practices and score outcomes – another powerful incentive for assessment providers to take their social responsibilities seriously (Fulcher & Bamford, 1996).

As reflected in the account presented here, language assessment as an academic field and as a professional endeavour has its institutional origins in the US, Britain and a few other countries, predominantly English speaking (Spolsky, 1995). It has tended to centre on the assessment of English as a foreign language internationally, English as a second or additional language for migrant groups, and on modern foreign languages taught in English-speaking countries. Today, its influence on institutional practice may remain limited, but it has spread to all parts of the globe and centres of language assessment expertise can be found in every region and in the assessment of a wide range of languages. Although the established centres continue to thrive, as the profession continues to expand, innovative techniques in assessment design and quality assurance are beginning to emerge from new sources.

Last words

We have discovered a great deal over the past century about how languages are learned and used. New fields of research such as neuroscience and computational linguistics regularly deliver new insights. For all that, our understanding of the intricacies of the process is still very limited. The quality of the information we can gain from language assessments is therefore unavoidably partial and uncertain. This makes it all the more important that we take full advantage of the resources we do have at our disposal – the PRICE elements of planning, reflecting, improving and working cooperatively – to generate the best evidence we can to inform our decisions.

There is a pressing need for a shift in attitudes towards assessment in language education: a shift that is only beginning to happen. Assessment is, as I hope this book makes clear, an indispensable ingredient in effective teaching and learning. Unfortunately, in teacher training it is often treated as a marginal component, poorly integrated with other modules and often relegated, like an afterthought, to the end of the course. As a result, teachers often know and care far less about assessment than about other aspects of teaching. Many feel poorly equipped to carry it out. Language textbooks do not generally provide them with the help they need, failing to match assessment activities with learning objectives in useful ways. Books that are designed to prepare learners for external tests have long been popular, but they typically offer little more than practice in test taking, with inadequate guidance on how to cultivate and develop learners' skills and understanding in ways that match the objectives of the test.

Teachers have much to learn from the quality standards employed in external tests and can benefit from learning about effective assessment design. Tests themselves can often provide information that is useful for teachers and learners: information that is too often under-exploited. On the other hand, external tests with their rigid, standardised conditions and delayed feedback do not provide a good model for classroom activity. Alternative forms of assessment are often more engaging and may be more useful and more enlightening about learning processes. Exploring the alternatives open to them is important to teachers' professional development.

Ultimately, the value of assessments depends on the people involved in designing, building, administering and scoring them and those who interpret the results. Good practice in language assessment, finding the most appropriate tools for each purpose, requires commitment and expertise. I hope that this book will encourage readers who are involved in language education to make that commitment and seek to learn more.

8 Commentary on tasks

Chapter 1

Task 1.1

There are many advantages claimed for both peer and self-assessment and a lot of teachers who use them become real enthusiasts. If you are new to these concepts and would like to try them, it is always a good idea to work with colleagues and to share ideas and experiences. Below are some of the advantages and concerns that are widely mentioned. You may well have thought of many others.

Peer assessment

Advantages

If students judge each others' work, they must develop an understanding of what makes performance successful. Students may discuss and agree on criteria with their teacher, or work together to understand published criteria. This will help them to better understand the qualities of their own work as well as the work done by other students.

It encourages discussion of what makes a correct answer or good performance. This promotes reflection and deep understanding of content.

It encourages students to take more responsibility for the learning that happens in the classroom. It encourages collaboration rather than competition and involves all students. Students who tend to 'switch off' when a teacher is talking can get more involved when engaged in peer assessment.

Disadvantages

Especially if students are unfamiliar with peer assessment, it can take a long time to train them to do it effectively. Teachers often underestimate how difficult this can be. Introducing peer assessment is best done in small steps. Once introduced, it should be done regularly, using consistent procedures.

Students may be reluctant to criticise their peers, or may try to award higher marks to their friends. Some may be embarrassed or reluctant to show their work to others. There is a risk that some students may be offensive or cruel in their comments. Teachers may need to manage the process by collecting and monitoring student comments before sharing them. In some contexts, it may be better not to make students responsible for grading decisions. Peer assessment can be used successfully without playing any role in grading.

Advantages	Disadvantages
Students may sometimes find their peers' feedback and explanations easier to understand than feedback given by their teachers.	Students may not feel confident about judging the work of others and often start by awarding everyone the same mark. Some may simply not be able to recognise the difference between good and poor work. In truth, finding out whether students are able to judge quality is one of the advantages of peer assessment – if they can't yet judge the difference, they may lack understanding of the subject and clearly need more training.

Self-assessment

Advantages	Disadvantages
It increases student self-regulation – essential if students are to make the most of opportunities to learn outside the classroom. It engages students in planning what they will learn, thinking about what they are doing well or poorly and how best to improve. It helps teachers and students to work together as partners in the classroom with shared goals for learning.	Self-assessment has many of the same disadvantages as peer assessment: it takes time and commitment to get it underway and students can need a lot of training, especially if they are new to the idea. They often lack confidence: 'if I knew the answer, I'd be the teacher.' It takes time for students to understand that rather than obtaining a grade, the objective is to develop their understanding. As with peer assessment, in some contexts it may be preferable to avoid using self-assessment in making grading decisions.

Chapter 2

Task 2.1

1   How long is it likely to take this person to learn to speak at an advanced level?
    This information would be useful to the person him/herself, as well as to teachers and to anyone who is thinking of paying for the language classes or study abroad that might be needed. Obtaining the information could involve an assessment of language learning aptitude. If available, it might be equally helpful to look at charts of how long it typically takes learners to reach an advanced level when studying this language in similar circumstances.

2   What sounds does this learner find it most difficult to produce?
    This will probably be of most interest to the learner and his/her teachers. This is a diagnostic purpose.

3   Is this learner going to benefit more from an elementary- or an intermediate-level language class?
    This would interest school administrators who need to put learners into suitable classes: placement purposes.

4   Has this student learned enough to progress to studying at the next level?

Again, this is likely to be of most interest to school management, teachers and learners. The purpose of any assessment would be to focus on achievement (and the emphasis is clearly summative rather than formative, although results could also be used to focus instruction on areas of weakness – formative diagnosis).

5   Has this student learned the definitions of the 20 words assigned as homework?

This is of interest to the teacher and student (and perhaps parents or others with an interest in the student's learning). This involves assessment of achievement (which is potentially formative if used to guide further study).

6   Does this person speak Chinese well enough to be able to work effectively with Chinese colleagues at our office in Beijing?

This would be of primary interest to employers. The focus is on proficiency – probably for selection purposes. Of course, the employee would also like to know the answer and might hope to gain some insights into how to improve in order to reach the level needed. There might be formative implications if the employer is planning to give the person some language classes.

7   Will this student be able to write effective essays in English when he/she studies at an Australian university?

This would probably interest the university authorities, who might use the information to decide whether to offer the student a place. Like number 6, this is a matter of proficiency. As with number 6, the answer to the question will also be of interest to the learner and perhaps to language teachers for aptitude and diagnosis – if the assessment can inform measures to improve his/her writing.

8   Has this learner reached a high enough level in Italian for us to award him/her an intermediate-level certificate?

This would be a question for the organization awarding the certificates. It is often a matter of achievement based on a defined programme of study, but certification can also be based on ideas about proficiency. There may be claims made on the certificate about what the successful assessees can use their Italian language skills to do in the real world.

Task 2.2

The government will need someone who is able to learn languages successfully and to a high level. They might use a language aptitude test to gauge this. Other sources of information could include evidence of previous language learning, such as achievement and proficiency test scores in one or more languages other than Russian.

Chapter 3

Task 3.1

- If you were asked to prepare a language assessment to use in a school, what would be your first step?
  At the outset, it is essential to be clear why (and whether) an assessment is needed. What information is sought about assesses? Can an assessment really provide that information? Who will use the information and how will they use it? Do the people commissioning the work understand the costs and benefits of creating good quality assessments and are they prepared to commit the necessary resources? An initial period of research investigating these kinds of questions can help you to avoid or minimise many of the problems that can occur later.

- What kinds of expertise do you think you would need? What other qualities are needed?
  The outline of the assessment cycle in Chapter 3 includes the essential roles needed to build and operate an effective assessment system. Expertise and ongoing commitment is needed in every area with documented procedures to ensure that the assessment functions successfully. Anyone given the task of developing an assessment system will need to have a good awareness of all aspects of the cycle. Because good assessments always involve collaboration, good communication is vital – and you will need a lot of resilience.

- What steps could you take to make sure you produce a good quality assessment?
  In Chapter 3, I suggest that it is helpful to think of assessments as working service systems that require ongoing attention and maintenance. It is important to agree to a timetable for building and implementing the assessment that takes account of all the elements of PRICE, but that does *not* include an end date. The commitment of resources must be for the long term.

- What factors might prevent your assessment from being as good as you would like?
  Answers to this question commonly include:
  Lack of resources: time; people; expertise; funding and organizational support.
  Staff turnover: people in key positions leave or change roles.
  Conflicting ideas about the purpose of the assessment.
  Lack of cooperation and communication among those involved.
  Complacency: lack of willingness to change and improve practices.

Task 3.2

- Make a list of the activities (such as preparing the assessment, taking the assessment, etc.) that might be involved in developing a language assessment system.
- What documents are used to guide or record each activity? Which people are involved in each activity?
  Compare your lists with the general list of essential roles and documents in the assessment cycle presented in Figure 3.1. In some cases, people and documents fill more than one of the roles described. In large organizations, teams of specialists may carry out each role.
- Are all of these activities essential? Which activities would be important in developing an assessment for use in the classroom?
  Chapter 3 argues that the quality of an assessment system, whether in the context of the classroom or of international examinations, rests on all parts of the cycle.

Task 3.3

There is no single correct answer to the question of whether all teachers should use the same assessments with their classes as it is partly a matter of local culture (the culture of the school involved as well as regional or national culture).

The advantage of using different assessments is that it may allow teachers greater freedom in deciding what to teach and greater creativity in deciding on the kinds of evidence to collect. Students in different classes may have studied different content: it would therefore be more appropriate to use tailored material to assess their achievements.

On the other hand, using the same procedures makes it easier to compare results. It also allows teachers to pool their resources and may make the overall programme appear more coherent to learners, managers, parents and other stakeholders. If important decisions are based on the results, using the same assessment procedures for everyone can appear fairer as it gives all students the same opportunity to demonstrate their abilities.

Task 3.4

This test will inform a *gate-keeping* decision: deciding who should be allowed to come to Denmark to live with their spouse or partner. The information seems to be intended mainly for those who might need to take the test (people who want to live in Denmark) or their advisers. It provides information on the test content, but does not really explain the rationale for the test or for the level of performance required. It does not explain, for example, why citizens of certain countries are not required to take the test.

Immigration decisions are among the most disputed uses of language assessments as they are often introduced for obviously political reasons. What objections do you think critics might have to this test?

Task 3.5

A teacher using this item in a class test would be able to decide for herself which responses to accept, but allowing scorers to take such decisions could lead to inconsistencies if the test were given to different groups of students.

Issues like these have to be considered and dealt with consistently and in accordance with the theory behind the design of the assessment. An assessment development team would need to anticipate the range of possible answers and decide which should be accepted. In this case, the range of possibilities is so great that it might make the scoring key unmanageable and so the item would probably have to be rewritten or rejected.

1 The answer to this question depends on the purpose of the test. How much does spelling matter in this context?
2 Many answers are possible. Share your ideas. What do others think of your suggestions?

Chapter 4

Task 4.1

Answers to the questions are given in the text.

It is possible (although unlikely) that the student who scores two points actually knows more words than the one who scores six, but is just extremely unlucky in the choice of words on the test. Over time, or with enough questions, this chance is reduced. The student who consistently achieves high scores on vocabulary tests over the course of year either has a good level of knowledge or an effective system for cheating.

Task 4.2

Were you surprised by the number of heads/tails you threw? In what ways do you think taking a language test is like tossing a coin?

Task 4.3

There are a number of reasons why your results might be better (more consistent) than Edgeworth's. First, the teachers/raters may have received some training in scoring essays for another assessment and made use of this experience. Second, if the teachers all work at the same institution, they might share ideas about what makes an essay worthy of a certain score. Most scoring systems, even ones that use detailed rating scales, rely on raters to come to some collective understanding of the meaning of different scores.

If the scores are all very similar, this may suggest that the teachers discussed the scores they awarded to each essay before recording their scores. Although it may make the scores appear more consistent, this is not good practice in assessment. Once the initial training and discussion is over, it is important to see how far people agree when they work independently.

Task 4.4

1   There is clearly a risk that the students who live in the city will have far more time to use the library than the others and so tend to perform much better. This may mean that the results of this project are inconsistent with other work done during the term. However, if all graded work is done this way, the advantage for the city children will be consistent and the results will be reliable, but biased. Other threats to reliability come from the choice of topics (some students will pick easy topics, others will choose very challenging topics) and from the very limited range of scores that are possible (a wider range of scores allows for more reliable results). Imposing more control on the task – setting one topic and giving everyone a set period working in the library – will improve reliability, but will reduce the level of responsibility it gives learners and could make the task itself much less interesting for them.

2   The recording and test questions are the same for everyone, but the administration and scoring will probably vary. One teacher may give his class unclear instructions; another might decide to play the recording twice. In scoring the responses, one teacher may be more flexible than another in accepting spelling mistakes. Issues such as these will lead to less reliable results. Improvements to reliability could be achieved by agreeing on standard administration and scoring procedures: developing guidelines.

3   This kind of incident could have an effect on the results of any of the assessees in the room. The noise of the falling chair and the following activity (including the return to the room 20 minutes later) probably distracted all the test takers, reducing the time they were able to focus on the questions. It might have been better to halt the test until the unwell student had left the room (and it may have been unwise to let him return, rather than taking him to get immediate medical attention). Luckily, there were two invigilators in the room so that one could accompany the student, but the incident may have distracted the invigilators, giving dishonest students the opportunity to share or copy

answers. It may have been better to contact a supervisor to replace the second invigilator. It is important to have clear contingency plans in the guidelines to deal with emergencies like this in the course of a test so that procedures are consistent and the impact upon results is minimised.

Task 4.5

Although it may seem reasonable to expect the language teacher to have an adequate command of the language she is teaching, at least two aspects of her employers' requirement raise questions about validity. First, the test being used is not designed to assess language for teachers of young children, but is designed to test the language used by adults in the workplace. The vocabulary used in the test centres around offices, meetings and business functions, while the language she is teaching mainly includes such topics as colours, animals, objects in the classroom and counting up to ten. The test includes sections assessing the ability to read and write; but in class the teacher spends most of her time speaking with the children. The curriculum calls for very little reading or writing. In other words, there are very clear differences between the kinds of language being assessed and the kinds of language needed in the classroom.

Second, the level of the test material and the score she is expected to achieve both seem much more challenging than the level of language she is expected to use with the children. She teaches only basic vocabulary and simple phrases, while texts on the test are very lengthy and complex. Her employers do not explain why a teacher of very young beginner learners might need to be so highly qualified in the language of business.

Task 4.6

Content validation of this item might involve expert judges deciding on whether or not this item is relevant to the purpose of the assessment. In this case, they could check whether this is a skill covered by the English reading curriculum. They might also consider whether or not learners who had completed the biology course would be likely to know the word without looking at the context. As the intention is to test whether the students can guess the meaning rather than whether they already know the meaning, it might be more appropriate to present a gap, or to use a fake or nonsensical word – *tunniscopic* or *banana* – rather than one that might be familiar.

Cognitive validation might involve asking assessees to report on how they arrived at their answers. Did you guess the correct answer (d) by using the context? Did you already know the answer? Did you work it out from your knowledge of another language? (It is based on a Greek word meaning *wheel*.) What other ways might assessees have to arrive at the correct answer?

Task 4.7

Experience suggests that most people do not respond to this kind of task as they would in a real-life situation. This is probably because it is not possible to reproduce all the conditions that are important influences on the kind of response people make in situations like this (such as how close a friend the person is, whether you are often late when you meet, the expression on their face, etc.) and because reflecting on what you might say and actually experiencing the situation can be very different. This is partly why it can be so difficult to connect test performance to real-life performance. Constraining the task so that assessees will actually need to respond with an excuse and deciding how to deal with unusual responses are matters for careful design and effective trialling of material.

The characteristics of acceptable responses could be decided by a panel of expert speakers of the language. They might consider trial responses and agree on a set of characteristics that would mark a response as adequate to satisfy the demands of the task.

There is no single answer to the final question – it will depend on the purpose of the assessment – but a consistent policy must be agreed and applied.

Task 4.8

1 *This is great work, well done!*
   This is positive and encouraging: the kind of comment that learners like to get, but as feedback it has very limited value. It is retrospective, giving the student nothing to do to improve their work. It focusses on the performance – great work – but does not explain what was good about the essay.

2 *In line 3, you made a mistake with your use of possessives. You wrote 'Marta is the best friend of mine' – the correct sentence is 'Marta is my best friend.'*
   This is specific and focusses on the student's performance, but does not require the student to think about how to improve. It might be more effective if it set the student a challenge. *Can you find and fix the problem with possessives in your second paragraph?* or *Can you correct this sentence? Look at the notes on possessives on p.62 of the textbook, if you need help.*

3 *Although your essay was generally good, I only awarded you a B grade because there were a few basic problems. Try to do better next time.*
   This encourages future improvements, but is too generic: it gives no clear guidance on the problems that need to be dealt with. As a grade has already been given, there is little reason for the student to try to improve the essay. Once students have been awarded a grade, they usually put aside or throw away their work and never look at it again.

4. *Your essay was well organised with clear paragraphs and you made effective use of examples to illustrate your ideas.*

This is task referenced and, unlike example 1, is reasonably clear about why the essay was successful. On the other hand, there may be steps the student could take to make the essay even better.

Chapter 5

Task 5.1

A wide variety of text types, including tables of contents, dictionaries and internet search pages, can be used to represent the range of reading tasks that assessees may need to master. For formative purposes, learners can be asked to report on how they read, timing themselves and explaining how they located answers to questions. With technology, it is now relatively straightforward to control the length of time that a text is available to the assessee. The ability to read quickly and selectively can be assessed by allowing less time than would be needed to read slowly and carefully. Scores on different kinds of reading tasks may help to reveal where readers are experiencing difficulties.

Task 5.2

Vocabulary and grammar are fundamental to all reading and the difficulties that readers experience can often be traced to one or the other, or to both. Understanding where the reader is experiencing problems in these areas can be very helpful for teaching and learning. Gaining insights into knowledge of vocabulary and grammar can help teachers and learners to choose appropriate reading material: texts that are likely to be easy for extensive reading that can help to build confidence, or more challenging texts that can be used to develop strategic reading skills in situations of incomplete comprehension. What can learners do when they face a text that they obviously cannot understand in detail?

Assessing conceptualization is more challenging than assessing vocabulary or grammar. Responses to tasks or questions will need to involve bringing together ideas from different parts of the text and understanding the relationships between them. In other words, assessees will probably need to summarise or restate the text in some way. The Task Types document for this book on the website (www.routledge. com/cw/rial) has suggestions for tasks of this kind.

Task 5.3

Considerations of practicality and efficiency are very important in testing and tests that focus on details are relatively straightforward to make. Tests of selective listening are necessarily less efficient because by definition, much of the recording must be irrelevant to the task. Interactive listening is challenging to assess because it is usually intimately linked to speech: it can be difficult to know whether a failure to respond appropriately involves difficulties in listening (understanding the input) or in speaking (formulating a response). It is also expensive to administer interactive assessments because the assessee, rather than simply listening to a recording, will need to have someone to interact with (at least until artificial intelligence is able to take on the role of the interlocutor).

Task 5.4

News reports often refer to people, places and events that are very familiar to most listeners and so do not need much explanation for local readers. Of course, international stories are likely to have fewer such issues, but even these often involve assumptions about what the readers already know about a story. The media choose the grammar and vocabulary they use according to the kind of listeners or viewers they want to attract. Popular shows may use an entertaining, idiomatic style; more serious shows may use a more formal style. Both may be difficult for language learners to follow.

Recordings can be made easier for learners by simplifying the grammar and vocabulary, slowing the rate of delivery, perhaps using more standard accents and by removing or explaining cultural references. This would probably involve re-recording the piece. This naturally limits (or changes) any claims the assessment developer can make about the assessee's ability to understand genuine news reports in the target language use domain.

Tasks 5.5 and 5.6

These tasks are discussed in the text of Chapter 5.

Tasks 5.7

It may be that the learners the test is intended for are all known to be skilled readers who will have no problem with understanding the three options. Even so, as listening is the focus of the test, it would be more appropriate if the item involved more listening than reading. The questions and options could perhaps be presented in spoken rather than written form.

It might be interesting – and useful for teaching – to discover whether learners who are unable to answer the question when they listen are able to give the correct answer when they see it in print: are their difficulties caused by an inability to process the sounds they hear, or by their limited knowledge of the language (regardless of whether it is written or spoken)?

Task 5.8

Reading Task 2 is intended to be more difficult than Task 1. The text is longer, uses a wider range of vocabulary and has longer, more complex sentences. The content is more abstract and the organization of the text is less straightforward.

The Task 1 text seems to be a kind of advertisement aimed at older, wealthy travellers who are looking for a quiet and luxurious holiday. The Task 2 text is more educational, concerning a famous case study in the history of psychology and language acquisition, but seems to be intended for a general readership rather than academic specialists. It could be from a magazine article or an introductory text book. Both texts seem accessible to a wide range of readers, although clearly more suitable for adults than young children. Neither seems immediately relevant to business and the world of work, or to the immediate needs of migrants. Both texts have been adapted for use in a test. The first seems to have been simplified as it includes far less descriptive detail than would be usual in this kind of text.

The items in Task 1 target specific points of information in the text. The reader needs to understand the individual propositions. Success generally depends on matching phrases in the items to phrases in the text: 'peace and quiet' matches 'relax and get away from it all.' Task 2 concerns coherence and the relationships between ideas. For example, finding the answer to 4 (D: 'However, this turned out not to be the case.') depends on recognizing the relationship between the ideas expressed in the sentences that precede and follow the gap.

Task 5.9

Task 1 is a Constructed response: Short response item involving dictation. The assessees are required to type the words they hear. It mainly assesses word recognition and grammatical knowledge. It involves both listening and writing.

Task 2 is a Selected response: Multiple choice item that involves choosing the correct response to a conversational prompt. It involves knowledge of grammar and vocabulary with a focus on question forms, although it may be possible for assessees to guess the answer by matching the word *room*, heard both in the prompt and in option B.

Both questions seem suitable for a very wide range of learners, although Task 2 is linked to an office setting by the use of words such as 'meeting room' and 'director.'

Chapter 6

Task 6.1

A test of the multiple meanings of the slogan would be very challenging to produce. Asking the test taker to explain it could elicit many different correct responses. As some learners might have been taught about this well-known slogan, success might depend more on taught knowledge than on the ability to understand it in context. If told that it is an advertisement, a learner might easily guess that its purpose is to encourage people to buy eggs, without appreciating the witty word play. Without the context, much of the meaning is lost.

Producing advertising slogans is a specialist task and for most learners, there is no clear reason to test the ability to write them. It could form part of a course on the language of advertising. The learners might be asked to create a slogan as part of a brief to advertise a certain product. In a vocational course, the quality of the slogans could be judged by a panel of potential clients or consumers.

Task 6.2

Both sentences contain errors, although most judges would agree that the first communicates more successfully. It is not really clear what the errors might actually be.

Should the correction of the first sentence be

(a) '*Eggs are one of the only foods that contain naturally occurring vitamin D*'? or
(b) '*Eggs are one of the only foods containing naturally occurring vitamin D*'?

In systems that count errors according to how many words are used accurately, correction (a) may be understood to identify two errors; correction (b) identifies one.

In some error counting systems, both would lead to a deduction of one point (one incorrect sentence). In others, errors would be judged for seriousness, but this re-introduces subjectivity and reduces reliability.

Task 6.3

Most raters find criteria such as range and accuracy easier to judge than fluency, interaction or coherence. The lowest scores tend to be awarded for accuracy. Studies have shown that raters often take account of factors such as body language or expressiveness that are not included on the rating scale they are using.

It is unlikely that the scores you awarded agreed completely with the scores provided by the test developer. The use of rating scales alone cannot assure that raters will all award the same score to the same performance. Raters often need extensive training with sample performances before they will be able to apply a rating scale in a way that is reasonably consistent with their colleagues.

Did you agree with the testing organization about which was the strongest and which was the weakest performance? Provided that most raters agree about the rank order of the performances, it is possible to make adjustments to scores that take into account the tendency of individual raters to be harsher (award lower scores) or more lenient (award higher scores) than the average rater. It is more problematic for assessment developers when raters disagree about which performances are better.

Task 6.4

Both writing tasks are based on input. The first involves understanding and relaying the information provided in the recording. This is not simply a matter of memorizing and repeating back, as the message is too long to memorise in full while listening. To succeed, the learner has to understand the message and be able to formulate a short, written statement to convey it. However, there is no requirement to consider who will read the message or to organise an extended sequence of ideas.

The second task involves much more language, both in the input text and in the expected response, but in this case it is all written language. The learner is expected to take information from the input text to create a different kind of text, written for a different purpose and for a different audience. This requires more awareness of the use of language for social purposes. The learner must advise the friend and use the form of an email to do this, organising the ideas appropriately. The task provides support by directing attention to key information (the notes) and providing an outline for the writer to follow ('include the following information').

Task 6.5

Speaking tasks
Describe them in terms of Bachman and Palmer's (2010) task characteristics framework. What are the main differences between them?

The first task is based mainly on visual input, although there is also spoken input from the examiner that includes the first part of the story, modelling the kind of response that is expected. The expected response will be a short, simple narrative on what is likely to be a familiar, concrete topic. The information expected in the response is all provided in the input so that a learner who is able to interpret the pictures should have all the information needed to respond.

The second task involves written input (the task instructions) and spoken input, providing the opening exchange in a conversation. The test taker needs to understand this opening exchange, then take on the role of one of the participants. In this task, the test taker is given their call sign and the input sets the context, but the test taker is not always given the information to be communicated in the response. The expected response involves conveying information in standard phraseology, the restricted code used in aviation.

The third task also involves a combination of (partly scripted) spoken and written information, but in this case, the instructions are spoken and the task is largely based on written prompts (although there are also spoken questions). The test takers are given time to prepare their responses and are expected to generate their own ideas in addition to the one they are given. The expected responses to this task will likely be much longer than in the other two tasks. There is some reciprocity between the input and response as the follow-up questions are connected to what the test taker has said.

Chapter 7

Task 7.1

Your answer will depend on which test you have chosen for the comparison, but you may have noticed that there were no multiple choice questions and no reading or listening comprehension tasks on the 1913 CPE. Tasks that involve stating rules, correcting sentence errors and composing sentences to demonstrate the meaning of given vocabulary items are no longer widely used. These were dropped following the criticism that knowledge of rules is not the same as being to apply them in real-world communication. Translation has been widely rejected because it is a specialised skill. Accurate word-for-word translation may misrepresent the overall meaning of a text while a reasonable rendition of the gist may be faulty at the sentence level. Literature has also fallen out of favour as educators have placed more emphasis on everyday communication.

Task 7.2

These items involve listening comprehension with multiple-choice questions, innovations that were introduced into language tests after the launch of CPE. The test takers are not expected to say or write anything; they simply mark the correct response to each item.

Task 7.3

Cloze tasks are very practical to produce. Finding suitable texts is not as easy as you might think, but once that has been done, each can produce large numbers of items. Critics have argued that the technique does not provide clear evidence that a reader has managed to understand a text in the sense that they are able to extract ideas or gain a sense of what the text as a whole might mean.

Task 7.4

Your answers will depend on the text you chose, but gaps that involve function words that signal grammatical relationships are usually much more clear-cut than gaps that involve content words. Specialist texts are more likely to require related content words. In fact, gap fill tasks are often used to test subject knowledge.

Task 7.5

These tasks clearly attempt to replicate university life. Listening to talks about university events and extracting information from bibliographies are both tasks that most students will encounter. The information the test takers are asked to find – such as when the tutor is available in her office, or which books cover which topics – also reflect realistic needs. On the other hand, there are features that are associated with testing, not with the target language use domain. For example, the items follow a multiple-choice format, time limits are in operation and the bibliography does not relate to a topic that most of the test takers will be studying.

Task 7.6

Translanguaging features in many real-world instances of communication. Tests that involve an element of translanguaging would reflect this fact and might encourage a change of direction in language teaching, making it more inclusive. On the other hand, it would further add to the complexity of contextually embedded assessment and could make it more difficult to identify areas of strength and weakness in the use of one target language. The success of translanguaging strategies in communication is highly contingent and depends on the contribution of all participants. It could be misleading to assume that an assessee who was able to communicate successfully with a group of sympathetic multilingual interlocutors would also be able to succeed with a less cooperative group of monolingual speakers.

Task 7.7

The use of a school test is unlikely to be suitable for this purpose. First, the school test is probably not based on the kind of communication expected of volunteer guides. It would be preferable to design a test for this purpose, based on the areas of the language (mostly spoken, involving exchanging information) expected of the volunteers.

The pass mark might be based on a standard setting exercise of the kind described in Chapter 6. Groups of experts with experience of working as, or with, volunteer guides could agree on a suitable level. If the mark is set too low, many of the guides may not provide a useful service, having a negative impact on the visitors' experience. Setting the pass mark too high would involve rejecting suitably qualified people and might result in too few guides being recruited.

The new assessment might encourage more people to learn languages, boosting local schools and improving international connections. On the other hand, it could, for example, increase tensions between social groups with different levels of access to language training.

Glossary

Partly because language assessment is such a diverse field, the terminology is used inconsistently. Even apparently fundamental terms such as **assessment** and **test** can take on somewhat different meanings for different writers working in different countries or different sectors. In some cases the same word can be used to refer to entirely different things. A **rubric**, for example, is used in the UK to refer to **task instructions** and other information given on a test paper about testing procedures. In the US it is often used to refer to **rating scales** or **descriptors** (scoring rubrics). In other cases, different terms refer to the same thing: one person's **proctor** is another's **invigilator**.

The short glossary offered here can provide only brief explanations of terms used in this book. A more comprehensive dictionary of language assessment will be a very helpful reference tool when exploring the literature. Here are three suggestions.

ALTE Members. (1998). *Multilingual glossary of language testing terms*. Cambridge: University of Cambridge Local Examinations Syndicate and Cambridge University Press.

Davies, A., Brown, A., Elder, C., Hill, K., Lumley, T., & McNamara, T. (1999). *Dictionary of language testing*. Cambridge: University of Cambridge Local Examinations Syndicate and Cambridge University Press.

Mousavi, S. A. (2012). *Encyclopedic dictionary of language testing* (5th ed.). Tehran, Iran: Rahnama Press.

ability
see **knowledge, skills** and **abilities** (KSA).

absolute score interpretation
(compare **relative score interpretation**) understanding the results of an assessment in relation to the performance expected of other individuals – answers the question 'How does this assessee's performance compare to that of other assessees?'

accommodations
adjustments made in assessment materials or procedures to take account of test taker characteristics (such as providing an amanuensis in a writing test for someone who has injured her hand).

achievement assessment
assessment of the knowledge, skills or abilities developed following a period of study.

analytic scale
a **rating scale** which includes a number of separate criteria to guide the assessor's judgements and so generates a number of different scores – e.g., a score for *grammar*, a score for *pronunciation* and a score for *task fulfilment*.

answer key
a form of mark scheme consisting of a list of responses that should be accepted as correct (or partially correct).

aptitude (language learning aptitude)
a natural or acquired predisposition to learn; a learner with high levels of language learning aptitude would be expected to pick up a new language more quickly than those with less aptitude.

assessee
a person whose knowledge, skills or abilities are assessed. Related terms include test taker, examinee and candidate. The word assessee is used here because the alternatives generally refer only to those who are taking tests, while this book is concerned with a wider range of assessment tools and techniques.

assessee (or test taker) characteristics
attributes of assessees that may affect their performance on an assessment. Some assessee characteristics (such as language ability) are **construct relevant**, others (such as temporary medical conditions) are not.

assessor
a person who assesses the performance of an assessee – a scorer, marker or **rater**.

assessment for learning or AfL
see **formative assessment**.

assessment literacy
awareness of effective assessment principles and ability to interpret assessment results among teachers, policy-makers and the general public.

assessment of learning
see **summative assessment**.

assessment review
following administration of an assessment, a systematic process of reflection on its qualities with a view to making improvements.

assessment use argument
a framework for interpreting performance on an assessment and linking this interpretation to decisions about the **assessee**.

authenticity
see **situational authenticity** and **interactional authenticity**.

behavioural objective
a description of specific behaviours on the part of learners that would demonstrate that intended learning has occurred.

bias
a pattern of results from an assessment that systematically and unfairly favours one group of assessees over another in a way that does not reflect their relative knowledge, skills or abilities.

blueprint
(compare **design statement**) like the assembly instructions for a building or piece of self-assembly furniture, sets out the content of the assessment in such a way that different **forms** of the assessment compiled according to the blueprint should give interchangeable results.

body of work method
a standard setting method that involves groups of expert judges assigning collections of student work (such as essays written on different themes) to performance levels.

Can Do statement
a description of a behaviour that is illustrative of a learner's functionality in a language. Can Do statements are popular as learning objectives and as descriptors that help to define levels on rating scales. An example of a Can Do statement is: '*Can ask for and give directions referring to a map or plan.*'

cloze test
a kind of gap fill activity. In a classic cloze test words are deleted at fixed intervals of a given number of words. The assessee is required to restore the missing words.

cognitive validity
an aspect of validity, closely related to the **interactional authenticity** of assessment tasks, concerned with the extent to which mental processes engaged by assessees resemble those required in the relevant **target language use domain**.

communicative language testing
an approach to language assessment that prioritised the performance of realistic tasks requiring language use.

computer adaptive test (CAT)
a test in which the difficulty of the items is automatically adjusted according to the test taker's level of success. Successful test takers are given more difficult items; unsuccessful test takers are presented with easier items until a stable estimate of ability can be generated.

concurrent validity
an aspect of **criterion-related validity** involving comparisons with alternative estimates of assessees' knowledge, skills or abilities (such as teacher judgements or results of other assessments) that are obtained at around the same time.

consequences
the intended and unintended effects of assessment use, including **impact** and **washback**.

construct (psychological)
an abstract attribute of an individual (such as 'intelligence,' 'job satisfaction' or 'language ability') that that cannot be directly observed or measured, but must be inferred from observable behaviour (such as performance on an assessment).

construct relevance
performance on any assessment will inevitably involve factors other than the intended construct (such as luck or fatigue on the part of the assessee). This means that part of

an individual's result or score on any assessment reflect these construct irrelevant factors. Assessment designers aim to minimise construct irrelevance.

construct representation
because of practical limitations, assessments cannot involve the full range of behaviour associated with a **construct**. This means that all assessments under-represent the intended construct to some extent. Assessment designers aim to include as broad a range of relevant tasks as possible to maximise construct representation.

content standard
(compare **performance standard**) sets out the range of what learners should know and be able to do. For example, it may be decided that learners should be able to 'produce texts on a wide range of subjects and explain a viewpoint on a topical issue giving the advantages and disadvantages of various options' (Council of Europe, 2001).

content validity
an aspect of validity that concerns the choice of test content and the extent to which this reflects informing theories of language ability in relevant **target language use domains**.

convergent validity
(compare **divergent validity**) in the multi-trait, multi-method approach to validation, this is the extent to which different assessments intended to measure the same construct give similar results.

criteria
in a **rating scale** criteria are the categories (such as *grammatical accuracy* or *task completion*) for which scores are awarded.

criterion measure
an alternative indication of an assessee's knowledge, skills or abilities that can be used as a touchstone when evaluating an assessment.

criterion-referenced score interpretation
(contrast **norm-referenced score interpretation**) the interpretation of scores in terms of a **performance standard** rather than in relation to the performance of other assessees.

criterion-related validity
an aspect of validity concerning the relationship between different indicators of an assessee's knowledge, skills or abilities. Criterion-related validity embraces both predictive and concurrent validity.

critical language testing
an approach that explores the role of language assessment in relation to the distribution of power in societies.

cut score
the score on a test that defines the boundary between two classes of assessee (such as *mastery/non-mastery, grade B/grade C* or *pass/fail*).

cycle of assessment
the cycle of activity involved in developing and refining assessments. A distinction can be made between the *operational cycle*, which involves building and delivering comparable **forms** of the same assessment, and the *developmental cycle*, which involves creating new **versions** of an assessment. In an efficient assessment system, the operational and developmental cycles are closely integrated.

decision
the primary purpose of most language assessments is to inform decision-making. Decisions range from on-the-fly choices about the content and pacing of a classroom activity to life-changing decisions about access to opportunities. In both cases, effective decision-making rests on the quality of the evidence and the ability or willingness of the decision-maker to interpret the evidence in a reasonable way.

descriptor
(on a **rating scale** or checklist) a written statement describing a level of performance.

design statement
(compare **blueprint**) a statement that explains the rationale for an assessment and the elements that are fundamental to its design (such as its purpose, the nature of the assessees that it is intended for and the theory of language that informs it).

diagnostic assessment
an assessment intended to identify particular areas of strength or weakness with a view to addressing these through interventions (such as additional classroom activities focused on areas of weakness).

dichotomous scores
item scores that have only two possible outcomes – typically, correct (1)/incorrect (0).

differential item function (DIF)
occurs when people with the same level of ability have different probabilities of success on an assessment item targeting that ability. DIF may occur for many reasons, but is a possible symptom of **bias** in assessment material.

discrete-point test
(see **skills/components**) a test made up of separate **items**, each targeting a distinct component of language ability.

discrimination
the extent to which an assessment or item is capable of distinguishing between more and less able **assessees**.

divergent validity
(compare **convergent validity**) in the multi-trait, multi-method approach to validation, this is the extent to which assessments having a similar format, but intended to measure different constructs, yield different results.

dynamic assessment
a set of approaches to assessment based on socio-cultural theory in which the assessor aims through the assessment process to improve the assessee's understanding or ability to function independently.

educational assessment
(contrast **proficiency assessment**) assessment intended to reflect or measure learning, it may be more **formative** or more **summative**.

evaluation
(in programme evaluation) the **assessment** of individual learner abilities is often contrasted with programme evaluation or judgements about the overall qualities and effectiveness of a language teaching programme. Inferences made on the basis of assessments often contribute to evaluation decisions. For example, teachers whose students all obtain poor results on end of year tests may be asked to attend retraining sessions.

evaluation
(in an **assessment use argument**) the link or bridge in the chain of argument that relates assessee performance to the result or score – tests the claim that the score is a fair and accurate reflection of the assessee's abilities.

examination
the term examination usually refers to a formal **test** administered by an official body (such as a government agency or university) that involves the award of a certificate with institutional, national or international acceptance. In some countries, public examinations may include forms of assessment other than tests, such as portfolios, projects or course work.

exercise
classroom exercises are activities carried out in class that may be used in assessment in more and less formal ways. Results may be recorded, but conditions are not as restricted or **standardised** as in **tests**.

exit assessment
an assessment employed at the end of a programme of study, often with a retrospective focus on the content of the preceding course. Exit assessments often focus on summative achievement.

expected response
(in test specifications) the nature of the language that the assessment designer anticipates an **assessee** will produce in response to a task prompt.

explanation
(in an **assessment use argument**) the link or bridge in the chain of argument that relates the assessment design to the **specifications** – a coherent theory of language ability that accounts for performance on the assessment.

face validity
the extent to which an assessment appears credible to non-specialists such as users, teachers and **assessees**.

fairness review
a formal review of assessment material to identify and eliminate construct-irrelevant features of assessment material that may disadvantage or offend certain assessees. Examples might include content that might be inaccessible for certain age groups; topics that might offend or upset members of certain groups; formats that might cause difficulties for disabled assessees.

feedback
the provision of descriptive information about the adequacy of assessee performance that is said to be useful in guiding improvement and fostering learning.

form (of an assessment)
(compare **version**) different forms of an assessment are intended to reflect the same specifications. Ideally, the results from two forms of the same assessment should be interchangeable.

formal assessment
formal assessments involve the systematic recording of results contributing to the award of scores and grades. They represent the opposite pole to **informal assessments**.

formative assessment
(contrast **summative assessment**) educational assessment that is intended to guide the teaching and learning process.

gate-keeping
the use of assessments to control access to opportunities, such as acceptance onto academic courses, jobs and immigration.

general purpose assessment
(contrast with **specific purpose assessment**) language assessments can be located on a continuum extending between those that are closely identified with very specific, often vocational, applications of language ability (such as language assessments for lawyers involving reading legal documents and writing legal opinions) to those that are designed to cover more generic language use – assessments of languages for general purposes.

generalization
(in an assessment use argument) the link or bridge in the chain of argument that connects the assessment result or score to the specifications. Generalization supports the claim that the result would be very similar if the assessee had taken a different **form** of the assessment based on the same specifications.

grade
in reporting the outcomes of an assessment, grades are often contrasted with **scores**. While scores are typically expressed as numbers, grades usually involve placing learners into relatively broad categories and often use a system of letters – A, B, C, etc. Sometimes grades and scores are used in combination so that an A grade might represent a score of 80 percent or above, a B grade is 70 to 79 percent.

guidelines for administration
a document or set of documents setting out how an assessment or assessment system is to be administered.

high stakes
see **stakes**.

holistic rating scale
a global **rating scale** used in awarding one overall score (or band, level or grade) to an assessee's performance.

impact
(compare **washback**) the impact of an assessment includes, but is not limited to, its washback. Where washback usually refers to the local effects of an assessment on people and practices associated with preparing for the assessment, impact also includes other social effects. Increasing the number of hours spent studying languages before a major examination would be an instance of washback; the profile of the workers chosen by an employer for international postings on the basis of a language test would be covered by impact. Impacts upon individuals are sometimes referred to as micro-impact and are contrasted with wider effects on society – macro-impact.

inference
users of language assessments are usually less interested in how well a learner has performed a specific task on the day of the assessment than in what this can tell them about wider questions – how much the learner has gained from a course of study or how well they are likely to be able to perform tasks that involve language use in the future. In either case, the user must be able to trust that they can infer what they need to know from the learner's result on the assessment.

This also implies that there must be some underlying ability that enables the assessee both to carry out the test task and to carry out the class of real world tasks that the user is interested in. It is this underlying ability that is measured by the assessment.

informal assessment
informal assessments represent the opposite pole of a continuum from **formal assessments**. The most informal assessments are conducted on-the-fly by teachers – the assessment conditions are not standardised, the outcomes are not recorded and they do not contribute to grades or scores.

input
(in **specifications** and task description) the material that the **assessee** is provided with (a recording to listen to and questions to read and answer; an essay **prompt**; etc.)

integrative test
(contrast **discrete-point test**) a test that simultaneously engages different aspects of language ability. A dictation test is integrative because it involves listening and writing and might involve pragmatic and phonological awareness, as well as knowledge of grammar and vocabulary.

intelligent tutoring system
a computer system intended to provide an element of **assessment for learning** by, for example, offering customised hints to help learners improve their performance or adjusting the sequencing of tasks according to a learner's level of performance.

interactional authenticity
(compare **situational authenticity**) the extent to which an assessee engages the same mental processes in an assessment task as in target language use in the world beyond the assessment.

interactionist formative assessment
assessment in which the assessor plays an active role, probing the assessee's understanding and helping the assessee to learn from the assessment as it progresses.

interventionist formative assessment
assessment that involves giving a pre-test, identifying the need for an intervention such as focused teaching, and a post-test to establish whether or not the intervention has been successful.

invigilator
a person who supervises assessees while they take a test. Also known as a proctor.

item
(compare **task**) the smallest unit that produces distinctive and meaningful information on an assessment – information that can be captured in the form of a single score, rating or description of performance.

item review
(in quality control) a review of assessment items, often informed by statistical and other evidence from trialling. The purpose of item review is to select the best material for inclusion in operational assessments.

item writing
the challenging process of preparing effective assessment material that matches the specifications.

knowledge, skills and abilities (KSA)
in this book, knowledge, skills and abilities are used as umbrella terms to encompass the range of constructs that assessments may be designed to address (see Chapter 1). In language education, a distinction is often made between knowledge of a language form, skill in using that form in communication, and the ability to achieve intended goals through

language. More generally, KSAs are used as a recruitment tool in trying to match the capacities of applicants to the demands of specific jobs.

low stakes
see **stakes**.

mastery learning
an educational approach that divides learning into a series of incremental steps defined in terms of tasks that learners should be able to perform as they make progress. Learners demonstrate their mastery of one specified task before progressing to the next.

measurement error
assessment approaches based on measurement theory borrow techniques from the physical sciences to quantify human attributes. This involves estimating the accuracy of the measurements that are made. The inevitable element of uncertainty involved can be estimated using a variety of statistical techniques and is referred to as measurement error.

mediation
in formative assessment, involves intervening either during or following an assessment to help learners develop their knowledge, skills or abilities.

method effect
the choice of any particular method of assessment or task type will have an effect on the results. If the assessment task characteristics closely match the characteristics of tasks from the **target language use domain**, method effects may not be seen to be problematic; but if assessment tasks are very different, evidence of method effects will undermine the **validity** of score interpretations.

minimal pairs test
minimal pairs are words that are phonologically similar, but differ by a single sound – such as *chip* and *tip*, or *bat* and *but*. They have been used in assessment to reveal how well assessees are able to discriminate between the sounds of a language.

moderation
checking and reviewing the work of an assessor or item writer by one or more colleagues. Moderation of rater judgements involves the checking of grading and scoring decisions; moderation of items equates to **item review**.

multiple trait rating scale
an analytic **rating scale** designed for use with a specific task.

multi-trait, multi-method validation
an approach to test validation based on the idea that as well as unrelated tests of the same ability giving similar results, tests of distinct abilities should give different results (see also **convergent validity**, **divergent validity**).

nested rating scale
the use of two **rating scales** in combination. In language assessment a scale describing task characteristics (*basic task* – *intermediate task* – *advanced task*) may be combined with one describing performance (*weak performance* – *adequate performance* – *strong performance*) and outcomes are reported as a combination of the two (*basic task* – *adequate performance*).

norm-referenced score interpretation
(contrast **criterion-referenced score interpretation**) the interpretation of scores in relation to the performance of other assessees rather than in terms of a **performance standard**.

observation
(as an assessment technique) assessment of a language learner's performance on a task that has not been prepared with assessment in mind.

overlap
(in washback) the extent to which teachers and learners perceive that an assessment reflects curriculum content or target language use or both.

peer assessment
learners act as assessors of each other's performance. The objectives of peer assessment usually include fostering improvement and giving learners insights into the qualities of successful performance.

performance assessment/performance test
an assessment that requires the assessee to carry out one or more tasks involving extended responses. Tasks are usually intended to be **situationally** and **interactionally authentic**.

performance standard
(compare **content standard**) the level of performance required for a given purpose (such as meeting graduation requirements or being certified as competent for a particular job). Often expressed as a **cut score**.

performance test
see **performance assessment**.

piloting
a form of **trialling**, usually referring to newly developed assessment material.

placement assessment
an assessment intended to group learners for the purposes of teaching or to match learners to the most appropriate course of study. Placement tests often have a **prognostic** function.

polytomous scores
(compare **dichotomous scores**) item scores that can involve partial credit or a range of possible outcomes – e.g., scores on an **item** that can range from one point to five points.

portfolio
a purposeful collection of a learner's work (typically pieces of writing) representing the learner's achievements and progress over time.

post-test (compare pre-test)
a test given at the end of a course or experimental treatment to establish how much change has occurred. Results are often compared with pre-test scores to calculate a difference or gain score for each rest taker.

practicality
an essential quality of any viable assessment that involves the provision of sufficient resources to sustain its operation.

predictive validity
an aspect of **criterion-related validity** that involves comparisons between assessment results and subsequent performance in the target language use domain. Examples include comparisons between results on **gate-keeping** language tests for university admissions and subsequent academic grades.

pre-test (compare post-test)
a test given at the beginning of a course or experimental treatment to establish a baseline for the measurement of change. The term pre-test, with or without the hyphen, is also used to refer to test forms used in pretesting.

pretesting
(compare **piloting**) a form of trialling, typically referring to material intended for inclusion on operational tests.

primary trait rating scale
a **global rating scale** designed for use with a specific assessment task.

proficiency assessment
an assessment that is external to any course of study and intended to reflect future performance (e.g., in a particular job or on an academic course).

prognostic assessment
an assessment that looks forward in time to predict the rate or extent of student learning.

progress assessment
(compare **placement assessment, exit assessment**) periodic assessment that tracks how far learners are advancing. Progress assessments often have both **formative** and **summative** functions.

prompt
a form of **input** that is intended to elicit a response from the assessee. Responses to the prompts are generally used as a basis for scores or grades that are taken to represent the assessee's level of the knowledge, skill or ability being assessed.

psychometrics
the field of psychological measurement. Psychometrics has involved the development of theories and practices that have been very influential in educational testing, but not all language assessments are constructed according to psychometric principles.

quality management
(of assessment systems) (see also **standards for language assessment**) steps that those responsible for an assessment take to ensure that its quality improves over time.

quiz
a low-**stakes** test administered in the classroom as part of a routine class.

rater
the **scorer** of extended performance responses.

rater reliability
the extent to which different **raters** agree in their ratings.

rater training
the process of training raters to make effective and consistent use of a **rating scale** to score performances.

rating scale
a hierarchically ordered set of categories designed to help **raters** classify performance on an assessment.

raw score
a total score on an assessment in its simplest form, before any **weighting** or other transformation has been applied.

rebuttal
(in an **assessment use argument**) a rebuttal offers an alternative explanation for the outcomes of an assessment, contradicting the claim that the test designer would like to make – e.g. that the results accurately represent the abilities of the assessees.

relative score interpretation
(contrast **absolute score interpretation**) understanding the results of an assessment in relation to a defined level of performance – answers the question: 'On the basis of his\her performance does the assessee seem qualified to carry out certain functions in the real world?'

reliability
the extent to which an assessment produces consistent and stable results.

revealing
a quality of assessments emphasised in some approaches to formative assessment. A good assessment should reveal more about the assessee's current state of understanding than whether or not he/she can provide a correct response.

rubric
see **task instructions** – also (**scoring**) rubric: see **rating scale/descriptor**.

scaffolding
the provision of support for the assessee in the course of an assessment that facilitates more successful performance, moving learning forward. Scaffolding may be progressively withdrawn as the learner gains the ability to perform independently.

score
a number that communicates the quality of an assessee's performance on an assessment.

scorer
a person or machine that assigns a score to the assessee's performance.

scoring rubric
see **rating scale**.

second language acquisition
the process of learning any language in addition to one's first language and the branch of applied linguistics concerned with this process.

self-assessment
the practice of learners reflecting on and acting as assessors of their own performance. Self-assessment is usually carried out for self-improvement rather than for grading or certification.

setting
the context in which a task is performed – covers features such as the location, the people involved and the time.

situational authenticity
the fidelity with which features of real life tasks are reproduced in an assessment task.

skills
see **knowledge**, **skills** and **abilities**.

skills/components
(see also **discrete-point test**) a model of language used in developing tests that regarded language as divisible into separate components that could be assessed independently.

socio-cultural theory
a theoretical perspective that emphasises the role of cultural and social factors on learning rather than internal biological and cognitive factors.

specific purpose language assessment
assessment based on the premise that different assessments should be based on an analysis of specific uses of language (such as the language of business or the language of medicine).

specifications
(see also **design statement** and **blueprint**) a document that sets out what is to be assessed and how an assessment should be conducted.

stakes
the stakes associated with an assessment may be high or low. A high-stakes assessment has important **consequences** for the assessee (such as access to job opportunities); a low-stakes test does not. The same assessment may be high stakes for some assessees, low stakes for others.

standard
see **content standard**, **performance standard**, **standard setting**, **standards for language assessments**.

standard setting
a range of techniques for determining appropriate **cut scores** on an assessment.

standardization
the process of training raters to interpret a **rating scale**. Following standardization, raters should all arrive at the same score for any assessee's performance.

standardised test
a test built to tightly defined specifications, administered to all assessees under the same defined and controlled conditions, and scored according to clear rules.

standards for language assessment
guidance for instilling and improving quality in language assessments. Examples include the International Language Testing Association's (2007) *Guidelines for Practice*.

summative assessment
(compare **formative assessment**) **educational assessment** that is concerned retrospectively with what has been learned.

table of specification
(compare **blueprint**) a way of representing content sampling in an assessment. Assessment activities may be mapped against curriculum goals or theoretical categories.

target language use domain
a term used by Bachman and Palmer (2010) to refer to situations outside language assessments in which people use language to carry out tasks.

task
tasks are carried out both in the real world or **target language use domain** and as part of assessments. Target language use tasks might involve visiting an online travel agency to purchase a ticket or talking to a friend to persuade them to go to a party. Assessment tasks might include reading a text and responding to a series of comprehension questions or role playing a conversation with a fellow student. An assessment task may include one or more related **items**.

task characteristics
(see also **task**) detailed descriptions of the features that define a task may be used to relate assessment tasks to real world tasks in support of claims of **authenticity**.

teacher conference
a meeting between a teacher and a learner in which performance on an assessment is discussed, often a programmed opportunity for **feedback**.

test
an assessment event especially set up to elicit a performance (usually within a predetermined time frame) for the purpose of making judgements about a person's knowledge, skills or abilities.

test taker characteristics
see **assessee characteristics**.

testlet
an assessment task made up of a set of items based on a common input (a recording or text).

trialling
(of assessment material) trying out assessment material as a means of obtaining evidence of its quality. Evidence may be qualitative (e.g., opinions gathered from assessees and teachers) or quantitative (statistics reflecting the difficulty and **discrimination** of the tasks).

unitary competence hypothesis (UCH)
the proposition that a person's ability to process and use a language involved a single underlying ability. Briefly popular in the 1970s, the evidence for the UCH proved to be flawed.

usefulness
a subjective judgement of the extent to which an assessment fulfils its purpose. A useful assessment must meet minimum standards of **practicality**, **reliability**, **validity** and beneficial **consequences**. Conclusions about test usefulness may be arrived at on the basis of an **assessment use argument**.

utilization
(in an **assessment use argument**) the link or bridge that connects the underlying theory that informs assessment design to the decision being taken about the assessee: 'Is the theory underlying the test relevant and sufficient to justify the decision?'

validation
the process of collecting evidence about the validity of the inferences that may be made on the basis of assessment results.

validator
a person who reports on the overall qualities of an assessment and its adequacy as a basis for making decisions.

validity
(compare **usefulness**) the extent to which the inferences about assessees made by the users of assessment results are justified by the evidence the assessment provides.

version
(compare **form**) a new version of an assessment results when substantial revisions are made to the **specifications**. The results from different versions of an assessment are not interchangeable.

wait time
the time between a teacher or assessor asking a question or setting up a task and expecting a response from an assessee.

washback
the effect of an assessment on the teaching and learning conducted in preparation for that assessment.

washback direction
a judgement as to whether the washback from an assessment is beneficial (positive) or damaging (negative).

washback intensity
the strength of the washback from an assessment, often associated with the importance accorded the results by learners, teachers and other stakeholders.

washback variability
the differential washback effects experienced by individual teachers, learners or others. One learner in a class may adjust her behaviour significantly to prepare for a test, another may make no changes.

weighting
transformation of scores on different tasks or components on an assessment to reflect their relative importance.

zone of proximal development (ZPD)
a concept introduced by Vygotsky (1986) to describe emerging abilities. The ZPD covers the distance between what a learner is able to do independently and what he is or she is not yet capable of doing. Within the ZPD, the learner is able to perform with guidance and mediation. This is where productive learning occurs.

Further reading

Introductory books

Cheng, L., & Fox, J. (2017). *Assessment in the language classroom*. Basingstoke: Palgrave Macmillan.

This book covers the range of assessment that teachers need to use in the classroom, including tests alongside less formal approaches. It offers many useful materials and examples of practice.

Douglas, D. (2010). *Understanding language testing*. London: Hodder-Arnold.

Concise, practical introduction to the processes of test development, scoring and analysis; and interpreting and using test results. Particularly strong on uses of computer technology. Offers some coverage of classroom-based assessment.

Hughes, A. (2003). *Testing for language teachers*. Cambridge: Cambridge University Press.

Standard and very readable introduction to testing principles and techniques. A good starting point for test developers, but does not cover alternatives to tests.

McNamara, T. (2000). *Language testing*. Oxford: Oxford University Press.

A concise introductory book that focuses on issues and controversies in language testing rather than on practical techniques.

O'Malley, J. M., & Valdez-Pierce, L. (1996). *Authentic assessment for English language learners*. New York: Addison-Wesley.

Designed for the working teacher, this book covers alternatives to multiple choice tests. It contains a wealth of photocopiable resources and practical procedures. Intended for teachers of English language learners in US schools, but most of the ideas might easily be adapted to other settings.

Wiliam, D. (2011). *Embedded formative assessment*. Bloomington, IN: Solution Tree Press.

Not specifically concerned with language assessment, but covering the full range of the school curriculum. Argues persuasively for the benefits of effective formative assessment: assessment for learning. Suggests a range of practical classroom assessment techniques.

The assessment cycle and assessment qualities

Association of Language Testers in Europe (ALTE). (2011). *Manual for language test development and examining: For Use with the CEFR.* Strasbourg: Language Policy Division.
    A free download from www.coe.int/t/dg4/linguistic/ManualtLangageTest-Alte 2011_EN.pdf This is a practical manual designed to accompany the CEFR, intended to help test developers to produce effective language tests that meet quality standards.

Bachman, L. F. (1990). *Fundamental considerations in language testing.* Oxford: Oxford University Press.

Bachman, L. F., & Palmer, A. S. (2010). *Language assessment in practice.* Oxford: Oxford University Press.
    These two volumes set out the authors' very influential approach to language assessment which has also developed over the 20-year period. The first is more theoretical, the second more practically oriented with illustrative examples of assessment development projects. These are for the more advanced reader.

Fulcher, G. (2010). *Practical language testing.* London: Hodder Education.
    A relatively comprehensive handbook that introduces potential test developers to the skills, knowledge and principles needed to build effective tests.

Weir, C. J. (2005). *Language testing and validation: An evidence-based approach.* Basingstoke: Palgrave Macmillan.
    Suggests a practical and flexible socio-cognitive approach to designing and developing language assessments and justifying their use.

Quality management

American Educational Research Association (AERA), American Psychological Association (APA) and National Council on Measurement in Education (NCME). (2014). *Standards for educational and psychological testing.* Washington, DC: AERA Publications.
    Comprehensive and widely accepted standards for the development and use of tests. Not always an easy read for the beginner. The standards are updated every decade and a new edition may be available.

Saville, N. (2013). Using standards and guidelines. In A. J. Kunnan (Ed.), *The companion to language assessment.* Hoboken, NJ: Wiley-Blackwell. Chapter 55.
    Introduction to the use of standards and guidelines in assuring quality in language testing. Covers a range of useful resources for test developers.

Statistics

Bachman, L. F. (2004). *Statistical analyses for language assessment.* Cambridge: Cambridge University Press.

Brown, J. D. (2005). *Testing in language programs: A comprehensive guide to English language assessment* (New ed.). New York: McGraw-Hill College.

Green, R. (2013). *Statistical analyses for language testers*. Basingstoke: Palgrave Macmillan.
  Bachman and Green both cover a range of techniques used in test validation. Brown provides a more general focus on the use of tests in language teaching contexts and is particularly interested in the use of criterion-referenced approaches that are compatible with standards-based education.

Collections of papers

Andrade, H. L., & Cizek, G. J. (Eds). (2010). *Handbook of formative assessment*. New York: Routledge.
  A collection of papers on formative assessment. Not specifically concerned with language education but covering principles and practices that apply to language classrooms as well as those for other subjects.

Coombe, C., Davidson, P., O'Sullivan, B., & Stoynoff, S. (Eds.). (2012). *The Cambridge guide to second language assessment*. Cambridge: Cambridge University Press.
  A collection of short, accessible introductory papers on a wide range of issues connected with language assessment and testing.

Kunnan, A. (Ed.). (2013). *Companion to language assessment*. New York: Wiley-Blackwell.
  A comprehensive four-volume set including 150 chapters on a broad range of issues associated with language assessment.

Assessing language knowledge, skills and abilities

Alderson, J. C. (2000). *Assessing reading*. Cambridge: Cambridge University Press.

Bejar, I., Douglas, D., Jamieson, J., Nissan, S., & Turner, J. (2000). *TOEFL® 2000 listening framework: A working paper*. TOEFL® Monograph No. MS-19. Princeton, NJ: Educational Testing Service.

Buck, G. (2001). *Assessing listening*. Cambridge: Cambridge University Press.

Butler, F. A., Eignor, D., Jones, S., McNamara, T., & Suomi, B. K. (2000). *TOEFL® 2000 speaking framework: A working paper*. TOEFL® Monograph No. MS-20. Princeton, NJ: Educational Testing Service.

Chapelle, C. A., Enright, M. K., & Jamieson, J. M. (Eds.). (2011). *Building a validity argument for the test of English as a Foreign language*. New York: Routledge.

Cumming, A., Kantor, R., Powers, D. E., Santos, T., & Taylor, C. (2000). *TOEFL® 2000 writing framework: A working paper*. TOEFL® Monograph No. MS-18. Princeton, NJ: Educational Testing Service.

Enright, M. K., Grabe, W., Koda, K., Mosenthal, P., Mulcahy-Ernt, P., & Schedl, M. (2000). *TOEFL® 2000 reading framework: A working paper.* TOEFL® Monograph No. MS-17. Princeton, NJ: Educational Testing Service.

Geranpayeh, A., & Taylor, L. (Eds.). (2013). *Examining listening: Research and practice in assessing second language speaking.* Cambridge: Cambridge ESOL and Cambridge University Press.
    These volumes (for the more advanced reader) provide insights into test design considerations from the point of view of testing organizations: The Educational Testing Service (for TOEFL) and Cambridge Assessment: English (for Cambridge English Key, Preliminary, First, Advanced, Proficiency).

Khalifa, H., & Weir, C. J. (2009). *Examining reading: Research and practice in assessing second language reading.* Cambridge: Cambridge ESOL and Cambridge University Press.

Luoma, S. (2004). *Assessing speaking.* Cambridge: Cambridge University Press.
    These books in the Cambridge Language Assessment series each explore the principles and practice of assessing language abilities in second language settings in relation to a specific language skill.

Purpura, J. (2004). *Assessing grammar.* Cambridge: Cambridge University Press.

Read, J. (2000). *Assessing vocabulary.* Cambridge: Cambridge University Press.

Shaw, S. D., & Weir, C. J. (2007). *Examining writing: Research and practice in assessing second language writing.* Cambridge: Cambridge ESOL and Cambridge University Press.

Taylor, L. (Ed.). (2011). *Examining speaking: Research and practice in assessing second language speaking.* Cambridge: Cambridge ESOL and Cambridge University Press.

Weigle, S. C. (2002). *Assessing writing.* Cambridge: Cambridge University Press.

Historical perspectives

Davies, A. (2008). *Assessing academic English: Testing English proficiency 1950–1989 – The IELTS solution.* Cambridge: Cambridge University Press.
    An insider's account of testing English for academic purposes in the second half of the twentieth century.

Fulcher, G., & Davidson, F. (2007). *Language testing: An advanced resource book.* London and New York: Routledge.
    Covers theoretical and practical issues, illustrating these with a collection of landmark readings from the language testing literature.

Weir, C. J., Vidaković, I., & Galaczi, E. (2013). *Measured constructs: A history of Cambridge English examinations, 1913–2012.* Cambridge: Cambridge University Press.

An insightful history of language testing focusing on practices at one of the oldest international language testing institutions.

Weir, C. J., & O'Sullivan, B. (2017). *Assessing English on the global stage: The British council and English language testing, 1941–2016*. London: Equinox.
Complementing *Measured Constructs*, this book relates the history of language testing at the British Council.

Emerging perspectives

Chapelle, C. A., & Douglas, D. (2006). *Assessing language through computer technology*. Cambridge: Cambridge University Press.
Explores the growing use of computer technology in language assessment and its implications for practice.

Knoch, U., & Macqueen, S. (2019). *Assessing English for professional purposes*. Basingstoke: Routledge.
Covers the assessment of language abilities for specific, typically vocational, purposes and the issues this raises.

McKay, P. (2005). *Assessing young learners*. Cambridge: Cambridge University Press.

McNamara, T., & Roever, C. (2006). *Language testing: The social dimension*. Oxford: Blackwell.
Critical perspective on the use (and abuse) of language assessments.

Papp, S. (2018). *Examining young learners: Research and practice in assessing the English of school-age learners*. Cambridge: Cambridge University Press.
Overviews of the issues involved in assessing the second and foreign language abilities of children and teens.

Journals

Two major international academic journals are concerned directly with language assessment:

Language Testing (published by Sage);

Language Assessment Quarterly (published by Taylor and Francis).

There are often papers on language assessment issues in a range of other journals concerned with the wider fields of applied linguistics, language education and assessment.

Other resources

The Language Testing Resources website maintained by Glenn Fulcher has a wealth of language assessment material with, among other things, video clips on key concepts presented by leading figures in the field, downloadable articles, reviews of tests and links to professional organizations and conferences: http://languagetesting.info.

Links to other language assessment resources and language test providers are given on the website for this volume (www.routledge.com/cw/rial).

References

ACTFL (American Council on the Teaching of Foreign Languages) (2014). *World-readiness standards for learning languages*. Actfl.org.

Alderson, J. C. (1988). New procedures for validating proficiency tests of ESP? Theory and practice. *Language Testing, 5*(2), 220–232.

Alderson, J. C. (1991). Bands and scores. In J. C. Alderson & B. North (Eds.), *Language testing in the 1990s* (pp. 71–86). Basingstoke: Modern English Publications in Association with the British Council.

Alderson, J. C. (1999). *Testing is too important to be left to testers*. Plenary Address to the Third Annual Conference on Current Trends in English Language Testing, United Arab Emirates University, Al Ain and Zayed University, Dubai Campus, May 1999.

Alderson, J. C. (2000). *Assessing reading*. Cambridge: Cambridge University Press.

Alderson, J. C., Clapham, C., & Wall, D. (1995). *Language test construction and evaluation*. Cambridge: Cambridge University Press.

Alderson, J. C., & Hughes, A. (1981). *Issues in language testing*. ELT Documents 111. London: The British Council.

American Council for the Teaching of Foreign Languages. (1999). *ACTFL proficiency guidelines – Speaking* (Rev. ed.). Yonkers, NY: Author.

American Educational Research Association, American Psychological Association, and National Council on Measurement in Education. (2014). *Standards for educational and psychological testing*. Washington, DC: American Educational Research Association.

Association of Language Testers in Europe. (2002). *The ALTE can do project (English version)*. Retrieved 20 September 2012, from www.alte.org/attachments/files/alte_cando.pdf

Association of Language Testers in Europe/ Council of Europe. (2011). *Manual for language test development and examining for use with the CEFR*. Strasbourg: Council of Europe.

Bachman, L. F. (1990). *Fundamental considerations in language testing*. Oxford: Oxford University Press.

Bachman, L. F. (2004). *Statistical analyses for language assessment*. Cambridge: Cambridge University Press.

Bachman, L., & Damböck, B. (2017). *Language assessment for classroom teachers*. Oxford: Oxford University Press.

Bachman, L. F., Davidson, F., Ryan, K., & Choi, I. (1995). *An investigation into the comparability of two tests of English as a Foreign language: The Cambridge-TOEFL comparability study*. Cambridge: Cambridge University Press.

Bachman, L. F., & Palmer, A. S. (1996). *Language testing in practice*. Oxford: Oxford University Press.

Bachman, L. F., & Palmer, A. S. (2010). *Language assessment in practice*. Oxford: Oxford University Press.

Baker, B., & Hope, A. (2019). Incorporating translanguaging in language assessment: The case of a test for university professors. *Language Assessment Quarterly*, 16(4–5), 408–425.

Baker, D. (1989). *Language testing: A critical survey and practical guide*. London: Edward Arnold.

Barker, F. (2013). Using corpora to design assessment. In A. J. Kunnan (Ed.), *The companion to language assessment*. Hoboken, NJ: Wiley-Blackwell. Chapter 61.

Baxter, G. P., & Glaser, R. (1998). Investigating the cognitive complexity of science assessments. *Educational Measurement: Issues and Practice*, 17(3), 37–45.

Bejar, I., Douglas, D., Jamieson, J., Nissan, S., & Turner, J. (2000). *TOEFL 2000 listening framework: A working paper*. TOEFL Monograph No. MS-19. Princeton, NJ: Educational Testing Service.

Bennett, R. E., Kane, M., & Bridgeman, B. (2011). *Theory of action and validity argument in the context of through-course summative assessment*. Princeton, NJ: Educational Testing Service.

Black, P. J., & Wiliam, D. (1998). *Inside the black box: Raising standards through classroom assessment*. London: Kings College London School of Education.

Black, P. J., & Wiliam, D. (2006). Assessment for learning in the classroom. In J. Gardner (Ed.), *Assessment and learning* (pp. 14–44). London: Sage.

Block, J. H. (Ed.). (1971). *Mastery learning: Theory and practice*. New York: Holt, Rinehart and Winston.

Bloom, B. S. (1968). Learning for mastery. *Evaluation Comment*, 1(2), 1–12.

Bloomfield, L. (1933). *Language*. London: George Allen & Unwin.

Brindley, G. (1989). *Assessing achievement in the learner-centred curriculum*. Sydney: National Centre for English Teaching and Research.

Brindley, G. (1998). Outcomes-based assessment and reporting in language learning programmes: A review of the issues. *Language Testing*, 15(1), 45–85.

Brindley, G., Hood, S., McNaught, C., & Wigglesworth, G. (1997). Issues in test design and delivery. In G. Brindley & G. Wigglesworth (Eds.), *Access: Issues in language test design and delivery* (pp. 65–85). Sydney: Macquarie University, National Center for English Language Teaching and Research.

Brown, D. (1983). Conversational cloze tests and conversational ability. *English Language Teaching Journal*, 37(2), 158–161.

Brown, G. R., Gillian, B., & Yule, G. (1983). *Discourse analysis*. Cambridge: Cambridge University Press.

Brown, H. D., & Abeywickrama, P. (2010). *Language assessment: Principles and classroom practices* (2nd ed.). White Plains, NY: Pearson Education.

Brown, J. D. (2005). *Testing in language programs: A comprehensive guide to English language assessment* (2nd ed.). New York: McGraw-Hill College.

Brown, J. D., & Hudson, T. (2002). *Criterion-referenced language testing*. Cambridge: Cambridge University Press.

Brown, G. R., Gillian, B., & Yule, G. (1983). *Discourse analysis*. Cambridge: Cambridge University Press.

Bruner, J. (1983). *Child's talk: Learning to use language*. New York: Norton.

Buck, G. (2001). *Assessing listening*. Cambridge: Cambridge University Press.

Buck, G. (2009). Challenges and constraints in language test development. In J. C. Alderson (Ed.), *The politics of language education: Individuals and institutions* (pp. 166–184). Bristol: Multilingual Matters.

Bunderson, C. V., Inouye, D. K., & Olsen, J. B. (1988). *The four generations of computerised educational measurement*. ETS Research Report Series. Princeton, NJ: Educational Testing Service.

Bygate, M. (1987). *Speaking*. Oxford: Oxford University Press.

Campbell, D. T., & Fiske, D. W. (1959). Convergent and discriminant validation by the multitrait-multimethod matrix. *Psychological Bulletin, 56,* 81–105.

Campbell, R., & Wales, R. (1970). The study of language acquisition. In J. Lyon (Ed.), *New horizons in linguistics*. Harmondsworth: Penguin.

Canale, M. (1983). On some dimensions of language proficiency. In J. W Jr. Oller (Ed.), *Issues in language testing research* (pp. 333–342). Rowley, MA: Newbury House.

Canale, M., & Swain, M. (1980). Theoretical bases of communicative approaches to second language teaching and testing. *Applied Linguistics, 1*(1), 1–47.

Carroll, B. J. (1980). *Testing communicative performance*. Oxford: Pergamon.

Carroll, J. B. (1961). Fundamental considerations in testing for English language proficiency of foreign students. In *Testing the English proficiency of Foreign students* (pp. 31–40). Washington, DC: Center for Applied Linguistics.

Carroll, J. B. (1963). A model of school learning. *Teachers College Record, 64,* 723–733.

Carroll, J. B. (1971). Problems of measurement related to the concept of mastery. In J. H. Block (Ed.), *Mastery learning theory and practice* (pp. 29–46). New York: Holt, Rinehart & Winston.

Carroll, J. B., Carton, A. S., & Wilds, C. P. (1959). *An investigation of cloze items in the measurement of achievement in foreign languages*. Cambridge, MA: College Entrance Examination Board.

Carroll, J. B., & Sapon, S. M. (1959). *Modern language aptitude test*. New York: Psychological Corporation.

Carter, R. A., & McCarthy, M. (2006). *Cambridge grammar of English: A comprehensive guide*. Cambridge: Cambridge University Press.

Chalhoub-Deville, M. (2003). Second language interaction: Current perspectives and future trends. *Language Testing, 20*(4), 369–383.

Chan, S. (2012). *Establishing the cognitive validity of EAP reading-into-writing tests*. Paper presented to the 9th Annual EALTA Conference, University of Innsbruck, Austria, 3 June, 2012.

Chapelle, C. A. (1998). Construct definition and validity inquiry in SLA research. In L. F. Bachman & A. D. Cohen (Eds.), *Interfaces between second language acquisition and language testing research* (pp. 32–70). New York: Cambridge University Press.

Chapelle, C. A., & Douglas, D. (2006). *Assessing language through computer technology*. Cambridge: Cambridge University Press.

Cheng, L., & Fox, J. (2017). *Assessment in the language classroom: Teachers supporting student learning*. Basingstoke: Palgrave Macmillan.

Chenoweth, A., & Hayes, J. (2001). Fluency in writing: Generating text in L1 and L2. *Written Communication, 18,* 80–98.

Cho, Y., & Bridgeman, B. (2012). Relationship of TOEFL iBT® scores to academic performance: Some evidence from American universities. *Language Testing, 29*(3), 421–442.

Cohen, A. D., & Olshtain, E. (1993). The production of speech acts by EFL Learners. *TESOL Quarterly*, 27(1), 33–56.

Coniam, D. (2009). Investigating the quality of teacher-produced tests for EFL students and the impact of training in test development principles on improving test quality. *System*, 37(2), 226–242.

Cook, V. (2008). *Second language learning and language teaching* (4th ed.). London: London: Edward Arnold.

Cooper, R. L. (1968). An elaborated language testing model. In J. A. Upshur & J. Fata (Eds.), *Problems in Foreign language testing*. Language Learning Special Issue. No. 3 (pp. 57–72). Ann Arbor, MI: Research Club in Language Learning.

Corder, S. P. (1971). Idiosyncratic errors and error analysis. *International Review of Applied Linguistics*, 9(2), 147–159.

Council of Europe. (1970). *A compendium of studies commissioned by the council for cultural co-operation: A contribution to the united nations' international education year*. Strasbourg: Author.

Council of Europe. (2001). *Common European framework of reference for languages*. Cambridge: Cambridge University Press.

Council of Europe. (2009). *Manual for Language test development and examining for use with the CEFR–produced by ALTE on behalf of the Language Policy Division*. Strasbourg: Council of Europe.

Council of Europe. (2009). *Manual for relating language examinations to the common European framework of reference for languages*. Strasbourg: Author.

Council of Europe. (2018). *Common European Framework of Reference for Languages: Learning, Teaching, Assessment. Companion Volume with New Descriptors*. Strasbourg: Council of Europe.

Cummins, J. (1979). *Cognitive/academic language proficiency, linguistic interdependence, the optimum age question and some other matters*. Working Papers on Bilingualism, 19, 121–129.

Cutler, A. (Ed.). (2005). *Twenty-first century psycholinguistics: Four cornerstones*. Hillsdale, NJ: Erlbaum.

Davidson, F., & Lynch, B. K. (2002). *Testcraft. A teacher's guide to writing and using language test specifications*. New Haven, CT and London: Yale University Press.

Davies, A. (1990). *Principles of language testing*. Oxford: Blackwell.

Davies, A. (2008a). Textbook trends in teaching language testing. *Language Testing*, 25(3), 327–347.

Davies, A. (2008b). *Assessing academic English: Testing English proficiency 1950–1989: The IELTS solution*. Cambridge: Cambridge University Press.

Davison, C., & Hamp-Lyons, L. (2010). The Hong Kong certificate of education: School-based assessment reform in Hong Kong English language education teacher. In L. Y. Cheng & A. Curtis (Eds.), *Language assessment for Chinese learners*. New York: Routledge.

Douglas, D. (2000). *Assessing languages for specific purposes*. Cambridge: Cambridge University Press.

Douglas, D. (2010). *Understanding language testing*. London: Hodder-Arnold.

Downing, S. M. (2006). Twelve steps for effective test development. In S. M. Downing & T. M. Haladyna (Eds.), *Handbook of test development* (pp. 3–25). Mahwah, NJ: Lawrence Erlbaum Associates.

Edgeworth, F. Y. (1890). The element of chance in competitive examinations. *Journal of the Royal Statistics Society 53*, 460–475.

Ellis, R., & Shintani, N. (2013). *Exploring language pedagogy through second language acquisition research*. Abingdon: Routledge.

Enright, M., Grabe, W., Koda, K., Mosenthal, P., Mulcahy-Ernt, P., & Schedl, M. (2000). *TOEFL 2000 reading framework: A working paper*. TOEFL Monograph MS-17. Princeton, NJ: Educational Testing Service.

Field, J. (2008). *Listening in the language classroom*. Cambridge: Cambridge University Press.

Foucault, M. (1975). *Discipline and punish: The birth of the prison*. New York: Vintage.

Fulcher, G. (1987). Tests of oral performance: The need for data-based criteria. *English Language Teaching Journal, 41*, 287–291.

Fulcher, G. (2003). *Testing second language speaking*. Harlow: Longman.

Fulcher, G. (2004). Deluded by artifices? The common European framework and harmonization. *Language Assessment Quarterly, 1*(4), 253–266.

Fulcher, G., & Davidson, F. (2009). Test architecture, test retrofit. *Language Testing, 26*(1), 123–144.

Fulcher, G. (2010). *Practical language testing*. London: Hodder Education.

Fulcher, G., & Bamford, R. (1996). I didn't get the grade I need. Where's my solicitor? *System, 24*(4), 437–448.

Fulcher, G., & Davidson, F. (2007). *Language testing: An advanced resource book*. London and New York: Routledge.

Fulcher, G., Davidson, F., & Kemp, J. (2011). Effective rating scale development for speaking tests: Performance decision trees. *Language Testing, 28*(1), 5–29.

García, O., & Wei, L. (2014). *Translanguaging: Language, bilingualism and education*. Basingstoke: Palgrave Macmillan.

Genesee, F., & Upshur, J. (1996). *Classroom-based evaluation in second language education*. Cambridge: Cambridge University Press.

Gough, P. B., Hoover, W. A., & Peterson, C. L. (1996). Some observations on a simple view of reading. In C. Cornoldi & J. Oakhill (Eds.), *Reading comprehension difficulties* (pp. 1–13). Mahwah, NJ: Erlbaum.

Grabe, W., & Stoller, F. L. (2019). *Teaching and researching reading*. 3rd ed. New York: Routledge.

Green, A. (1998). *Verbal protocol analysis in language testing research: A handbook*. Cambridge: Cambridge University Press.

Green, A. B. (2007). *IELTS washback in context: Preparation for academic writing in higher education*. Cambridge: Cambridge University Press.

Green, A. B. (2012a). *Language functions revisited: Theoretical and empirical bases for language construct definition across the ability range*. Cambridge: Cambridge University Press.

Green, A. B. (2012b). Placement testing. In C. Coombe, B. O'Sullivan, P. Davidson, & S. Stoynoff (Eds.), *The Cambridge guide to language assessment*. Cambridge: Cambridge University Press.

Green, A. B. (2014). *The Test of English for Academic Purposes (TEAP) impact study: Report 1—Preliminary questionnaires to Japanese high school students and teachers*. Tokyo: Eiken Foundation of Japan. www.eiken.or.jp/teap/group/pdf/teap_washback_study.pdf

Green, A. B., & Hawkey, R. A. (2012). Re-fitting for a different purpose: A case study of item writer practices in adapting source texts for a test of academic reading. *Language Testing, 29*(1), 109–129.

Green, A. B., Unaldi, A., & Weir, C. J. (2010). Empiricism versus connoisseurship: Establishing the appropriacy of texts for testing reading for academic purposes. *Language Testing, 27*(3), 1–21.

Grice, H. P. (1975). Logic and conversation. In P. Cole & J. L. Morgan (Eds.), *Syntax and semantics: Speech acts* (Vol. 3, pp. 41–58). New York: Academic Press.

Gronlund, N. E. (1989). *Stating behavioral objectives for classroom instruction* (4th ed.). New York: Palgrave Macmillan.

Halliday, M. A. K., & Hasan, R. (1976). *Cohesion in English*. Harlow: Longman.

Hamp-Lyons, L., & Condon, W. (2000). *Assessing the portfolio: Principles for practice, theory, and research*. Cresskill, NJ: Hampton Press.

Harlen, W. (2007). *Assessment of learning*. London: Sage.

Hawkins, J. A., & Filipovic, L. (2012). *Criterial features in L2 English: Specifying the reference levels of the common European framework*. Cambridge: Cambridge University Press.

He, A. W., & Young, R. (1998). Language proficiency interviews: A discourse approach. In R. Young, & A. W. He (Eds.), *Talking and testing: Discourse approaches to the assessment of oral proficiency* (pp. 1–24). Amsterdam: Benjamins.

Henning, G. (1987). *A guide to language testing: Development, evaluation, research*. Rowley, MA: Newbury House.

Hill, K., & McNamara, T. (2012). Developing a comprehensive, empirically based research framework for classroom-based assessment. *Language Testing, 29*(3), 395–420.

Hughes, A. (2003). *Testing for language teachers* (2nd ed.). Cambridge: Cambridge University Press.

Hughes, R. (2010). *Teaching and researching: Speaking* (2nd ed.). London: Longman.

Hymes, D. H. (1972). On communicative competence. In J. B. Pride & J. Holmes (Eds.), *Sociolinguistics. Selected readings* (pp. 269–293). Harmondsworth: Penguin.

Hymes, D. H. (1974). *Foundations in sociolinguistics: An ethnographic approach*. Philadelphia: University of Pennsylvania Press.

International Language Testing Association. (2000). *Code of ethics*. Birmingham, AL: Author.

International Language Testing Association. (2007). *ILTA guidelines for practice*. Birmingham, AL: Author.

Jakobson, R. (1960). Closing statement: Linguistics and poetics. In T. Sebeok (Ed.), *Style in language* (pp. 350–377). Michigan: The MIT Press.

Johnson, K. E., Rehn-Jordan, S., & Poehner, M. E. (2005). The TOEFL trump card: An investigation of test impact in an ESL classroom. *Critical Inquiry in Language Studies, 2*(2), 71–94.

Johnson, M. (2001). *The art of non-conversation: A re-examination of the validity of the oral proficiency interview*. New Haven, CT: Yale University Press.

Kane, M. T., Crooks, T., & Cohen, A. (1999). Validating measures of performance. *Educational Measurement: Issues and Practice, 18*(2), 5–17.

Khalifa, H., & Weir, C. J. (2009). *Examining reading: Research and practice in assessing second language reading*. Cambridge: Cambridge University Press.

Kim, H., & Elder, C. (2009). Understanding aviation English as a lingua franca: Perceptions of Korean aviation personnel. *Australian Review of Applied Linguistics*, 32(3), 23.1–23.17.

Kim, J., Chi, Y., Huensch, A., Jun, H., Li, H., & Roullion, V. (2010). A case study on an item writing process: Use of test specifications, nature of group dynamics, and individual item writers' characteristics. *Language Assessment Quarterly*, 7(2), 160–174.

Klein-Braley, C. (1985). A cloze-up on the C-test: A study in the construct validation of authentic tests. *Language Testing*, 2(1), 76–104.

Koda, K. (2005). *Insights into second language reading: A cross-linguistic approach*. Cambridge: Cambridge University Press.

Krashen, S. D., & Terrell, T. D. (1983). *The natural approach: Language acquisition in the classroom*. London: Prentice Hall.

Kunnan, A. J. (2004). Test fairness. In M. Milanovic & C. Weir (Eds.), *European language testing in a global context* (pp. 27–48). Cambridge: Cambridge University Press.

Lado, R. (1961). *Language testing*. London: Longman.

Leech, G. (1983). *Principles of pragmatics*. London: Longman.

Leung, C. (2007). Dynamic assessment: Assessment for and as teaching. *Language Assessment Quarterly*, 4(3), 257–278.

Leung, C. (2010). Language teaching and language assessment. In R. Wodak B. Johnstone, & P. Kerswill (Eds.), *The Sage handbook of sociolinguistics* (pp. 545–564). London: Sage.

Leung, C., & Lewkowicz, J. (2006). Expanding horizons and unresolved conundrums: Language testing and assessment. *TESOL Quarterly*, 40(1), 211–234.

Levelt, W. (1989). *Speaking: From intention to articulation*. Cambridge, MA: The MIT Press.

Lightbown, P., & Spada, N. (2012). *How languages are learned* (4th ed.). Cambridge: Cambridge University Press.

Long, M., & Robinson, P. (1998). Focus on form: Theory, research, and practice. In C. Doughty & J. Williams (Eds.), *Focus on form in classroom second language acquisition* (pp. 15–63). Cambridge: Cambridge University Press.

Lowe, P. J. (1982). *ILR handbook on oral interview testing*. Washington, DC: DLIA Oral Interview Testing Project.

Lumley, T. (2005). *Assessing second language writing: The rater's perspective*. Frankfurt: Peter Lang.

Luoma, S. (2004). *Assessing speaking*. Cambridge: Cambridge University Press.

McCall, W. A. (1922). *How to measure in education*. New York: Palgrave Macmillan.

McKay, P. (2005). *Assessing young learners*. Cambridge: Cambridge University Press.

McNamara, T. (1995). Modelling Performance: opening Pandora's box. *Applied Linguistics*, 16(2), 159–179.

McNamara, T. (1996). *Measuring second language performance*. Harlow: Longman.

McNamara, T. (2000). *Language testing*. Oxford: Oxford University Press.

McNamara, T., & Roever, C. (2006). *Language testing: The social dimension*. Oxford: Blackwell.

McNamara, T., Knoch, U., & Fan, J. (2019). *Fairness, justice & language Assessment*. Oxford: Oxford University Press.

Meddings, L., & Thornbury, S. (2009). *Teaching unplugged: Dogme in English language teaching*. Peaslake, Surrey: Delta Publishing.

Messick, S. (1989). Validity. In R. L. Linn (Ed.), *Educational measurement* (3rd ed., pp. 13–103). New York: Palgrave Macmillan.

Miller, D. M., Linn, R. L., & Gronlund, N. E. (2012). *Measurement and assessment in teaching* (11th ed.). Upper Saddle River, NJ: Prentice Hall.

Mitchell, R., Myles, F., & Marsden, E. (2012). *Second language learning theories* (3rd ed.). London: Edward Arnold.

Morrow, K. (1979). Communicative language testing: Revolution or evolution? In C. J. Brumfit & K. Johnson (Eds.), *The communicative approach to language teaching* (pp. 143–157). Oxford: Oxford University Press.

Moss, P. A. (2003). Reconceptualizing validity for classroom assessment. *Educational Measurement: Issues and Practice* 22(4), 13–25.

Munby, J. (1978). *Communicative syllabus design*. Cambridge: Cambridge University Press.

Murphy, R. I. L. (1982). Sex differences in objective test performance. *British Journal of Educational Psychology, 52,* 213–219.

National Education Examinations Authority (NEEA). (2018). *China's Standards of English Language Ability*. Beijing, China: Higher Education Press & Shanghai Foreign Language Education Press.

North, B. (2000). *The development of a common framework scale of language proficiency*. New York: Peter Lang.

Ockey, G. J., & Wagner, E. (2018). *Assessing L2 listening: Moving towards authenticity* (Vol. 50). Amsterdam: John Benjamins.

Oller, J. W., Jr. (1979). *Language tests at school*. Harlow: Longman.

O'Malley, M., & Valdez Pierce, L. (1996). *Authentic assessment for English language learners*. New York: Addison-Wesley.

Oskarsson, M. (1980). *Approaches to self-assessment in Foreign language learning*. Oxford: Pergamon.

O'Sullivan, B., & Green, A. B. (2011). Test taker characteristics. In L. Taylor (Eds.), *Examining speaking: Research and practice in assessing second language speaking*. Cambridge: Cambridge University Press and Cambridge ESOL.

Paulson, E. J., & Henry, J. (2002). Does the degrees of reading power assessment reflect the reading process? An eye-movement examination. *Journal of Adolescent and Adult Literacy, 46,* 234–244.

Pawlikowska-Smith, G. (2000). *Canadian language benchmarks 2000: English as a second language – For adults*. Toronto: Centre for Canadian Language Benchmarks.

Pennycook, A. (2001). *Critical applied linguistics: A critical introduction*. Mahwah, NJ: Lawrence Erlbaum.

Perelman, L. (2012) *Construct validity, length, score, and time in holistically graded writing assessments: The case against automated essay scoring (AES)*. In C. Bazerman, C. Dean, J. Early, K. Lunsford, S. Null, P. Rogers, A. Stansell (Eds.), *International advances in writing research: Cultures, places, measures* (121–132). Fort Collins, CO: WAC Clearinghouse, Anderson, SC: Parlor Press.

Perren, G. (1967). Testing ability in English as a second language: 3. Spoken language. *ELT Journal, 22(1),* 22–29.

Pimsleur, P., Reed, D., & Stansfield, C. (2004). *Pimsleur language aptitude battery: Manual 2004 edition*. Bethesda, MD: Second Language Testing, Inc.

Poehner, M. E. (2008). *Dynamic assessment: A Vygotskian approach to understanding and promoting second language development*. Berlin: Springer.

Poehner, M. E., & Lantolf, J. P. (2005). Dynamic assessment in the language classroom. *Language Teaching Research, 9(3),* 1–33.

Pollitt, A. (1991). Giving students a sporting chance: Assessment by counting and judging. In J. C. Alderson & B. North (Eds.), *Language testing in the 1990s*. London: Modern English Publications in Association with the British Council (pp. 46–59).

Popham, W. J. (1978). *Criterion-referenced measurement*. Englewood Cliffs, NJ: Prentice Hall.

Popham, W. J. (2001). Teaching to the test. *Educational Leadership, 58*(6), 16–20.

Purpura, J. (2004). *Assessing grammar*. Cambridge: Cambridge University Press.

Read, J. (2000). *Assessing vocabulary*. Cambridge: Cambridge University Press.

Rea-Dickins. (2001). Mirror, mirror on the wall: Identifying processes of classroom assessment. *Language Testing, 18*(4), 429–462.

Roach, J. O. (1945). *Some problems of oral examinations in modern languages: An experimental approach based on the Cambridge examinations in English for foreign students*. University of Cambridge Examinations Syndicate: Internal report.

Rost, M. (2013). *Teaching and researching listening*. 2nd ed. London and New York: Routledge.

Saville, N. (2013). Using standards and guidelines. In A. J. Kunnan (Ed.), *The companion to language assessment*. Hoboken, NJ: Wiley-Blackwell. Chapter 55.

Selinker, L. (1972). Interlanguage. *International Review of Applied Linguistics, 10*(3), 209–231.

Shohamy, E. (2001). *The power of tests*. Harlow: Longman.

Shohamy, E., Donitza-Schmidt, S., & Ferman, I. (1996). Test impact revisited: Washback effect over time. *Language Testing, 13*(3), 298–317.

Sinclair, J. M., & Coulthard, R. M. (1975). *Towards an analysis of discourse: The English used by teachers and pupils*. Oxford: Oxford University Press.

Spaan, M. (2007). Evolution of a test item. *Language Assessment Quarterly, 4*(3), 279–293.

Spolsky, B. (1977). Language testing: Art or science. In G. Nickel (Ed.), *Proceedings of the fourth international congress of applied linguistics* (pp. 7–28). Stuttgart: Hochschulverlag.

Spolsky, B. (1995). *Measured words: The development of objective language testing*. Oxford: Oxford University Press.

Stobart, G. (2006). Validity in formative assessment. In J. Gardner (Ed.), *Assessment and learning*. London: Sage.

Stobart, G. (2008). *Testing times: The uses and abuses of assessment*. Abingdon: Routledge.

Strevens, (1965). *Recent British developments in language teaching*. In Kriedler, C (ed.) Report of the sixteenth annual round table meeting on linguistics and language studies. (pp.171-180), Washington, DC: Georgetown University Press. ERIC Document No. ED013047.

Strömqvist, S., Holmqvist, K., Johansson, V., Karlsson, H., & Wengelin, Å. (2006). What keystroke logging can reveal about writing. In K. Sullivan & E. Lindgren (Eds.), *Computer key-stroke logging and writing: Methods and applications* (pp. 45–71). Amsterdam: Elsevier.

Swain, M. (2001). Examining dialogue: Another approach to content specification and to validating inferences drawn from test scores. *Language Testing, 18*(3), 275–302.

Takala, S., & Kaftandjieva, F. (2000). Test fairness: A DIF analysis of an L2 vocabulary test. *Language Testing, 17*(3), 323–340.

Taylor, W. L. (1953). Cloze procedure: A new tool for measuring readability. *Journalism Quarterly, 30*, 415–433.

Teasdale, A., & Leung, C. (2000). Teacher assessment and psychometric theory: A case of paradigm crossing? *Language Testing, 17*(2), 163–184.

TESOL. (2006). *PreK-12 English language proficiency standards.* Alexandria, VA: Author.

Tonkyn, A., & Wilson, J. (2004). Revising the IELTS speaking test. In L. E. Sheldon (Ed.), *Directions for the future* (pp. 191–203). Bern: Peter Lang.

Traynor, R. (1985). The TOEFL: An appraisal. *ELT Journal, 39*(1), 43–47.

Trinity College London. (2009). *Syllabus – From 1 February 2010.* London: Author.

Upshur, J. A., & Turner, C. E. (1995). Constructing rating scales for second language tests. *English Language Teaching Journal, 49*(1), 3–12.

Urquhart, S., & Weir, C. (1998). *Reading in a second language: Process, product and practice.* London: Addison Wesley Longman.

Valette, R. (1967). *Modern language testing: A handbook.* New York: Harcourt. Brace Jovanovich.

Van Lier, L. (2006). *The ecology and semiotics of language learning: A sociocultural perspective.* Berlin: Springer.

Vojak, C., Kline, S., Cope, B., McCarthey, S., & Kalantzis, M. (2011). New spaces and old places: An analysis of writing assessment software. *Computers and Composition, 28*(2), 97–111.

Vygotsky, L. S. (1986). *Thought and language.* Cambridge, MA: The MIT Press.

Walsh, S. (2011). *Exploring classroom discourse: Language in action.* Abingdon: Routledge.

Wang, Z., Zechner, K., & Sun, Y. (2018). Monitoring the performance of human and automated scores for spoken responses. *Language Testing, 35*(1), 101–120.

Weigle, S. C. (2002). *Assessing writing.* Cambridge: Cambridge University Press.

Weir, C. J. (1983). The associated examining board's test of English for academic purposes: An exercise in content validation events. In A. Hughes & D. Porter (Eds.), *Current developments in language testing* (pp. 147–153). London: Academic Press.

Weir, C. J. (1993). *Understanding and developing language tests.* Hemel Hempstead: Prentice Hall.

Weir, C. J. (2003). A survey of the history of the certificate of proficiency in English (CPE) in the twentieth century. In C. J. Weir & M. Milanovic (Eds.), *Balancing continuity and innovation. A history of the CPE examination 1913–2013.* Studies in Language Testing 15. Cambridge: Cambridge University Press.

Weir, C. J. (2005a). *Language testing and validation: An evidence-based approach.* Basingstoke: Palgrave Macmillan.

Weir, C. J. (2005b). Limitations of the council of Europe's framework of reference (CEFR) in developing comparable examinations and tests. *Language Testing, 22*(3), 281–300.

Weir, C. J., Hawkey, R., Green, A., & Devi, S. (2012). The cognitive processes underlying the academic reading construct as measured by IELTS. In L. Taylor & C. J. Weir (Eds.), *IELTS collected papers 2: Research in reading and listening assessment.* Cambridge: Cambridge University Press.

Weir, C. J., Vidakovic, I., & Galaczi, E. (2013). *Measured constructs: A history of the constructs underlying Cambridge English language (ESOL) examinations 1913–2012.* Cambridge: Cambridge University Press.

Wenger, E. (1987). *Artificial intelligence and tutoring systems: Computational and cognitive approaches to the communication of knowledge.* Los Altos, CA: Morgan Kaufmann Publishers.

White, R. (1998). What is quality in English language teacher education? *English Language Teaching Journal, 52*(2), 133–139.

Widdowson, H. (2003). *Defining issues in English language teaching.* Oxford: Oxford University Press.

Wiggins, G. (1998). *Educative assessment: Designing assessments to inform and improve student performance.* San Francisco: Jossey-Bass.

Wilds, C. (1975). The oral interview test. In R. L. Jones & B. Spolsky (Eds.), *Testing language proficiency* (pp. 29–44). Arlington, VA: Center for Applied Linguistics.

Wiliam, D. (2011). *Embedded formative assessment.* Bloomington, IN: Solution Tree.

Winke, P. (2013). Eye-tracking technology for reading. In A. J. Kunnan (Ed.), *The companion to language assessment.* Hoboken, NJ: Wiley-Blackwell.

Xi, X. (2012). Validity and the automated scoring of performance tests. In G. Fulcher & F. Davidson (Eds.), *The Routledge handbook of language testing.* New York: Routledge.

Index